There's
a
Hole
in my
Bucket

Royd Tolkien

There's a Hole in my Bucket

A Journey of Two Brothers

Little

Published by Little A, Seattle.

www.apub.com

Amazon, the Amazon logo, and Little A are trademarks of Amazon.com, Inc.,
or its affiliates.

ISBN-13: 9781542027571
ISBN-10: 1542027578

Cover design by Emma Rogers

Printed in the United States of America.

For Mike.

Contents

Foreword

I was never going to be able to write a book like this on my own. Not because I can't write. And not because, shall we say, I struggle with motivation. But because, as much as I try to find humour in as many places as possible, there is a core element to this book that is as raw and painful to me now as it has ever been.

Like a songwriter 'moving on' before penning emotional couplets about his or her recent heartache, it seems to me that it's just a lot easier to write some things from the outside looking in. I'm still very much inside the loss of my brother, Mike. Don't get me wrong, I have tried to put it into words on numerous occasions, and some bits are easier than others. But even now, if I had to try and tell the whole story myself, I'd still feel the surge of a scream inside me, a cry of anguish that would confound the spell-check, a torrent of grief and rage jostling for ascendancy.

And yet I wanted to get this book out of me and exorcise the ghosts. I wanted to share the journeys that Mike and I went on, together and apart. But I needed help. I needed someone I could absolutely trust with my barest emotions (not something I find easy at the best of times), someone with empathy and understanding who could become my voice.

The stars aligned and I struck gold. The phantom wordsmith behind these pages is someone who shared some of this journey with me. He became a part of the journey. First appearing as the hairy cameraman tasked with filming my exploits, Drew became a close friend and it is him I owe for bringing my story to life.

I want to reassure you, the reader, that the purpose of this foreword is confessional. I want to be candid. I stand behind the sense, the sentiment and the truth of everything you are about to read. I just wanted you to know that even the writing of the book has been a part of my journey, and of a shared journey. As much as the events themselves, the painstaking process of recounting, discussing and describing has been a cathartic release. Tears and laughter have gone into writing this book, and if I can inspire anything like the same in you, that is all the reward I need.

PART ONE

THE BEGINNING AND THE END

Walking the Plank

I won't lie, I'm bloody terrified.

I'm standing on the right end of a gangplank that sticks out ten or so feet from the top of a cliff. I say 'right end' because the other end, the utterly 'wrong end', comes to a sudden halt a couple of hundred metres above what could arguably be described as a picturesque canyon, complete with a charming river bubbling serenely along its bottom. I can't appreciate that right now. As far as I'm concerned, despite the obvious metaphor, I'm staring right into the abyss. A terrifyingly literal, figurative, actual abyss.

I've got straps, buckles and a harness that goes between my legs. There are clips and carabiners and a rope or two that look far too thin to take my weight (the fact that I even need a safety rope makes me feel even more unsafe), all attaching me to some enormous washing line that stretches across the increasingly unattractive canyon to the cliff face on the other side.

'Smile for the camera,' a cheeky Kiwi voice rings out. What camera? Where? And what on earth is there for me to smile about? I look around like an idiot, putting on my best dry-mouthed grin for posterity.

'Are you sure this is safe?' I ask moronically, desperately, hoping these mad Kiwis might magically decide that, in fact, it isn't, then sensibly suggest we all go back into Queenstown for a nice cup of coffee and a . . .

'Piece of cake, mate.'

'Yes please.' Everyone deserves a last meal, surely.

It's just a zip wire. Easy, right? Except this is The Fox, the world's highest cliff 'jump', and it's no ordinary zip. The plan is I will run, yes run, off this creaky plank and hurl myself onto the mercy of the inadequate looking thread that attaches me to the wire. Then, almost immediately, that wire just ends. It ends. I will fall off it and, in an ideal world, be caught by a secondary wire before rocketing over 450 metres of worryingly thin air to the other cliff, all 200 metres above the rocks and river at the bottom of what I've now decided is the most revolting looking canyon I've ever had the misfortune of gazing upon.

Hang on, back up. Fall?

Now, I've already done a few 'jumps', bungies and what have you, so you'd think this would be a cinch. And that's exactly what I thought. It's a zip wire, how hard can it be? Well, it turns out it's a lot harder to pluck up the courage to run off a cliff than it is to step (even reluctantly) from a bungy platform. Part of me wonders if it might be easier if I just get on my belly and slowly crawl to the edge, clinging to the gangplank with my fingertips before ungracefully dribbling off at the last possible moment.

But it's not just the run. It's the drop. The fall. I am supposed to willingly charge off a cliff with the full knowledge that I'm effectively going to then simulate falling off a zip wire. Who thinks this stuff up?

I won't lie, I'm bloody terrified.

'Shout Mike's name as you jump,' someone yells encouragement from behind me.

Mike.

That's why I'm here.

I'm here for Mike.

Because Mike died.

If you've read the blurb of this book, you'll already know a little about Mike. Mike was my brother. He died of motor neurone disease and left me a bucket list of things to do on his behalf. I had no idea what they would be until just before I had to do them, but if I tell you that hurling myself into that canyon wasn't the hardest thing he made me do, well, you get a hint of what made him tick.

'Just run and scream Mike's name,' comes another shout.

I get it. The shaking fear in me steadies in that moment, and I can feel Mike. If he was here now I'd be getting it right in the neck. I've already given it the full bravado treatment on the way up here, swaggering and clowning about, doing anything but face the reality of what I'm about to do. If Mike was here and he saw me fannying around, fearfully vacillating like this, I'd never hear the end of it. And if he was in my place . . . well he wouldn't be in my place. He'd already be on the other side. He wouldn't have hesitated for a moment. He'd probably have thrown himself off backwards while giving me the finger and laughing. And if we'd managed to get here when he was sick, he'd probably have found a way to do it in his wheelchair. If he was here now, I'd have already done it too. Anything rather than give him ammunition to ridicule me for days.

I feel his name in my throat. I'm going to do it. I have to do it now. I sure as hell can't shout his name and then chicken out. I wish he was here. The whole emotional gravity of this journey drags my feet downwards, screams at me to stay safe, stay alive, stay in control. But that's not what Mike wanted. He wanted me to surrender to the lack of control and to really live.

Channelling my inner lemming, I open my mouth, the 'M' of his name already forming, and I run.

'MIIIIIIIIIIIIIIIIIKE,' I scream at the top of my lungs. I'm not sure if the 'K' really comes out. I'm too busy flailing like a rag doll.

Then I'm caught, jarringly, by the second zip line. And as I slide out in the sunshine across the canyon, I laugh. Euphoric.

Where Are the Brakes?

We had donkeys when I was a small boy. We had all sorts. Mum and Dad loved animals. The donkeys were rescues. We also had chickens, sheep, pigs and a particularly mean and fractious greylag goose we named Smoky Joe.

'Mum, make it go faster. Make it go faster,' I goaded Mum cockily, repeatedly. Eventually Mum had enough of my lip and gave the dear old beast of burden I was riding a little crack across its rear with a riding crop. The donkey lurched forward like a possessed greyhound, with me suddenly clinging on for dear life, screaming.

And then it rammed its front hooves into the ground and stopped. On a dime. I didn't. Instead, I hurtled less than gracefully over the top of its head and fell into a crumpled heap on the ground.

'Don't be so stupid, Royd,' a voice in my head spoke up once the shock had subsided. 'Don't ask for things you can't handle. Sedate is safe.'

◆

Mike was five years younger than me, though by the time he was eight it already didn't matter. He endured the usual trials of a younger brother, inheriting all my old clothes. He got my primary school uniform, and old pairs of jeans all covered in patches, that no longer fitted me. My first bike became his first bike.

Long before Mum and Dad got divorced, we grew up on a smallholding on the outskirts of Halkyn, a little village in the wilds of North Wales. There wasn't much to the village: just a pub and a shop and a sprinkle of houses. Dad, when he wasn't running his printing business, was the backbone of the local countryside committee, and Mum, who had been a nurse right up until Mike came along and spent much of her time involved with CND and fighting injustice with the likes of Amnesty International, had lots of local friends who were all into horsey stuff. They were both active in the local community; they would sometimes put on fundraisers in one of our outbuildings, or 'the big shed' as we used to call it, hosting discos or bonfire parties that people from the village would attend.

Mandy, our sister, is a year and a half older than me, so closer in age to me than Mike was. We played together when we were young, when Mike was too small, and formed a club with our best friends that had its meetings in the loft above the pigsty. But Mandy grew up faster than me, as girls do, and she hit her teenage years at a time when I still had years left of being an annoying kid. Our adventures and treasure hunts didn't last as long as I wanted.

When I was thirteen, Adam and the Ants did a gig at the local leisure centre. I was a massive fan, as was Mandy. Her friend's dad was the manager at the leisure centre, so she got invited to the gig and to go backstage.

'Brilliant, I can't wait to go,' I said excitedly when I heard the news.

'Oh, you can't go,' Mandy told me. 'You're too young.'

I was gutted. It wasn't fair. And it only added insult to injury when, after the event, she revealed to me that I could have gone after all as there had been an area set aside where younger kids could hang out. She just about redeemed herself though, by getting Mr Ant to sign her programme for me.

That was about the time we stopped doing much together. She went on and did teenage girl things, finished school and went to art college and all that grown-up stuff. I resented her being older, more rebellious and able to do things I couldn't yet do. We didn't drift apart or anything; she just wasn't a kid any more.

Fortunately by then, Mike was old enough to start getting stuck into the things boys enjoyed doing.

◆

As an adult, I'm a big fan of rural living. My house in Wales is my ultimate sanctuary. You'll probably catch me a few times, when faced with some adventurous bucket list task, wishing I was back here drinking a cup of tea in my garden. Weirdly, it was just this kind of secluded and peaceful upbringing I wanted for my son, Story. But when I was a child, especially a young teenager, I was hugely frustrated by our remoteness. I felt trapped. I had to rely on my parents to take me places, like to friends' houses, which didn't happen as often as I'd have liked.

I stayed a few times with my best friend at the time, Richard, who lived in a town a short drive from us. He lived on an actual street, where actual kids would play until nine in the evening. And we'd watch TV. What luxury! We weren't allowed to watch much television at home. I used to go to school on a Monday and listen to everyone talking about *Tiswas* or Kenny Everett or whatever else they had seen over the weekend, and not have a clue what they were banging on about. Home was more about feeding the animals and doing chores.

I don't want to come across as if I don't value my childhood. I do, immensely, now at least. I'm just trying to convey how isolated we were. As kids, we didn't have any friends in the village, a sad state of affairs not helped by the fact that Mum's own religious upbringing and continued faith meant we went to the nearest Catholic school, which was in a different town, in a completely different direction, where no one in my area went. And I hated it.

To be fair, the primary school was decent. But high school was dramatically worse. I started there with my best friend but, by the cruel and fickle whim of fate, we got put in different classes. I got stuck in the lower one, filled, naturally, with all the troublemakers. The path of least resistance, characteristically now my favourite path of all, was not to try and achieve academically, but to remain anonymous amongst the ranks of the naughtier kids. I'm over six foot now but I really was a late bloomer, the runt of the litter, barely five-foot-sod-all until I was nineteen. And considering I left school at fifteen, I was the weedy kid for the duration.

Mike's school route was similar to mine. He went to the same primary (dressed in his hand-me-down uniform) and did a whole year at the same high school (which he surprisingly really loved) before my parents saw fit to better his education and send him to a private school. It was one of those military-type schools that insist on everyone shining their boots and parading around like little soldiers. I found out much later that Mike resented being pulled away from his friends at the other school, and hated the new one.

For me, being the short-arse around school made it easier to keep a low profile (pun intended) but, like most schools, bullying was an issue. It wasn't terrible, but it was enough to instil in me distaste for violence of any kind. I loathed the constant sense of peer pressure. I would sit and wistfully gaze out of the window of North Block during science class, doing my level best to ignore the lesson and instead look across the fields to the hill on the horizon near where my home was, wishing I was there.

Wishing I was there with Mike, playing.

◆

I suppose if we had gone to the local school instead of the Catholic one, and if we had known more kids our own ages in the village, and if Mandy hadn't gone off and started menstruating and doing whatever teenage girls do, Mike and I might not have been as close as we were. I might have even considered hanging out with (or 'looking after') my little brother as a royal pain in the proverbial. But I didn't. So I'm grateful for all of it. I'm grateful for growing up and not knowing many people, for going to the shit school, and for Mandy becoming an adult before we did. Because what I got instead was a brother.

As soon as Mike was old enough, we were off. We were outside at any and every opportunity, playing, riding our bikes and climbing trees. Where we lived was on its own little hill, and from that hill you could look over the Wirral and Liverpool and the coast. And to go anywhere you had to go down that hill, a serious incline for kids' bikes.

I don't know if Mike was overly aware of the age difference between us, but he quickly worked hard to make it count for nothing. He was either desperate to prove himself to his big brother, or he was just bloody fearless. I had the edge over him physically for a while, but what he lacked in stature (even relative to little me) he made up for in gusto. So when we set off down that hill on our bikes there was an explicit dare to not use our brakes. Yeah, right! Remember the donkey? I'd be hunched over the handlebars, slowing my progress to a comfortable speed while he sped off like a rocket, not slowing until after he'd hit the cattle-grid at the bottom with a great rattling sonic boom.

Beyond that was the lake. It used to be surrounded by lead mines, and the run-off from the mines made the water horribly polluted. We used to throw stones there, testing our accuracy by trying to hit whatever target was nominated. That was something I was better at for a while, being that much older and stronger. But the more the physical gap between us diminished, the more competitive we became. Mike always had to climb higher up a tree than me, higher than I deemed prudent. At some point, as the years went by, he decided he hadn't really fully climbed a tree until his head was up above the topmost leaf.

And yet somehow he never fell. Nothing bad ever happened. Sure, there was the odd scrape, a cut here and a bruise there, but no broken bones. And everything became a competition. Who could throw further? Who could climb higher? Who could marinate and bake the toughest champion conker? Who could go faster on their bike? Who could pull the longest wheelie? I might have done okay at the wheelies on my Tomahawk (think Chopper, but cheaper), but I couldn't keep up with him. Because he dared to go faster. He dared to climb higher. He dared to push himself. We became closer and closer as we grew older, and more and more competitive.

And for the most part, Mike outdid me.

◆

I had asthma when I was a child, and the odd allergy – to horses of all things, which was less than ideal on a farm. Mike was similar, though even less noticeably. Neither of us had much in the way of medical complaints as kids, but the one big one for Mike, when he was around ten, was a meningitis scare.

The worst part of it was him needing to have a lumbar puncture, a spinal tap, to test for viral meningitis. I remember sitting in the waiting room of the local cottage hospital . . . that description says it all really; it was definitely more cottage than hospital. I'm sure everyone there was fully qualified and excellent at their jobs, but it felt at the time, listening to Mike's screams of agony from the next room, that some part-time nurse had hurriedly read a book that morning on how to perform the procedure and was botching and sweating their way through it. I could hear the terror in Mike's voice, and the whole experience was something that was going to come back to haunt us.

He was fine, it turned out. It wasn't viral meningitis. It was nothing a good old course of antibiotics couldn't sort out. But what it left him with was a lifelong phobia of needles.

And that was it, until November 2010. At the age of thirty-five, having barely been sick a day in his life, Mike got ill. He had a really high temperature and a rash for about four days, along with flu symptoms, and he made a slow recovery. It was odd, given his clean bill of health for most of his life, but it wasn't life changing by any means.

A month later, Mike began to feel a strange cramp in his left calf muscle. Again, when he told me, I thought nothing of it. We've all had cramp. You stretch it out, wait a bit and it goes. That said, it's usually associated with exercise and, despite Mike's active lifestyle, this cramp didn't seem related to anything strenuous. Just pointing his foot or squeezing his toes seemed to escalate into his left calf seizing up, and it wouldn't go away. And even when it did, it came back. Always in the same place.

It continued for several months, to the point that it became aggravating for Mike. But it still wasn't particularly worrying. He wondered if it might be some hang-up from the fever he had gone through in November, and eventually went to see his GP. As I recall, the doctor gave him some muscle relaxants or something similar and sent him on his way.

They didn't work. The cramp continued for six months, as did the visits to the doctor and the seemingly random drug prescriptions, before other symptoms began to appear that affected his hands and arms. He started feeling like his hands were getting weaker. But still, dramatic as that may sound, none of us were overly concerned. I mean, I feel like my hands are weaker now than they were. I'm pretty sure I've got arthritis in my thumbs from excessive Candy Crush playing. But that's life, right? I'm not going, 'oh no, what's happening to me?' and neither was Mike at that point.

We had no idea then that in four years, Mike would be gone for ever.

Chief Rocka

I hear my name being called.

'Mike's brother, Royd, is going to say a few words.' That's Mary, officiating at the funeral. The words wash over me, echoey and vague.

Mike is gone. I have just helped bring his coffin into a packed crematorium to the rapping strains of *Chief Rocka* by Lords of the Underground. What a tune. Our friends got it. I saw several heads nodding along to the beat, reluctant smiles on sad faces. We've all lost our Chief Rocka, our main man.

A few words. How can I say goodbye to Mike in just a few words? But then again, I'm not sure I can summon the strength to utter even one.

I move towards the pulpit, towards the few stairs that lead up to it. It's now. It has to be now. The silence is stifling, draped like a shroud over the congregation. I can feel every pair of eyes on me, but I can't look at anyone. I can sense the collective assumption that this is going to be beyond awful. *Hold it together Royd*, hundreds of people seem to be willing me. *Hold it together.*

A chair creaks. Someone sniffs. A muffled cough echoes around the room. It has to be now. Focus. This matters. It really matters. I just want it to be over. I want to shatter this cloying quiet.

I find the first step and lift my foot from the mud I feel like I'm walking in. The second step waits for me.

It has to be now.

I kick my other foot forward, hard into the side of the step. Bang. And I'm falling. My momentum carries me forwards, and down. I crumple onto the remaining steps and my head bangs into the side of the pulpit. The crash thunders around the room.

I lie there, hidden from the congregation, feeling the silence somehow intensify. Nobody knows what to do, or think.

I did it.

◆

I remember Mike calling his best mate, and asking him to come round.

'I can't today, Mike.' Ali was on speaker. 'I'll come round tomorrow.'

Mike grinned at me and lifted the phone closer to his mouth. 'Erm, I'm dying, mate. Today would be good.' Humour was his means of glossing over the stark terribleness of what he was going through.

Mike and I never talked about him dying. Not since the day we found out he had motor neurone disease. So we hadn't made any plans for the funeral. There were no decrees from Mike, no outlandish requests or detailed playlists. Mike had been all about living, until he just couldn't do that any longer. He died at 10.20 in the morning on 28 January 2015, and then it was over to us. We knew him well, and we knew what he would have wanted.

There was a two-week backlog at the crematorium, presumably because of the Christmas period, so we were given the option of having his funeral on either the twelfth or the fifteenth of February. It was a no brainer. Mike's birthday would have been the thirteenth:

his fortieth birthday. We didn't want Mike to be buried at forty, having passed away at thirty-nine, it just felt odd, so we immediately opted for the earlier date.

The two weeks passed quickly. Numbly. There was a lot to organise, but everything was done in an emotional vacuum. We arranged for an elegant wicker coffin, sorted the flowers, the music, the venue, and I tried to put pen to paper and write my public farewell to my brother.

We all wrote to him privately as well. The letters went in his coffin with him, along with a leaf I had plucked from the tree above Bilbo's house on the Hobbiton set in New Zealand when Mike and I went there, and a piece of dragon's gold. Yes, actual dragon's gold. Okay, let me qualify that one. On the same trip, we visited the set of *The Hobbit*, which was filming at the time. I was lucky enough to have been involved in *The Lord of the Rings* films so had met Peter Jackson then, but it was all new and exciting to Mike. After meeting Peter, we bumped into my close friend, Jed Brophy, who was playing the dwarf, Nori. Jed had asked Peter at some point how much he wanted him to be 'in character' on set.

'Look, Nori's a thief,' Peter had told him in his soft Kiwi tone, 'so be a thief. But if you steal anything, you need to do it under my nose and not let me catch you.'

Jed handed me a piece of gold from Smaug the dragon's horde. One of many he had successfully pilfered. So that went in Mike's coffin as well.

◆

A few days prior to the funeral, Mike's girlfriend, Laura, handed me a piece of paper. Laura had only been with Mike for a year before he got ill, and stuck with him when many others would have run for the hills. To my mind, Laura is an angel.

'Mike wanted you to have this,' she told me.

It was the first task on the bucket list that Mike had prepared for me. I knew about the list, but had no idea what was on it. He had started writing it at the beginning of his illness, and originally it was all the things he wanted to do, before, you know . . . He had wanted us to return to New Zealand together, where he had decided most of the tasks needed to happen, and where he wanted me to experience all the things that he could no longer physically undertake.

But the thing about MND (motor neurone disease) is that it doesn't hang about. It's a rapid and steady decline with only one possible outcome. So when travel became impossible for Mike, we decided I would do it alone.

And he wanted it filmed.

'You make films, Royd,' he told me. 'Make a film of this.'

The list became something he bequeathed to me. Something I needed to complete. A documentary that needed to be financed and crewed and shot and edited and delivered. It was something dear to Mike's heart, not because he wanted to live on after his death, not a vanity project or some mechanism to posthumously stitch me up. It was born from what he went through with MND, an unspeakably horrible and lonely experience. It was meant as a way to let people know about this disease, to raise awareness and address the negative and often dismissive attitude of the medical profession to a condition that comes with such a bleak prognosis. It was about finding a way to get much-needed help and support to sufferers, and to their families.

I would do anything Mike asked of me. I knew about the list and I could only imagine the terrors he had in store for me, but I was determined I would make it happen somehow. I couldn't fail him. And apart from anything else I already yearned to hear Mike's voice again, something reading the tasks on the list would provide.

But it wasn't something I was thinking about in the lead-up to Mike's funeral.

◆

We'd been offered the chance to see him in his casket, and I had debated with myself whether or not that was something I wanted. Something I perhaps needed. After all, my last memory of his face was when I tried to close his eyes after turning his breathing machine off. Seeing him lying in peace might have replaced that image that I carry with me to this day, might have offered me some kind of closure. But I decided against it. Mike hadn't been able to lie flat for pretty much a year before he died, let alone sleep in a bed. It didn't feel right that I should see him lying in a coffin. It wouldn't have made sense. It wouldn't have been Mike. And maybe I just wanted to deny myself that closure. Maybe I needed the pain.

We actually had two funerals for Mike. The first one, in the morning, was held in the chapel of rest at the funeral directors. The whole family was there. Mum, Dad, Mandy and her children, Jacob and Megan, Story, Mike's son, Edan, and other members of the extended family. The moment I saw Mike's coffin, I crumbled. I lost all control of the words that came out of my mouth and I very nearly collapsed. And I cried. Uncontrollably. I was devastated. This was happening. It had been taken out of my hands. Out of everyone's hands. I hadn't seen Mike since he died. I stood at the back, feeling faint. Feeling how everyone's individual grief seemed to amplify everyone else's.

It was a beautiful service. Mike's wicker coffin was classy and chic. The flowers were exquisite. The younger members of the family were able to express their grief and be supported, free to move around the room. Jacob and Edan comforted each other while Megan handed out white roses. Story read *Bilbo's Last Song*. It was intimate and private. And what got me most wasn't Dad crying – I'd never seen him cry before, but it just seemed inevitable that he would – no, what got me was seeing Chris, Mandy's husband, in floods of tears. Somehow it made it all hit home. The room was replete with pain and loss and heartache.

After that, we waited at Mike's house. It was surreal being there, suited and booted and shedding tears, without Mike. The hearse came, and we crept after it in a quietly shocked and incomprehensible silence to the second funeral at the crematorium. I had no idea how many people would be waiting there for Mike, and for us. Ten, maybe? A hundred?

Loads! A great crowd of people had gathered outside, and were waiting in solemn silence for their Chief Rocka. We got out of the car and for a while there was a peculiar 'us and them' moment that didn't sit right with me, so I went over to them. There were a lot of my friends and Mike's friends there, all looking at me awkwardly, not knowing what to say or do. I remember seeing Scottish Ali there, a friend of mine and Mike's who I hadn't seen in years. In the instant I saw his face I pictured him as I had last seen him, before any of this happened, out partying and drinking and loving life with Mike and me. And it just broke me. I walked into his open arms, held on to him and sobbed.

Then everyone was invited inside. The family waited until last, and Mike's coffin was loaded onto a gurney. We wheeled him solemnly into the crematorium. Dad led the way, followed by me and Story, Edan, Laura, Chris, Jacob and Mike's best mate Ali.

And *Chief Rocka* blared out of the speakers . . .

In the front pew, I fumbled in my pocket to make sure I had the piece of paper with my speech on. And the other piece of paper. The beginning of the bucket list.

I read the words, Mike's words.

'1. The Funeral Trip. Please make a tit of yourself before you speak. Trip over and make it really dramatic. Make everyone laugh for me and lighten the moment.'

Perfect.

◆

I pick myself up from the floor. I'm not really hurt, but it was an even more spectacular trip than the one I had intended. I really did lose my balance. That's method acting for you. I did it. You're welcome, Mike.

The room feels frozen in time. I look around. Most people are looking down. They can't even look at me. They're all thinking, 'Royd has just made a horrible moment completely unspeakable.' I feel their pain for me. There's a scent of panic in the air, a room full of mourners wondering if they should come forward and offer me some kind of support. Thankfully I prewarned Dad and Story.

'Are you okay?' Mary rushes towards me from the sidelines, arms outstretched to pick me up, but I'm already standing. My legs feel strong. I feel an unexpected sense of clarity, of purpose. Maybe even control.

I hold up my hands and offer her a sheepish, apologetic smile. I turn to everyone else, mutely reassuring them. I'm fine. I'm good. And I am. I actually am. So I milk the moment. Mike has somehow turned me into a performer at the exact moment I would otherwise have been irretrievably dumbstruck. I slowly reach into my jacket pocket and pull out my speech. I unfold the piece of paper and settle before looking out at the shell-shocked faces again. Finally, I pull out the other piece of paper, the one that says in big letters for everyone to read 'TRIP OVER', and I hold it up high.

'That's what Mike wanted me to do,' I say as I breathe out a great lungful of relief.

There's a second of quiet while the penny drops, and then the room laughs with me.

Thank you Mike. Without this, without me having to look like a tit, I wouldn't have been able to stand up here now and say what I want to say. You gave me that. And thank you for making everyone here laugh. For uniting us. From beyond the grave. I get it, you're gone – but we're here to remember your life, not your death.

What's next?

Ashes and Thongs

I look better in clothes than I do naked. It's that, not the fact that it's below freezing and I'm on the side of a snow-covered mountain that bothers me right now. I wish I'd gone to the gym like I planned. Brad Pitt in *Fight Club* is what I was aiming for, but it's sure as shit not what I've got.

I was expecting one of the tasks on the bucket list to involve me showing some flesh, but it didn't have to be quite so early on, did it? It's not something I like to do. Mike and I never changed in the same room, both maintaining a competitive pretence that each had the better body than the other. It's rare that I even strip off and jump in a swimming pool. And it's pure vanity, I admit it. Nothing more. I'm no potato, but since I'm currently being filmed by my friends, I really wanted whoever might end up watching this to say, 'wow, what a body – I'll have some of that!'

So while I fully intended to go to the gym, I'm also predisposed to laziness. And vain and lazy don't mix well. I've just spent ages getting everyone in position to film this, to film my disgusting body. And yes, it is mighty cold too. Bonus!

I should explain. I'm currently in Avoriaz, in the French Alps, on a slope with my snowboard, wearing boots and a coat. And not much beneath it except a snug leopard-print thong. Aside from that, perhaps in the spirit of dubious anonymity, I'm wearing sunglasses and a lovely shocking pink cowboy hat. Oh, and I have a pair of fluffy handcuffs attached to my wrist.

I knew there would be a task to complete here, in Avoriaz, and I knew it would be horrible. It wasn't going to be 'Go on Royd, have an amazing day snowboarding and maybe learn a new trick.' Obviously. But a thong? Really?

This is Mike stitching me up.

Thanks Mike.

◆

Both Mike and I were keen skateboarders in our early twenties. We had a friend called Cleggie, in Chester, who built a mini ramp in his back garden. So we honed our skills there. Well, Mike did. Mike being Mike, he would always have to ollie the highest and jump the biggest gap. I never even dropped in on the ramp. I would bottle it. I just didn't have Mike's nerve. Any time I did try anything, my ankles usually paid the price. Because I was nervous. Mike, always fearlessly airborne, never suffered anything worse than the odd bruise or scrape.

When we were kids and it snowed, we'd be straight outside to make a toboggan run. There were hills all around us at home. We'd make ramps and jumps and little stunt courses. Mike was the first to buy a snowboard. Having never been on one before, he just stuck it on his feet like it was the most natural thing in the world and set off down a hill. I, of course, didn't bother. It just seemed crazy, strapping yourself to a glorified plank and sliding perilously down a snowy slope.

But years later I came to it. I built up my confidence and I loved it. I started going on snowboarding trips with a group of friends and we went every year for about fifteen years. We began with a

24

few trips to Chamonix, in France, but soon switched to Avoriaz. It's a nice cheap holiday: a simple package deal that includes the flight from Manchester to Geneva, transfer to the resort and basic self-catering accommodation. All you need. Well, all that and snow, which never seems to be in short supply.

I'd never gone with Mike. He boarded occasionally with his friends but had never been to Avoriaz with me. His strange cramping seemed to have fizzled out, so I suggested that we combine forces and make a big trip of it.

Avoriaz is gorgeous. Vehicles aren't allowed in the town, just horse-drawn sleds and the odd Skidoo. The centre of the town is compact and full of bars and, being something of a regular, I knew all the best places to go. There were ten of us, and as soon as we'd settled into our accommodation we hit the bars. There's just something about this place. It brings out the absolute lush in all of us. A couple of hours in and we were all mullered. Mike, generous as ever, seemed to be constantly at the bar getting the rounds in. Our efforts to beat him to it just resulted in even more drinks, to the point there seemed to be an endless supply of beer and shots, Jägerbombs and the disgustingly medicinal tasting Fernet-Branca.

Eventually we decided to go to a club a couple of doors down. Some of the group decided they'd had enough and crawled off home. Probably a wise decision, but the rest of us were having way too much fun. We carried on drinking, and dancing, and laughing. Mike happened to end up dancing next to a girl. Too close to her, apparently, as her boyfriend took offence and muscled his way between them. Pretty inebriated by now, Mike was amused by this display of machismo. At this time nobody had a clue just how ill Mike was, but I think we all sensed something wasn't quite right. Even then there was a subconscious group mentality of protectiveness towards him. So, at this point when Mike's friends, Ali and Slick, saw what was going on, they got up and put themselves between him and this guy.

Mike just shrugged it off and headed to the bar, but Slick somehow attracted the attention of the French bouncers. They decided to chuck him out. Slick's not a big guy, and these two bouncers were enormous, so it wasn't going to end well. Long story short (since there are a few alcohol-induced gaps in my memory), we all ended up out in the snow-covered street trying to prevent Slick getting the crap beaten out of him. Well, not all. Mike and a friend of mine, Andy, were still at the bar. Eventually I persuaded the bouncers to let me go back in briefly to get our coats and the rest of our party, and I found Mike and Andy standing at the bar with a long line of shots.

'There's been a bit of trouble,' I explained. 'We have to go.'

'But we just got these shots,' Mike grinned at me. And him and Andy looked at each other and proceeded to neck about five Jägerbombs each. And we all know that's never a good idea, especially when you're about to go outside into the freezing cold air.

Trudging through the deep snow back to the apartment, it was clear Mike was really quite drunk.

'I'm gonna puke,' he groaned, then, 'I can't puke,' and finally, 'I need to puke.'

So Andy climbed on Mike's back and started trying to force his fingers into his mouth. 'This will make you puke,' he laughed.

And that was just the first night.

When we hit the slopes the next morning it was glorious. The weather was sublime. I got a real kick out of showing Mike places that I knew, places that meant something to me. It was the same later in the year when we went to New Zealand together.

26

Mike and I had slightly different approaches to snowboarding. For him it was all about having the best gear. Mike and Slick were fiercely competitive about that. So Mike had this amazing board that he had bought especially for this trip. And then there was me. I had some hand-me-down board borrowed from a mate of mine, but that was fine with me. You could stick a plank of wood on my feet and it wouldn't make a huge difference. While Mike was always intent on the more extreme aspects of, well everything really, I prefer to enjoy my downhill journey. I like to stop at various points and enjoy the amazing views, maybe roll a cheeky cigarette and have a drop of my homemade damson gin from my hip flask. Sure, I might do the odd mini (and I mean tiny) trick on a little bump on the slope if I know where it is, but I genuinely have no need for fancy equipment. It would be utterly wasted on me.

That's not to say that Mike and I weren't competitive. We were. Always. It's an unwritten (but well-established) rule that if someone stacks it in front of you on the slope then it is your absolute mission to approach them as fast as you can, then stop really hard and spray them with as much powdery snow as humanly possible.

Mike ended up on his arse quite a lot that holiday. And I dutifully sprayed him with half a mountain of snow. For a while I revelled in the fact that, for once, I was better at something than him. He didn't snowboard as much as me, so why shouldn't I be? On one particular slope Mike was the last in our group to come down, and seemed to be having trouble getting to his feet.

'Do you want me to come up and help you?' I shouted mockingly up the hill, enjoying the moment.

'No, no. I'm good,' came back the irritated reply.

A while later, and still no Mike carving through the snow. 'You sure you don't want to ask me for help?' I called out.

'No, I'm all good.'

We waited.

'Mike?'

'I'm coming.'

And we waited.

'Mike, do you need help?'

'No!'

And we waited some more.

'Just bloody GO!' I shouted, and Mike's laughter rolled down the icy slope towards us, closely followed by him on his board.

The thing about snowboarding, for those who don't know, is that it's a bit of a schlep to get on your feet sometimes. It's a technique, and it takes a little effort and a little strength. You start on your arse then put your hands behind you, push up with your arms and legs at the same time, all while trying to stay balanced and not end up on your arse all over again. It also helps if you don't have some tool of an older brother sliding up to you and showering you in snow.

Mike got frustrated. He started finding it difficult to get up after a fall. Eventually I realised that waiving the unwritten rule of snow showering was a necessary kindness. It was funny the first few times, but became rapidly less so. I started helping Mike instead. Well, I offered to help him. Fiercely independent as ever, he pushed me away and wanted to do everything himself. He'd never needed my help before.

'I can do it,' he said. And the next time, 'I'm good. I just need to—'

In the end, reluctantly, he held out his hands and let me help him up.

Mike was getting weaker. We didn't think it at the time though. We just thought he was rusty and out of practice. We assumed if we'd stayed a bit longer he would have got it, and inevitably out-snowboarded all of us. He accepted more help as the holiday

28

went on, but there was never a sense of 'something's wrong with me'. It was more frustrating than concerning, and he was fine in the evenings, as we trudged through the deep snow of Avoriaz town to the bar to get hammered all over again.

One morning my friends and I set off early, planning to touch base with Mike and his friends at lunchtime. Avoriaz is massive, one of the biggest linked lift areas in the world. My friends and I have been there about ten times and we're still doing runs we've never even seen before. So the odds of Mike and I just bumping into each other were extremely slim.

We had been snowboarding most of the morning and had noticed a lift we hadn't taken in the ten years of going there, to a part of the valley we'd never visited. In the spirit of adventure, we climbed aboard the lift and began the slow ascent towards the undiscovered snow. It was a long slow climb, over a road and alongside a huge expanse of steep forest to the right. The usual piste, our most likely destination, was to our left.

And then I heard something, something I really didn't expect to hear, drifting up to me from way down to the right amongst the trees. Mike laughing. It was faint at first, which made me question my ears. Then, clear as a bell, Mike's roar of laughter.

'Mike!' I shouted. And he called back.

It turned out they had taken this same random lift and, on reaching the top, had ventured in the opposite direction of the piste and down into the trees. Into virgin, deep, powdery snow. When we got to the top we followed their tracks and found them in a clearing in the forest. It was a picture-perfect location, rich in unspoiled swathes of deep powder. How Mike and his friends managed to just stumble across it on their first visit to Avoriaz, I'll never know. But how we found them there that day was against all probability. Even if I'd phoned him and had precise directions, I could never have found them. It was his laughter that led me there. The sun came out and the sky was an electric blue. We hung out, messed about, did tricks and drank my damson gin.

It was that day that we clung to during Mike's illness. Even though he had struggled physically there, it was because of the time we shared in Avoriaz that his snowboard was always leant up against the wall in his house, while he sat nearby in his wheelchair. It gave him hope right until the day he passed away. He would look at that board and convince himself that one day he would get back on it and go back to that same place with me, and have another perfect day.

He never did.

◆

I had my 'Mike moment' yesterday, the real reason I wanted to come back here to Avoriaz. I'm here with friends, some of the same friends who were here with me and Mike. We all went out into the mountains yesterday to that secret spot and scattered some of Mike's ashes. We passed around the damson gin and remembered that amazing day we had all had together. As you'd expect, it wasn't easy to find. It snows differently every time. But we found it. And it was just as I remembered.

I have a few small caskets of Mike's ashes. I ordered them in specially from America, and the funeral director put some of Mike's ashes in them for me. There're a few places that meant a lot to Mike, and I want to be sure he gets to go back to them. So now he's back in Avoriaz with me. With us. He's here but he's not here.

Okay, okay. I know you're all waiting for me to take my coat off and reveal this magnificent leopard-print thong and my disgusting body. I'm already getting funny looks and laughs just because of this pink cowboy hat, so the thought of baring nearly all is distinctly unappealing. You'd think I might have borrowed Mike's all-singing and all-dancing board, the one that he kept next to him, his inspiration, the one that's a billion times better than my crappy old thing. I went to Avoriaz once while he was ill and thought he might appreciate me giving it a run.

'I could take your snowboard,' I suggested.

'No way,' came the predictable response. 'You'd wreck it.'

It was like he didn't trust me with it. Like it was too good for me. Like only he could handle such an incredible piece of engineering. 'You stick to your wooden plank, Royd,' he might as well have said.

I'm procrastinating. It's cold, and there're people around. People with eyes. People who will see me nearly naked. But I have to do it. For Mike. That's all I need to remember; I'll do anything for Mike. I can't not do it.

I stand up and slide out of my coat. The slope is really icy. If I fall, this is going to hurt. Since there's little point hanging around, I set off, albeit slowly. Well, nobody said I had to do this at speed, did they? Good, because I can't do speed. Don't fall. Don't fall. Everyone is looking at me. Don't fall. I wish I'd gone to the gym. Don't fall. DO NOT FALL.

And then, after the initial nerves, everything is suddenly okay. It doesn't matter that I look ridiculous in this thong, that my arse is hanging out in the chilly Alpine air for everyone to see. It doesn't matter that I'm not Brad Pitt. I feel a grin stretch over my face. It's not bad at all. I look for the cameras. There's one. I head towards it, and shift my weight, turning the board in a gentle arc in the snow.

'Arse shot!' I shout gleefully as I turn my back to the camera. I bend forward to stop the board, and give it a tasty close-up.

31

I straighten up. Wow, I feel great. I feel liberated. You know what, I couldn't care less that I'm basically naked and on show to half of Avoriaz. I've done it. Tripping over at Mike's funeral was one thing, and it was a while ago. That was a whole different experience, something I had to do on a day that didn't feel real. This, though . . . this is different. This is what the rest of the list might feel like.

And I've done it. I didn't want to do it. I really, really didn't want to do it. But it wasn't that bad. I can do this list. What's next? I can do it. No sweat.

Yeah, you keep telling yourself that, Royd.

Down the Rabbit Hole

Mike's experiences in Avoriaz made him realise that something wasn't quite right. We hadn't thought much of it at the time, but Mike's mounting frustration at finding it difficult to stand up on his board eventually became a genuine concern.

Back home, Mike began ramping up his efforts to get to the bottom of the worsening weakness in his legs and arms. He saw his doctor and was soon getting bounced around a whole gamut of medical professionals for all kinds of tests. Nobody seemed to offer any kind of diagnosis or even air a suspicion as to what the cause of his symptoms might be. Instead he found himself being referred on and referred on. He saw doctors, neurologists, physiotherapists, you name it. He even tried going private in the hope that somebody might at least explain the results of the copious tests he was enduring.

One of the many, many, many shit things about motor neurone disease is that there is no single test for it. You only get a diagnosis for MND by ruling out every other possible disease and ailment that could fit the bill. Hence the ton of tests. So not only were we still a long way off putting that particular label on Mike's condition, we weren't even entertaining it as a possibility. Like a lot of people, I imagine, I had only heard of MND because of Stephen Hawking. We certainly never considered that Mike could have it.

All these medical professionals, and nobody seemed to talk to anyone else. Mike became hugely exasperated at the lack of clear answers, at having to explain his symptoms over and over again to new people who, it seemed, had either not been sent any of his notes or just hadn't read them. That was how it felt anyway. He would return to his doctor time and time again, downcast, and ask who else he could see, what else he could try. The system just felt so slow. And through all this he'd be given this pill or that pill, various medications that he was told might work, but never did.

Mike turned to the internet, with all its freely available and dangerously dubious self-diagnostic medical expertise, and in the absence of any professional opinion, he thought he could have Lyme disease. That, or it was all some strange knock-on effect from the fever he'd had the year before. And then the next week . . .

'I think it might be MS,' he told me on the phone. I was working in London at the time.

'It's not MS, Mike,' I told him.

'I think it could be. The symptoms are the same.'

'It's not MS,' I repeated. I could hear the fear in Mike's voice.

A good friend of ours, a photographer called Keith, had passed away with MS a few years earlier. We saw first-hand what he went through, so I knew Mike was afraid. I explained to Mike that even if it was MS, which it wasn't – I was pretty sure Mike's symptoms weren't the same as Keith's – then we would deal with it. People can deal with it. There's plenty of treatments for it. There's medication for it. It's not always a terminal illness. I told Mike everything would be fine. Even if it was MS, which it wasn't, then he could take all the pills available. It would be rubbish, but he wasn't going to die. 'It'll all be okay,' I told him.

That's what I said, but I think deep down I was worried too. I was certainly becoming more protective of him, if only still at a fairly subconscious level. He came to see me in London a while before that and we went out drinking with a load of friends. Usually Mike would be standing at the bar hammering back shots (*à la* Avoriaz) and getting blind drunk. Instead he sat quietly to one side and barely touched a drop. His legs felt weird and weak.

'I'm going to go back to the house with Mike,' I told the group. And, bless them, they packed up and came back with us. I think that was the first time I felt properly protective of him. I had helped him to his feet in Avoriaz but this was different. Something wasn't right.

'We'll get through it,' I promised him. Yes, we. I'd be there to help him. MS be damned.

◆

Of course, it wasn't MS.

Mike's GP read out a letter to Mike from one of the neurologists he'd seen. That's it. He just read it out. I don't think he had even read the letter beforehand.

'Oh,' he said with apparent surprise. 'It says here you've got a working diagnosis of motor neurone disease.'

Thanks for that. You'd think the neurologist might have delivered the diagnosis himself, or at least written the letter to Mike directly instead of to his GP. Or you'd think someone fully equipped, a specialist in the subject perhaps, might have wanted to break the news gently and be there to answer the slew of inevitable questions. But no. All Mike got was a clumsy and thoughtless delivery, like a throwaway reference to the fact that it might rain tomorrow.

Mike phoned me to tell me the news. 'It's not verified yet, but, well . . . I was told this, and now I'm going to tell you this. Google it, but don't *google* it.'

Motor what?

35

'Don't go down some rabbit hole reading about it, because it's not a pretty picture.'

I went straight to Google and started reading.

It was awful. Desperately awful.

I was shell-shocked. Had we really just gone from thinking the worst case scenario was MS to this?

To motor neurone disease.

Mike was fucked, the horrible reality hit me. I went numb. Two to three years. That's it. That's what it amounted to. Two to three years more of Mike. *I don't want this shit,* I thought. *I don't want this shit in my life, but it is in my life. And it will change – it already has changed – my entire life.*

Everything collapsed in an instant with that diagnosis. It was real, and nothing in my life had prepared me for what was to come. I was terrified, raw, on the edge, close to tears, angry and couldn't be more lost.

It should be me, I want it to be me, I thought, the words resounding in my head. *That's not true, but I certainly don't want it to be Mike.*

I took the train home in a daze, in a whirlwind of devastating emotion, my heart thumping in my chest, my breath stuck in my closing throat. I couldn't believe what was happening.

To me. To us.

To my dear, dear lovely brother.

◆

Later that day, 5 April 2012, at 6.12 p.m., Mike and I found ourselves alone on my driveway. The rest of the family – Dad, Mandy, Laura, Edan and Story – had just left, having had an oddly restrained, ordinary and very 'English' discussion about comfortable topics, about almost everything and anything but the elephant in the room. Mike's diagnosis.

There on the driveway, we couldn't avoid it any longer, so we talked. We talked about the terrible, devastating and unbelievable immensity of what was happening. We talked about Mike not being around to see his son grow into a man, about Mike not being there for the rest of us when we need him. We talked about Avoriaz, already realising that we would never get to do that again. Everything was going to be stolen from him, as he would gradually be stolen from us.

We both broke down and wept uncontrollably. We held each other tight and let our emotions go. We cried heartbreaking and painful tears. I held my tough, handsome, caring, loyal little brother in my arms, and we felt the terror overwhelming us. That's the only time we acknowledged the unavoidable fact. Mike was going to die. And it would be sooner rather than later.

From that point on I had to be strong, while silently weeping.

Moel Famau

I'm up the mountain. Up Moel Famau. The highest peak in Flintshire, where I live, and where Mike lived.

We used to come up here and mess around. Off the main track a bit there are some great places to hide. We used to dig ourselves into the undergrowth and wait until people walked past, then make weird bird calls, just to see their confused reactions. Then we'd giggle quietly to ourselves. This wasn't when we were kids. It wasn't even that long ago really. And when we weren't acting like children, we were climbing trees and looking for gold. Mike was fascinated by Welsh gold, and had a notion it could be found here, around Moel Famau. We used to look through the streams for quartz, a good indicator for the presence of gold.

I'm wearing Mike's green coat. Sitting against a tree. Like always. I've been up here almost every day for more than a year and a half, no matter the weather. Sometimes I talk to Mike. Sometimes I just sit here in silence. The occasional days I've had to go to Mandy's near Manchester or wherever, I've made a point of being up here before I go, even at six in the morning. Sometimes I come up here for five minutes, sometimes half an hour, sometimes several hours. I've brought up coffees, breakfasts, lunches. I've been here at dawn, sunset, morning, noon, afternoon and night. And I sit here, by this tree, on the side of the mountain. Sometimes people walk past where I quietly sit, and they never notice me, and I remember me and Mike making bird noises. And I have a quiet little giggle to myself.

I'm up the mountain.

Because this is where most of Mike's ashes were scattered.

◆

Mike really wanted to go to Machu Picchu. It was his dream destination. When he was ill, he and Laura watched a programme about it on TV. It was one of the very rare occasions when he actually acknowledged there was something he would never do, a place he would never go.

'You never know,' Laura said optimistically. 'One day you might.'

But Mike knew he wouldn't and said so. At least not in his physical form.

Mike didn't leave any instructions about where his ashes should be scattered, apart from Machu Picchu. I had the small caskets made because I knew there would be other places he'd want to be. But as a family we wanted there to be somewhere local to us that we could visit. Somewhere a little closer than the top of the Andes.

Moel Famau was the obvious place.

It was several months after the funeral. I had picked Mike's ashes up from the funeral director and kept them in my spare bedroom for a while, which was weird in itself. We waited for Mum to come up from Oxford, then all gathered together at the foot of the mountain – Mum, Dad, Edan, Mandy and Chris with Jacob and Megan, Laura, Mike's mate Ali, Story and me.

With the sun beaming through the trees, we set off from the car park. I tried to remember the best spot: the place Mike and I had hung out. I knew we had to turn off the main track and down a little side path about a third of the way up. Mike and I used to cut through there towards the forestry tracks where the public never went. I remembered a view looking out over the valley. It would be perfect, I thought. Both Mum and Dad weren't overly agile then, so the walk was sedate. Mum was also in the early stages of dementia. I was with her when I recognised the little crossroads.

'I think we need to turn off here,' I said. Story, Edan, Jacob and Megan had all charged off ahead of the rest of us and were probably halfway up the mountain by then. Chris and Ali volunteered to go after them and bring them back. Dad was still behind us, with Laura and Mandy, so I led Mum along the small path.

It didn't take Mum long to get a bit agitated. She was confused, wondering where everyone had disappeared to, and clearly didn't think much of my dubious organisational skills.

'Wait here, Mum,' I told her patiently. 'I'll sort it.'

She found a place to wait and sat down on a log while I scouted a bit further ahead, intent on finding the spot I had in mind. I felt sure it was just a little further, so I pushed on through the undergrowth. But it wasn't. Further on was useless.

I turned back and found Mum again, just as the others all started arriving. And when I saw her, sitting peacefully on that log, in this little clearing, I suddenly realised that we were already there. Mum had found it. I had been so intent on some image in my head that I hadn't even noticed how beautiful it was, accessible yet hidden, the ideal location.

We all cried. We said a few words. And we all took turns sprinkling some of Mike's ashes at the foot of a tree. I'd never scattered human ashes before, but it wasn't what I expected. I thought they would come out as some fine, dusty cloud that would silently disperse on the breeze in some serene, symbolic and spiritual experience. Instead, as I held the big tube full of Mike's remains, I could hear and feel in my hands and arms the brutal and rattling vibrations of unburnt chunks (I suppose of bone) as they tumbled free with the ash. Bits of Mike. And in the moment, I was horrified. It just felt so wrong.

The moment passed and, amidst the tears, we all shared a farewell to Mike. I spread the ashes from one of the smaller caskets as well, then glued the box, with a brass plaque bearing Mike's name, to a sturdy rock that we placed beneath the tree. We said goodbye to Mike, and returned down the mountain, still grieving but a little lighter.

I went back up Moel Famau the day after. Back to that place. I went the next day as well. And the one after that. I went every day. It got me out of the house. It got me out of the funk I was in, out of the rut of sitting at home grieving. It got me a little fitter too.

I don't believe that the spirit remains where you scatter a person's ashes. I didn't go there to talk to Mike or be near him. Not to begin with. I found solace there. I found peace. I found escape. I found a place to bury my head in the sand and let life pass me by. It was my crutch, my way of not having to do anything, my way of not moving on.

And, in time, it did become the place I would go to be with Mike.

◆

Today I'm here to say goodbye to Mike. And to thank him. I'm here to break a habit. I won't be here tomorrow. Tomorrow I fly to New Zealand. I will begin my journey away from here, away from Mike. But I know this trip will bring me closer to him as well. Yes, I am finally going to complete the bucket list he left me.

Over a year and a half. That's how long it has taken to get the documentary green-lit. I had been getting to the point where I thought it might never happen. Producers and financiers have come and gone, promises have scattered on the breeze, and my hopes have waxed and waned to the point I have become exhausted with the effort. It's heartbreaking enough trying to raise money to make a film of any size, a road paved with continual knock-backs and disappointment, but when the film is as intimate as this one is to me, every bump in the road felt personal, felt like it might derail me entirely. At one point I considered trying to get to New Zealand under my own steam, to maybe film everything on my phone. But that's not what Mike wanted. He wanted it done properly. As did I. And that takes money. Not a lot, but a lot more than I've got. I've been increasingly angry, sad and frustrated at my apparent inability to get this film funded, at the prospect of my not being able to fulfil Mike's wishes. But here we are. Finally. It's happening.

I roll a cigarette, feeling tears gathering in my eyes. It's nearly time. I need to go. This habit of being up here, of not moving forwards, it's not a good thing. I'm stagnant, stuck in a particular phase of grief that I just can't escape.

I don't want to go. I don't want to leave Mike. And I'm nervous as hell. I have no idea what's waiting for me over in New Zealand. A load of things that will scare me, for sure. And a load of things that will make me look like a total muppet. And another load of things that will force me to reluctantly recognise some kind of emotion within myself – I'm so numb. But most of all, hopefully, some things that will bring Mike back to me again, if just for a moment. I can't tell you how much I long to hear his voice in the text of the list. I don't want to go, but I do want to go. It's complicated, okay?

Thank you, Mike. Thank you for the bucket list. Thank you for getting me out of this, for sending me on this horrendously scary trip. Thank you for leaving me a way back to you.

'Thanks, Mike,' I say out loud. I stand up and pull my coat, Mike's old green coat, close around me in a kind of embrace. It's time I went back down the mountain. I've got a train to catch to London.

It's hard to leave. It's hard to break this habit. And if the documentary had taken another year to get funded, I'd still be coming up here every day. It's hard. And it costs me two bloody quid every day to use the car park!

'Bye, Mike.' I turn and begin my descent, and my tears flow as much with joy at the prospect of my imminent journey as with sorrow at leaving this place. Leaving Mike.

PART TWO
THERE AND BACK

Fly, You Fools

It's 3.57 a.m.. I'm not convinced I've slept yet but if I have, it's been in fits and starts. In a few hours I'll be up and on my way to Heathrow. And then on to New Zealand, via Los Angeles. This is really happening.

And I'm nervous as hell.

◆

It's light and I'm sucking down a morning cigarette with my already cold coffee. The sun's out, but it's definitely still winter here. At least I'm flying into summer.

Drew, who I met for the first time last night at our accommodation near the airport (seems nice enough, if a little hairy), turns the camera on. One of the million things that kept me up last night was wondering how I'd react to being filmed the whole time. Up until now, like in Avoriaz, it's just been the odd thing caught on phones. Now we're actually making a film, finally doing what Mike wanted me to do. And I still haven't been to the gym.

I've been filmed a few times but I'm always prepared, whether it's an interview in a studio, a convention or talking to the press during *The Lord of the Rings* and *The Hobbit* premieres. You know it's coming, you know it's a few questions you've likely been asked before and you know it won't last long. In the dark sleeplessness of last night I imagined having a camera, this camera, being shoved in my face, obtrusive and artificial, but it doesn't feel that invasive at all. It's just this guy, Drew, with a camera, and a beard. Who cares what he's doing? I did just wave at him, which I'm probably not supposed to do, but to be honest I'm a bit more preoccupied with my anxious excitement at the prospect of going back to New Zealand.

Besides, there's only so much establishing footage he needs. The bucket list doesn't start until we get there. But hey, carry on filming me loading the taxi, why don't you?

◆

Heathrow already. I look at my phone. What was really a forty-minute drive seemed to last barely two. We unload our luggage, and all the camera kit, and walk into Terminal 2. Cue more pointless establishing shots, and footage of me walking.

I'm led to a check-in area. It's particularly quiet and free from crowds and queues. As I approach, I see someone I know. Roxy. What are the chances? I rush up and give her a big hug. Roxy works as cabin crew for Air New Zealand. We have mutual friends in LA, so I've met her a few times there when she's on a layover. It's wonderful to see her.

While our gear is checked in and our documents scrutinised, I excitedly explain to Roxy what I'm doing here. Out of the corner of my eye I notice Drew has the camera up on his shoulder and aimed at us. Bit much, mate – I'm just having a chat with an old friend of mine.

'Anyway, I've got something here for you, Royd,' Roxy says out of the blue. And she looks a little uncomfortable. I'm not surprised. I don't suppose she wants to be filmed.

'What is it?' I ask, trying to ignore the camera.

'It's from Mike.' She straightens up, suddenly looking all official in her Air New Zealand uniform with the nice hat and everything.

Mike.

I should have known. That's why Drew's filming. And Roxy knew exactly why I was here. Oh, the deceit.

'Last time we went to New Zealand,' she begins, and just those first words send a tsunami of emotion through me, 'I was struggling with my walking, using a cane to help steady myself.'

Mike.

'Get into the spirit of the journey by dressing up as Gandalf.'

Do what now?

'Embrace the character. Tell people they shall not pass constantly, and block their path with your wizard staff,' Roxy finishes, a sympathetic smile on her lips.

I'm already crying.

Actual tears. Just as an aside, despite what you may think from what you've already read, I am really not a crier. Before Mike got ill, I rarely cried. I'm just not an outwardly emotional, crying kind of person. Before I left Wales I told myself that I would not, at any point on this hopefully magical journey, ever be anything other than myself. I don't want to play up to the camera (unless I'm being silly), or force an emotion if there isn't one. I cried on the driveway the day Mike got diagnosed. I cried at his funeral. And I've cried occasionally in private. Other than that, nothing. I couldn't cope with the sheer awfulness of everything. I hated losing control to my grief. So I bottled it up. I pushed it down. And I was pretty sure, up until a moment ago, that I had no tears left in me.

I mean, I'm not sobbing, but that really got me. Just those first words. 'Last time we . . .' It wasn't even the mention of Mike's cane. Just his words. About him and me. About us, together. How did I go from Mr I-don't-cry to having my tears captured for posterity on a documentary camera? My first reaction to getting emotional is normally to hide away in a corner somewhere. It most certainly is not to stand in an airport terminal in front of a load of strangers and airline representatives.

I wipe my cheeks harder, trying to will the tears back into their ducts, to suck them back into me. Enough. But all I can think about is Mike. And . . . hold on . . . do what?

I have to dress as Gandalf!

◆

Mum read us *The Hobbit* when I was about nine years old. Without ceremony. There was no sense of 'you must listen carefully to this book because your great-grandfather wrote it'. To us, and to her, it was just another book that she picked off the shelf, although I imagine she felt the same family pride as I did when I did the same for Story. I vaguely understood that a relative of ours had written it, but we certainly didn't hold him in any higher esteem than any other relative, so I thought little of the fact.

My first day in English class at high school was a different experience. My teacher, for some inexplicable reason, made me stand up in front of the entire class, then introduced me as the great-grandson of the man who wrote the book we'd be studying that year. *The Hobbit*. I didn't know why we were studying a book written by some relative of mine. I didn't know anyone else had even heard of it. I certainly didn't know why I had to be singled out and humiliated in front of a class full of strangers. But I did start to realise that this little book was a bigger deal than I'd previously understood.

I first became aware of The Tolkien Society in my early teens. The society has been going for over half a century, and was formed through the literary fandom of Tolkien's works. J. R. R. Tolkien himself was the first president, and when he died the title was passed on to his daughter, Priscilla. Every year, in Oxford, the society gathers at what they call the Oxonmoot. Oxon, because of Oxford, where Tolkien studied and taught. Moot is a Saxon word, something to do with assembling for a debate. Basically, the Oxonmoot was, and is, a throng of fans gathering to discuss his various literary works, drink a load of beer and wine, and hang out at The Bird and Baby, where the man himself liked to go for a pint or two. Nowadays the society encompasses an appreciation for the films as well, but back when I was a teenager it was all about the books.

Mum and Dad used to take me and Mandy (and Mike when he was old enough) down to Oxford every year for the Moot, and we'd stay at Prisca's modest house in Summertown. Prisca (how I refer to my Great Aunt Priscilla) would deliver a witty speech to the assembled guests and have them roaring with laughter. And on the Sunday she would host a kind of open day at her house for new members. My job was usually to man the bar, a trestle table on the small driveway outside her garage, laden with red and white wine. And of course, when nobody was looking, I'd neck whatever I could!

As we got older we got more involved in the evening festivities as well. I'd see fans dressed as characters from the books, having sword fights and getting up to all manner of Middle Earth-y shenanigans. Each year my eyes opened wider to the extent of the fandom. Meeting these people, who came from all over the world, made me gradually realise how far and wide and deep the love for Tolkien's work reaches. At some point I'm sure only the Bible had sold more copies than *The Lord of the Rings*, presumably only because hotels don't tend to put a copy of Tolkien's book in every room. Maybe they should.

We even began opening up our little farm in Wales for 'Summer Moots', and members of The Tolkien Society would come and spend a long July weekend with us. They'd camp in the fields, go mushroom picking, have bonfires and tell stories. They'd set off fireworks and have sword fights in full costume. That was a lot of fun for me as a teenager. My favourite character from the books was, without a doubt, Aragorn. So I'd join in with the sword fights, then go and steal their beer and wine and get drunk with my friends . . . don't get me wrong, I'm not a habitual alcohol thief, just an opportunist!

Long-term members of the society get to choose a Tolkien-esque moniker to be known by, and there was one old guy who had adopted 'Gandalf' as his. He would turn up on a Triumph motorbike with a sidecar fittingly laden with fireworks, and put on bombastic displays over the fields around our farm, all culminating in an ear-shattering explosion from a huge pyrotechnic that he would hurl high into the air. When everyone had gone I'd try and scrape together pinches of gunpowder residue, then gleefully set a match to them.

I enjoyed the Moots. I got used to the fandom, and it was a comfortable and fun environment to be in. But apart from that annual event, the fandom really wasn't in our faces all the time. Sometimes, when I was a teenager, I'd anonymously go into a book-shop and see a line of the books there, and I'd get a warm fuzzy feeling: pride at knowing that my great-grandfather wrote them.

◆

And now I have to dress up as one of his most enduring characters. Well, that's embarrassing! I mean, I've done my share of conventions and fan appearances and whatnot, but I never dress up for them. That's for the other people, like actors, to do. The extent of fancy dress in my life has been limited to brief turns at parties as Adam Ant or Heath Ledger's Joker. And I love superheroes, but I've never ever dressed up as Superman or Spiderman or any of them. I just wouldn't. And I certainly wouldn't dress up as Gandalf.

Gandalf! What a great task. What a clever move from Mike. What a start to the journey.

One of the producers, who I thought was here just to see me off, presents me with a big bag. 'It's Ian McKellen's actual costume from the films, so be careful with it,' he tells me.

I'm sorry, what?

'Oh, and there's this too.' He produces an eight-foot tubular container. 'And it's Ian McKellen's actual staff.'

This is going to look amazing on camera!

◆

Well it would have done.

It turns out the cameraman, Drew, must be a wanted man in the US. Or rather, very much unwanted. God knows what he's done, or hasn't done, but apparently his ESTA (Electronic System for Travel Authorisation) had been mysteriously revoked. They won't even let him layover in LA on the way through to New Zealand.

'Fucking Trump,' was the last thing I heard him grumble before I headed off to go through security to the departure lounge. He trudged off towards the ticket desks with the producer to try and find a flight going the other way round the world. I'm sure he'll be fine. Plus, to be honest, it saves me being cooped up with him on a plane for the best part of a day having to 'get to know' him. Not that there's anything wrong with him, probably. It's me. I'm not big on meeting new people. And I don't want to feel like I have to open up. To be fair, Drew's not loud, over-opinionated or in-your-face, which are traits I shy away from. He's very much absorbed in the camera and his craft and it feels like I may get along with him. Time will tell.

Meanwhile, I've got Sir Ian McKellen's costume to put on, and no cameraman to film it. The show must go on. I'm shown into a lovely private room near the departure area so I can change. I can't believe I've got the actual costume, and the actual staff. Peter Jackson had to have authorised it to be sent over for me. What a lovely gesture. And so very trusting!

So that means Peter, probably along with lots of other people I know in New Zealand, know that I'm on my way. They will know that I am finally fulfilling Mike's wishes and doing the bucket list.

When Mike died, I didn't talk to a lot of people. I didn't tell people. But the news of his death spread quickly, and there was a huge outpouring of support from the Tolkien community, from people involved in the films, from fan sites, from friends of mine and Mike, from people who had only met Mike briefly but had felt a connection. Peter and Fran, his wife, sent an enormous bunch of flowers. And now this. Gandalf's costume.

Of course Mike probably meant for me to go to a fancy dress shop and find some half-arsed wizard outfit, a thin grey sheet, pantomime hat and silly-looking cotton-wool beard. He wouldn't have envisaged this. I pull on the thick grey under-trousers and slip the braces over my shoulders. The robe goes on over the top, and the hat . . . what a hat. As embarrassing as this is, at least I'll look good.

The nerves are kicking in now. I have to go out in public like this and let people see me. I have to perform. Cringe. Well, at least the people who see me won't know I'm a Tolkien. That would be really awkward. It's no big deal, I tell myself. It's fine. Just enjoy it. If I enjoy it, people will laugh, and it will be fun. I remind myself that Mike's failing body was a costume he was forced to wear. He had no choice, no control, and he couldn't take it off. At least, after a while, I'll be able to take this wizard guise off and go back to being me. Right, let's do this. I'm not just dressing up as Gandalf. I'm going to become Gandalf.

The costume fits great, but the beard is a bit of a bugger. It looks amazing, as you'd expect, but the thing about proper film beards is they are lovingly and carefully stuck onto actors' faces with a special glue, by professional make-up artists. I don't have any glue, and I certainly don't have a professional make-up artist. What I do have, though, is double-sided sticky tape.

◆

I'm standing, feeling somewhat awkward, in the doorway to the plane. I'm in full Gandalf mode, with his whopping great staff in my hand. There was an announcement made in the departure lounge to inform some of the other passengers that a member of the Tolkien family is dressed up as Gandalf and wants to greet them as they board the plane. I realise they have to be forewarned, since they'll be filmed (albeit on smartphones, thanks to Drew!), but did they really need to say I was a member of the family?

I start sweating. Nerves. And a hot costume. Mostly nerves, if I'm honest. I feel the tape on my face start to surrender to the clamminess and curl away from me, so I push the beard back into my cheek. Stay there, damn it! Here they come.

'You shall not pass!' I boom at the first of the line of Tolkien enthusiasts that head down the gangway towards me with their hand luggage. They laugh. This isn't so bad.

'YOU shall not pass,' I repeat, altering the emphasis a little and earning myself another laugh and a few smiles from the next group. I grin, and wave them on. This is quite fun.

'You shall not . . .' I begin saying to a pleasant-looking couple. 'Oh go on then, on you go.' I revert to my normal voice. And get a laugh. Royd, you're a bloody natural. I turn my head and look into the plane after the people I've just admitted. 'Fly, you fools,' I bellow heartily at their delighted and laughing faces.

Oh, there goes a bit more beard.

After the initial stampede of those happy enough to be caught on camera, I take my seat on the plane, which just happens to be right next to the door. So now everyone else who is boarding (unless they are turning left to business and first-class) is getting an eyeful of me anyway. The beard is hanging by its last bit of tape, so I take it off. Now I just have a few bits of tape stuck to my face. It's not a good look.

'Oh wow, it's Dumbledore,' someone says as they pass me.

'No, no, I'm Gandalf,' I turn my head and call after them. It turns out that the rest of the passengers not only don't know I'm a member of the family, but they apparently also have no idea who I'm supposed to be.

'Look, Mummy, it's Dumbledore,' a little boy beams at me.

'Actually, I'm Gandalf,' I smile back at him.

Nothing. Fine. I'm Dumbledore, then. Have it your way, kid. He's not the last either. I get several more happy recognitions for my supposed appearances in the Harry Potter films and eventually give up correcting people.

I suppose I have removed the beard, so now I just look like a mediocre Gandalf (which is a real shame given the pedigree of the costume) who has just had a messy breakfast of sticky tape. The rest of the passengers who file past me, those who missed the memo that I was related to Tolkien, probably at best just think I'm some sad geek who is so excited to be going to New Zealand that he's prepared to go the whole long, long way in full costume. I shrink down into my seat.

'Royd,' a member of the cabin crew approaches me. 'Would you like to go up to the cockpit? The pilots would love to meet you.'

'Yes please,' I jump up, liberated from my embarrassment. Time for some awesome selfies!

◆

I'm watching some programme about New Zealand to get myself in the mood. Well, I was trying to. Then some lunatic throws himself off a bridge with an elastic band tied to his ankles, and I feel nauseous just watching it. Who would want to do that?

'Ladies and gentlemen we do apologise for interrupting your in-flight entertainment,' a man's voice cuts through the rock music and screams of excited terror blaring in my ears.

No, please do interrupt.

'However, you may have noticed we have our very own wizard onboard the aircraft today,' the announcement continues.

Oh God, here we go. What now?

'He is the great-grandson of J. R. R. Tolkien and he's called Royd Tolkien.'

I press the headphones to my head, to hear him better. I bet there's a whole bunch of people kicking themselves now for thinking I was Dumbledore.

'Royd's brother sadly passed away two years ago of motor neurone disease and Mike left Royd a bucket list to fulfil in his honour and we are about to announce number four on the list. Now this is written in Mike's own words, so here you go Royd.'

I brace myself.

'You need to invite people to have a picture with you. You must get thirty-nine photographs. You need to capture no less than thirty-nine laughing faces please. Thirty-nine, the number of years I loved you, bro.'

I smile. There's already a smartphone trained on me, so I smile. But I'm twisted inside, hurled into thoughts and memories of Mike again. It's the number that gets me. A stark reminder of his all-too-short life, of how young he was when he was taken from me. From us. I feel like I've just been kicked in the chest.

And I hate selfies. I never take them. Well, unless I'm sitting in the cockpit of a plane dressed as Gandalf. That was cool. But generally, selfies really aren't my thing. Nor is going up to complete strangers and embarrassing myself. At least I can kind of hide behind my costume.

Again, the passengers have been gently encouraged to volunteer, so I am not short of willing participants. Everyone is lovely, smiling and excited and happy to be in a photo with me. I let them hold the staff if they want to, snapping away with my phone. Some of the cabin crew even get in on the action.

Not everyone wants to be a part of it. The odd misery-guts looks away as I pass, even more embarrassed than me perhaps, or really not a fan of *The Lord of the Rings*. Such people do exist. A couple of people pretend to be asleep but I sneak a selfie anyway, with a big grin on my face. One man seems so wrapped up in whatever he's watching or listening to that he doesn't see the six-foot Gandalf with a bloody great staff leaning over him.

'Excuse me,' I say politely. 'Excuse me, would you like . . .'

Nothing. Oh well, you can't please everyone.

Someone wants to take a selfie on their phone as well as mine. Sod it, go for it. And another. Sure. I realise that I'm going to appear on several Facebook profiles dressed as Gandalf. But that's okay. I'm making people happy.

I quickly lose count of how many selfies I've taken. This is easy.

What a start to my journey. Thank you, Mike.

◆

If you've ever flown into the US, you know that their immigration procedure can be pretty intimidating. You might even be aware, since they sometimes like to remind you of the fact, that an immigration officer is allowed to refuse entry to anyone for any reason they like. They don't have to ask a manager, or follow any kind of legal procedure. They can effectively take one look at you and just decide they don't like you. And when that happens, that's it. You're going back home on the next plane out of there and you don't get so much as a whiff of American soil. And these immigration folk aren't exactly renowned for being happy-go-lucky cheerful chaps.

I'm not dressed as Gandalf anymore. I took the costume off halfway across the Atlantic. But I am carrying the staff. Eight feet of faux wood wizard's staff. And I'm in the massive queue for immigration, suddenly very aware that what I'm proudly clutching must look like one heck of a weapon. It's one thing the cameraman having to go the other way to New Zealand, but I'll look like a right numpty if I get refused entry at this stage.

'What's that?' My thoughts are disturbed by an American accent. It's just one of the immigration guys who's marshalling the crowd into the various queues, or lines as they say there. And he's pointing at the big hunk of elaborately carved wood with a gnarly big crystal on top. He's pointing at Gandalf's staff. In my hand.

'It's a prop from a film,' I say as meekly as I can.

'Oh yeah?' he comes back at me. 'What movie?'

'Um . . . *The Lord of the Rings*.' I smile. Be friendly, I tell myself. I'd tell him to be friendly too, if I thought he'd listen. 'It's Gandalf's staff.'

'No way! What, like the actual staff from the movies?' Maybe he is friendly!

'Yeah. From the actual films. I'm taking it back to New Zealand.'

'Oh man, really? I love those movies. Big fan. Jeez, do you think I could hold it?'

Well I wasn't expecting this. 'Sure,' I say, sensing a connection. I hand him the staff and he grips it, revelling in the moment.

'That's so cool. Man, I wish I could take a selfie with it, you know, but there's no phones allowed in the hall. You can't take pictures in here.'

'Ah . . . that is a shame.' I wait for him to hand me the staff.

'Come with me,' he announces, then leads me past the enormous lines of people right up to the front and next in line at passport control. I thank him profusely, and ready myself for the next trial.

Of course the immigration guy at the booth looks pretty much as scary as any immigration guy you can imagine. He's a burly sort with a face that looks like it's rarely troubled by smiles. He's dealing with someone else at the moment, but I notice him look up and clock me. Yeah, he clocked the staff too. I could still be on the next plane home. In fact, he seems far more interested in me than he is in the probably dodgy person he's about to let in because he's too distracted looking at this stonking great pylon in my hand.

He stamps the passport he's barely even looked at and beckons me forward. I walk up to him, trying desperately not to look even half as sheepish as I feel.

'What's that?' He's looking at the staff. Here we go again.

'It's a prop from *The Lord of the Rings*,' I tell him as straightforwardly as possible. I notice the first guy is still lingering nearby, looking at me, smiling. He's still thrilled that he got to hold it. Maybe I'll let him have another go before I get put on a flight back to London.

'From the actual movies?' burly face asks me.

'Yes. It's Gandalf's staff.'

'No way, for real?'

'Yes, the actual one Ian McKellen used in the actual films. I'm taking it back to New Zealand.'

'Man I wish we could take pictures in here. I'd love a selfie with it.' I think he's smiling now. This is great! Behind me, his buddy is grinning and nodding. I think I've just made their day.

'Passport,' he holds out his hand. I stand there, relief washing over me as he peruses my documents.

'Tolkien huh? You related in any way?' I don't think he expects the answer to be yes.

'I'm his great-grandson.'

'No way. That's cool. That's amazing.'

BANG. His stamp thumps on the page of my passport and he hands it back to me.

'You have a great stay in the US, sir. And a great trip. God bless you.'

Well that was easy. I should carry a staff with me every time I go to America.

Scarab

I've just about got over the jet lag. After LA, it was another long and sleepless journey to the other side of the world, but here I am in sunny Auckland. I've been here a few days now, and it feels good to be able to wear just a T-shirt. Of course, the jet lag quickly gave way to a stinking cold that still bugs me now. Like most men, I'm miserable with a cold. You get these little sachets of liquid vitamin C here that you squirt into your mouth; I've been downing them like shots of tequila at a bachelor party. I just want to get on with Mike's bucket list.

Drew made it, via Dubai and Australia. He'd already been here twelve hours when I arrived and was fully rested and ready for action. I'm fairly immune to the camera being on me now and, apart from this irritating lurgy, I'm also primed to have a task delivered to me at any moment. I'm in a constantly heightened sense of anticipation. The tears in Heathrow airport surprised me. I didn't think I had any more in me. And if I did, I didn't think they'd come quite so readily. So I'm in a state of nervous excitement, trying to prepare myself for what I now realise really is going to be an emotional rollercoaster. This is the first time I've been in New Zealand since I was here with Mike, and I feel his absence acutely.

◆

After Mike got his working diagnosis of motor neurone disease it became a mission to do as much stuff as we possibly could, while we still could. While he still could. And high up on the list of essential travel was a long overdue trip to New Zealand. Mike had always wanted to come here, but never had. By that point I'd been around ten times. I was here for *The Lord of the Rings*, *King Kong*, *The Hobbit*, for a film I produced that I did post on in Wellington, for various premieres and so on. Any excuse to come, really. Because I just love it here, and I knew Mike would too. Every time I went I'd bombard him with pictures or FaceTime calls and say, 'Hey Mike, look at me on this amazing beach' or 'Hey Mike, look at me having a tour of Weta Workshop. Wish you were here'. Laughing crying face emoji.

And I did, really. I just enjoyed the opportunity to rip the piss out of him and make him feel jealous. He was married. And Edan was young. He (and I) would have thought he still had all the time in the world to make the trip. He'd go when it was more convenient. When Edan was older. When he had more time on his hands.

A friend of mine suggested I email some of the people at Air New Zealand who I'd met at one of the premieres, and see if they might be able to get a bit of a discount for me and Mike. Cheeky, I know, but there's no harm in trying, right? My scruples had been on holiday since Mike had been diagnosed, and since I would have done anything I could to get Mike there and show him all the places I love, I sent the email. It turned out the timing was pitch perfect. And the name Tolkien helped too. I got a surprisingly swift reply. It just happened that they were in the last stages of pre-production on a *Hobbit*-themed air safety video and would be delighted if we'd both take part in it.

Air New Zealand flew us first-class all the way from London for nothing. Yeah, I said that in a bragging kind of 'do you know who

I am?' tone, so you're probably thinking I'm being a dick, but hold on a minute. Mike was already getting weaker by this stage. He was getting 'drop foot' too. That's when your feet droop because you haven't got the strength to keep them upright any more. And when that happens, you tend to trip more and you fall forwards. And you haven't got enough strength in your arms to break your own fall. So even a flat floor becomes a dangerous trip hazard.

So as well as the walking stick, Mike also had mechanisms attached to his shoes that provided enough spring in his step to control the foot drop. A bit. They didn't take away the risk, but they mitigated it. So for Mike to have the luxury of a lie-flat bed on the plane was simply wonderful. And I was so excited to be going to New Zealand with him. All I wanted was to take our minds – his mind – off the horrible news that we were still very much reeling from.

Normally, when I fly into Auckland, the first thing I do is get straight on another plane and head down to Wellington. But Mike and I had business in Auckland first. We had an air safety video to be in. We had a couple of days to acclimatise, during which we met up with a few friends I know there and hung out. Normally we'd have hit the bars and got trolleyed as per, but Mike had already begun to be quite considered about doing anything that might exacerbate what he was only just starting to go through. Despite what you may think, I'm not a big drinker, and nor was Mike. It's a social thing, so when we saw friends or went on holiday we would cut loose a bit. And for full disclosure, I'm pretty much hanging on to the floor after half a pint of piss-weak beer, so don't be under any delusions that I'm Oliver Reed.

So we went on gentle walks and met friends in cafés. After a couple of days we got picked up from the hotel and taken to the massive aircraft hangar where the filming was taking place. Much of the film industry in New Zealand, everything from facilities to crew, has grown out of Peter's *Lord of the Rings* empire. And everyone works on everything. So when we got there it turned out that the first AD (Assistant Director) was also the first AD on a film I produced in Fiji, and she had worked on *The Lord of the Rings* and *The Hobbit* as well. There were other crew members and people appearing in the video who I had met before, and who had been involved in lots of the same things. So it was a familiar, friendly atmosphere.

The basis of the video, and if you want to see it then it's easy to find on YouTube, was a plane full of hobbits, dwarves, elves, Gandalf, Gollum, the odd wraith and so on, all off travelling on a plane to Middle Earth and being given the standard safety instructions you get on most planes. Obviously, it was way better than all the other safety videos, not least because Mike and I were in it. I mean, if you blink you might miss us, but it's a crucial part of the narrative concerning the stowing of hand luggage.

I got kitted up in Martin Freeman's borrowed hobbit feet with the invaluable help of one of the Weta Workshop make-up artists. Bloody great feet, twice the size of my own and considerably hairier. They were so realistic (assuming you know what hobbit feet should look like, which I do) and surprisingly comfortable. I sat on an aisle seat on the packed plane, with Mike next to me. I'm not sure why, but the Eye of Sauron got the window seat. Now that I think about it, perhaps this experience was Mike's inspiration behind the Gandalf task. Here we were, members of the Tolkien family, me wearing Bilbo's feet, sitting on a plane full of people dressed as characters from Middle Earth. Awkward. But very funny.

Our little cameo was the part of the announcement that tells passengers to stow their hand luggage under the seat in front of them if there's no room in the overhead lockers . . . you know the drill. The camera would track up the aisle to reveal me and Mike, then follow my hands down to the floor as I place my bag under the seat in front of me, hilariously revealing my massive feet as they push it into place. And I then had to look into the camera and give a cheeky little hobbit smile. It went something like this:

Take one. The camera is moving. Here it comes. Be natural.

'Chin,' Mike says next to me, and I laugh.

'Cut.'

Take two. Here we go. Nice and relaxed.

'Suck your belly in,' Mike whispers. I corpse again.

'Cut.'

Every time the camera started moving towards us Mike would feel it necessary to correct my slouch, to remind me that my chins were showing, to prompt me to suck in my gut and push my chin out. I'm not sure what take they ended up using – there were quite a few – but I guarantee the first few had me grinning like a fool, wound up by Mike. That was a good day.

◆

Overlooking Auckland harbour in the blazing sunshine, I am handed an iPad and told to press play on the open video file. I sniff loudly. This sodding cold can do one. Okay, here we go. I press play and an alphabetic grid appears on the screen, with a search bar above it. My heart immediately feels like it might burst. It's a screen recording of Mike's words being entered via the Apple TV search function. Even before the first letters begin to appear, I feel a painful wrench in my gut and my throat tightens. This is too much.

The cursor moves awkwardly around the screen, painfully slowly. Really painfully. Even though it has been sped up a little.

Y

o

u

Mike's words start to appear in the search bar. I'm overcome already.

n

e

e

d

I have to pause. I have to explain.

◆

As Mike's condition declined, his lungs weakened. There came a point when he could only really speak on an out breath. It would take a while, and I'd have to listen carefully as the laboured words were whispered out, a few at a time. Soon, though, his lungs simply weren't strong enough to sustain him without help. He needed a breathing assist, a mask that he had to wear at all times. The mask fitted airtight around his nose and mouth, and was connected to a machine that knew when he breathed in and out. Every time he needed to breathe in, it would give him a little boost. And every time he breathed out it would help draw the air, and the toxins, out.

He could still talk, on an out breath, for another month or two. I'd lean in close to him when he spoke, trying to read his lips through the mask as well as hear the words. But the effort of talking made him more and more breathless, so the number of words he could manage became fewer and fewer. Sometimes he would make fun of my bad hearing.

To make life easier for everyone, I developed a shorthand system. I had a list of important questions I would ask him, rather than wait for him to struggle to get the words out. If he needed something I would go through the list. Did his mask need adjusting? A gap in the seal was the first thing to rule out. I needed to make sure his breathing assist was working perfectly. If it needed adjusting I had to take the mask off him and get it back on as quickly as possible as Mike couldn't breathe without it. If the mask was okay, I'd carry on down the checklist. Was something tickling him? Did he need adjusting in his wheelchair? Did he need the toilet? Was he hungry? Thirsty? All the obvious things. And if it was none of those, I'd try to make out his words as he spoke on his shallow out breath into the mask. Sometimes it was really hard, especially for a half-deaf git like me. He'd look at me, exasperated, like I was an idiot. Then Laura would come over and he'd exhale a few barely intelligible words.

'He wants you to change the channel,' she'd say simply, or whatever it might have been, and he'd look at me with eyes that wanted to roll, like I was a right pillock.

Talking became harder and harder for Mike. He needed to put all his energy into just breathing. The checklist of potential emergencies became longer. But once that list was exhausted, there were still things Mike wanted to say. We tried using an optical viewer hooked up to a computer that would track Mike's eye movement. Basically his eyes would become a cursor on the screen, but that didn't work. His eyes were too weak to accurately control the cursor. By then he could barely move a muscle in his body. Sign language was never really an option. His hands became tightly frozen in claw-like poses, victims of muscle loss and restriction to his tendons. He could barely move his head. And he couldn't speak.

Realising that his eyes, even if they lacked the strength and focus to operate the optical viewer, were still our best bet at maintaining communication, I came up with a plan. We used to watch a lot of Apple TV, so I decided that its search function was the simplest way to enable Mike to say something to us. I'd have the remote and would sit and look at Mike while he looked at the screen. He'd move his eyes left, right, up, down and blink when he wanted me to enter a letter. It was a slow and difficult process for Mike.

But that's what it came to. For the last few months of his life, Mike could only speak to us slowly, one letter at a time. And even in that time, his eye movements became more laboured and difficult for him. A blink would require huge effort on his part. Such a simple, tiny movement still requires neurones to fire. If he needed something, I'd move into his sight line rather than him have to try and move his face or eyes towards me. Anything to make his life easier, knowing how much effort it took him to just blink his way through a very short message on the Apple TV.

It came to the point that he would even sleep with his eyes open, which was upsetting and shocking to see. It reminded me of Keith, who had died from MS. I remember going into the palliative care home he was in, just the day before he died. I walked past the open door of his room, saw this emaciated, skeletal figure lying on the bed and didn't recognise him. He was lying on his back, his wide-open eyes seemingly fixed on the ceiling. Leaning over and looking down at his face, I realised he was asleep. After a moment he woke up without a movement, and I saw in his motionless eyes the bizarre transition between sleep and consciousness.

So the whole Apple TV thing evolved through necessity. You do what you have to do to communicate. You improvise. You make things up. You adapt. But I can't look at it now. If I'm ever at someone's house and they have Apple TV, I have to leave the room if they go to search for something. I don't say anything. I'll make some excuse, like going outside for a smoke. I just can't look at that screen.

◆

My hands holding the iPad tremble.

'You need . . .' it has slowly spelled out in the manner that Mike used to communicate with me. Mike's words. What do I need? I squint through moist eyes.

69

a
n
e
w
t
a
t
t
o
o

A new tattoo. I smile a bittersweet smile, feeling broken.
Utterly broken.

I
t
h
i
n
k
y
o
u
k
n
o
w
w
h
a
t
y
o
u

n
e
e
d
t
o
d
o
h
e
r
e
R
o
y
d

I do. I know exactly what I need to do here. And it shatters my heart to remember our week in Chicago. To remember what a great time we had there.

A
r
e
m
i
n
d
e
r
o
f
m
e

The scarab. The symbol of rebirth and resurrection. The only tattoo Mike had. It was fitting then, for him. And it is fitting now. For me.

e
t
e
r
n
a
l
l
y

What a gift. Mike has spoken. It hurts, remembering. I put the iPad down and let out a long, deep sigh. And breathe.

◆

I'd been to Chicago alone, when I was seventeen. I was halfway through a two-year course in prop making and scenery for the local theatre. It was something I'd dreamed about, inspired by the sword- and costume-filled experiences of our Summer Moots in Wales and the Triumph-riding Gandalf and his fireworks, a passion fed by *Fangoria* magazine, where I first hungrily read about Peter Jackson and his early films, *Bad Taste* and *Braindead*. I loved those films and desperately wanted to get into that world.

But my Uncle Philip, who lived in Chicago, confused matters somewhat when he spread his big map of America across our dining-room table one Christmas. The map awoke in me a more demanding and immediate desire. As he pointed out where he lived, and all the other places that I'd barely even heard of but wanted to see, I realised that I needed to travel. I needed to explore. Life in Wales felt parochial and suppressed and I was suddenly and painfully aware how much of a world there was out there. So I applied for a visa.

A month or so before the end of the first year of my course, Mandy produced a letter that had come for me from the US Embassy. This is it, I thought. This is the potential big change in my life. Either I would be refused the visa and would (happily) carry on and finish my course at Theatr Clwyd and see where that path took me. Or I'd be granted the visa and I'd go on an almighty adventure to America. In anticipation, I'd already saved up the air fare and was more than ready to get my first real taste of independence.

I got the visa, and within a month I was in Chicago. That's when I met Dave and Mary, who became good friends of mine. I worked a lot with Dave, who was a carpenter, around Chicago and I got to travel around the country too, taking the fabled Greyhound buses to Tennessee, Texas, Mississippi, all over the place. Over the years, I've been to America loads, more times than I've been to Europe. I've been to Florida with mates, LA a bunch of times, and I even did three months in the late nineties as a camp counsellor in Virginia.

I made a great friend in Virginia, Marcus, who was also from the UK and had got on the same Camp America placement as I had during the summer of '88. Ten years on, Marcus decided he wanted to go back and do it all over again. We hatched a plan. I would go over and spend a week with him there, and catch up with other friends I hadn't seen in a decade, and then we would go north and spend another week in Chicago. And I wanted Mike to come with me.

Mike had never been to America. We'd never even been on a trip abroad together at that point. He was stuck working in a paint shop in Mold. His usual zest for life was muddied and stifled. I took months trying to persuade him to come with me, expounding the merits of the trip and promising him a fantastic time. I didn't expect him to agree to come, so was pleasantly surprised and excited when he finally did.

We spent a week in Virginia then headed up to Chicago with Marcus. I'd got a tattoo on one of my earlier trips to Chicago. It was a depiction of the winged serpent, Aztec creator god, Quetzalcoatl. Dave used to have one painted around the tops of the walls of a cactus shop he'd had in New York in the sixties, and had replicated it on the floor of his Chicago apartment. You could only really see it fully from the top of a ladder. I loved it. The design came from an old book on Aztec designs that Dave eventually found and gave to me, and which I still have. I wanted to get another tattoo from that book when I went back with Mike. And Mike, being Mike, decided that he wanted one as well.

At the time, Mike was really interested in Egyptian culture and mythology, so he spent a fair bit of time before we left refining the design he wanted. He settled on a winged scarab beetle, symbolising self-creation and rebirth. Scarab beetles roll balls of dung into their egg chambers to provide the larvae with food when they hatch. The larvae feast and appear as fully developed scarabs, earning the species a symbolic reputation for spontaneous creation and resurrection. I totally reworded that from Wikipedia.

Dave took us to this cool tattoo parlour in Bucktown, one of the 'fruitier' parts of Chicago. I had my design, intended for my shoulder, and Mike had his scarab beetle, which he wanted right across his back. Mike had never had a tattoo, so I gleefully told him how much it was going to hurt. The anticipation alone had me sweating already.

When it came to it, we sat side by side with a tattooist each. Mike whipped his top off. He had to, he was getting his back done. I guffawed at his physique and casually rolled my sleeve up. I got to keep my shirt on! And then the needles got to work. And boy, did it hurt. It always does. I mean, there's a weird addictive quality to this particular pain, as anyone who's had a tattoo knows – but it really does hurt.

I looked over at Mike, leant forward on his chair, calm as you like, getting this enormous winged scarab pricked all across his upper back and shoulders. He'd not even broken a sweat. In fact, he looked totally unfazed. It had to hurt, surely! Don't forget Mike had a real thing about needles. But there he was, with millions and millions of the buggers jabbing into his back over and over and over, and he looked like he could quite easily take a nap. I tried my best to put up the usual competitive front, desperate to out-cool him, but of course he won that race hands down. I was sticky with sweat by the time I was done. Not only that, my tattoo was finished in about a tenth of the time it took Mike to get his done, and it didn't look anywhere near as good as his. His looked amazing.

Outdone by Mike. Yet again.

◆

'I need to phone Mandy,' I say. I know what Mike wants me to do, but I'm just not prepared.

It's dick o'clock back home but thankfully Mandy answers, and I explain the situation to her. I need her to send me a picture of the scarab design. Her and Chris, both talented designers, had helped Mike draw out and refine his original design. Apparently my appointment at the tattooist is this afternoon. She's on it right away, groggily firing up the computer and promising me an imminent email.

'Sent,' she says. 'Can I go back to bed?'

'Sure. Thanks Mandy.' My phone emits a little incoming ping.

'Good luck, Royd.'

The next decision is where to have the tattoo. There's no way I'm having it on my back, for two reasons. Firstly, that was Mike's thing. This isn't about copying him, it's about remembering him. Secondly, and far more importantly, it would have to be a big bloody tattoo if I had it there, and I'm way too much of a wimp to get something like that done.

My left arm is already tattooed with the Aztec design I had done in Chicago with Mike. My right lower leg has the winged serpent. I think about it as we drive into downtown Auckland, and settle on the inside of my left wrist. I want to be able to see it myself, but not necessarily have it constantly on show. I tend to keep my spare hair-bands there, so they will provide a little cover for the tattoo. It can be there for me to look at when I want to, but not be in anybody's face. Also that will mean it can be pretty small. And it should hurt less having it done there. Sorted. Decided.

We pitch up at the tattooists, and I'm quietly buzzing now. A bit like the needle that's about to be stuck into me a zillion times. It's a short wait. Pretty soon I'm lying down with an inked outline of Mike's scarab ready and waiting on my left wrist. The buzz of the needle begins.

I was wrong. Utterly wrong. It hurts big time. I must have bony wrists. Every time that needle hits the bone it hurts like hell. It's a nice pain, but it's still a pain. And now I have a camera I have to look cool for. I smile down the lens at Drew, hoping the high definition won't show the sweat that's starting to bead on me.

Amidst the delicious pain of the needle repeatedly jabbing into my flesh, I feel a thread, a connection back to Mike. I look down at the emerging beetle, its wings outspread, then close my eyes. I can picture Mike, his smiling and calm face resting on the back of the chair he is leant over, the same design being etched into his back.

And an hour or so later I'm done. I'm inked. I look down at my own version of Mike's tattoo. It's such a strong link to him. I feel great. Hang on, I really do feel great. Somehow this whole experience has shocked my system into finally recovering from that lingering bloody cold. Or it's a weird coincidence. Either way, I feel amazing. I've ticked off my first task in New Zealand, and I am good to go. I'm ready for more. Bring it on.

◆

I look at that tattoo now – and I mean now, here in Wales, not the contrived now of New Zealand and the bucket list – and I absolutely love it. I love the way that, even if I look down at the top of my arm, I can see the very tips of the wings just curling up from underneath, peeking out. Any way I look at my wrist I can see a part of it. I can immediately tell that it's there. Always. Eternally. Just like Mike wanted. Anyone who sees it always comments on it, remarks how beautiful it is, and you know what . . . it always gives me a reason to talk about Mike. I can say as little or as much as I want. Most of the time it's enough to just say it was my brother's design, it was the tattoo he had on his back. It's a nice way of me being able to introduce Mike to other people. It keeps me joined to Mike, keeps a little of him here with me. For ever.

Yeah, I reckon I nailed that task.

Samson

I'm going to swear, and I don't care who hears me. I'm going to swear a lot. I lower the iPad, fully aware that I have an idiotic look of disbelief and fear on my face, and try to hide it with a smile.

'Shave my fucking hair off?' I begin. That's what Mike just tasked me to do. 'Fuck off. I'm not going to shave my . . . I can't shave my hair off! Literally, shave my hair off?' I shake my head, my head of glorious thick long dark HAIR. My precious hair. Okay, it's dyed and it's tied back so it doesn't annoy me, but still. 'What a wanker! I can't fucking shave my hair off so early on!'

'Your hair's too long. Shave it off.'

Mike's words!

This really is a stitch-up. Standing by a tree near our Jucy Snooze hotel, I have nowhere but everywhere to run. But I'm gobsmacked. If I'd really tried to figure out what Mike was going to put on the list, I probably would've guessed this, but I didn't, so I'm reeling. Did it have to be so early on in the process? I have to be on camera, for fuck's sake!

Okay, I'm done swearing. Back story time.

I got to play a ranger in *The Return of the King*. An extra, yes, but a ranger nonetheless. I'd read somewhere that filming was coming to an end on *The Lord of the Rings* and thought I'd chance my arm and see if I couldn't have a peek at what it was like on set.

So I emailed a friend of mine, Tracy Lorie (unfortunately not with us any more), who happened to then be the head of publicity at New Line Cinema, and asked if there might be any way I could visit the set.

She replied almost immediately with words to the effect of 'oh my word, of course you can. I didn't think you wanted to, but yes, you're more than welcome. I'd love to see you over there. But you're going to have to be quick. They finish filming in a month.'

I was there, a week later, excited to get a glimpse of what little I might be allowed to see, really expecting nothing more than that. Instead, I ended up being fitted for a costume and playing a ranger handing out spears in Osgiliath. Since I was, albeit very briefly, close to the camera, I needed a wig. And a good wig at that. So I ended up wearing Viggo Mortensen's wig. I had Aragorn's hair flowing over me!

Well, that vague resemblance to Aragorn sat well with me. I liked the look, so I started growing my hair out. It's been growing ever since, and it's long. Thick, luscious and beautifully long. I should probably mention that Mike had long hair too for a while. He used to wear it in a ponytail until he decided it looked silly and got sick of it. Me, I use a hair-band. I don't actually want all this hair over my face and getting in the way, so I scrape it back and tie it up. It's so thick that when I tie it back it sits in a great bouffant bun at the back of my head. I shave patches away underneath so it sits better.

I haven't been to a proper hairdresser for twenty or thirty years. If I ever feel the need I just hack the odd bit off with some scissors. I've shaved bits of it, dyed it all kinds of colours and almost always worn it scraped back. Mike thought that was idiotic, and ribbed me for years. But I like it. It's my thing. It's me. And I'm on camera – I need to look good. It's one thing completely failing to go to the gym then having to take my shirt off, but I just can't have a shaved head for the rest of the documentary. I'm relying on my hair. It's my safety net. If I do have to get semi-naked again, at least my hair would look good. Right?

Wrong. This is Mike flipping two fingers at me. 'Got you at last,' he'd say with a grin. He's been banging on at me for years to get it cut. And now, when he knows I have no choice, when he knows I have sworn to do whatever he's put on the list, now he drops this on me. I should have known. When Mike was compiling the list I was extra careful not to remind him of any fears I had, or things I really didn't want to do. Spiders is the big one. I never mentioned spiders to him, because I am absolutely terrified of them. Unlike him – he would carefully remove any scary spiders from the house while I ran about screaming like a tit.

I knew some of the list would be a source of amusement to Mike. At my expense. 'Look, about this list,' I said to him, a few months before he passed. 'I'll do whatever's on it, but it can't be, you know, like *Dirty Sanchez*.'

To clarify, I was referring to the Welsh version of *Jackass*, which is similar, but on steroids. 'You can't just tell me to walk into a restaurant and take a dump on a table in front of diners.'

And I remember Mike, wearing his mask and at this point unable to talk, looking up at me with those big expressive eyes of his as if to say, 'You'll do whatever I tell you to do, Royd.' But I don't want to be on camera for the rest of the list with no hair. There must be a compromise.

'I'll do it, but I'll do it last,' I suggest. 'I can get a razor and on the last day I'll just do it myself.' Seems like a solution to me.

But nobody's having it. Drew offers me a wistful shake of his hypocritically overly-haired head. Apparently that's not in the spirit of the list. My desperation soon dissipates into sadness. Fine. I have to do it. That was the deal I made with Mike. If he says do it, I do it. I'm actually going through the five stages of grief. That's how traumatic this is to me.

Denial. No, never going to happen.

Anger. No way, I'm not going to shave my hair off.

Bargaining. I'll do it, but I'll do it later, okay?

Depression. This sucks.

Acceptance. Fine, let's get it done.

I cycle through those five stages, on repeat, every few minutes on the way to the hairdressers. I'm still in shock, still uncertain if I have the ability to go through with this. I'm angry, sad, desperate. I'm doing it, not doing it, doing it. It's all I've got. It's me. What am I without it? But Mike says shave it off. Damn it. I have to. But I can't!

We're early, so we grab a coffee. Fat lot of good that will do. I could have used a shot, though. I decide to FaceTime Story back in the UK. He's actually flying over in a few days, but for now he's back home, and it's late. He's a night owl, so I'm sure he'll still be up. And I need some perspective, so tough.

'It's only hair,' he helpfully points out after I've explained the situation to him. Easy for him to say with his short hair. Where's his empathy? 'It'll grow back. Think of it as a new beginning too. You're finally on this important journey which will bring positive changes to you. And also, stop being a wimp!'

He's right. Damn it. He's my son, he's younger than me; he shouldn't be the one imparting wisdom, advising me correctly. But he's right. It is only hair. It will grow back. And this journey will hopefully change me and get me out of the funk I've been in. Of course I think of Mike. How can I not? What he went through, he went through with the awful knowledge that it wouldn't get better. So what if I cut my hair off? It's nothing compared to what Mike endured. It's less than nothing. Let's do this.

Walking up the stairs to the salon, however, I'm already back-tracking, already lapsing into feeling sorry for myself again. I might as well resign myself to the fact that I will never get another girl ever again. It's a disaster.

'How are you?' asks the 'executioner' as I walk in.

'I'm not good,' I answer like a spoiled teenager, dragging my feet, head down. This is the moment I'd disconsolately kick a can down the road if I could.

I insist on doing the first bit myself. I need to own this. I look in the mirror at what is about to be the old me, and turn the clippers on. The angry buzz they make sends a wave of panic over me. I can't do this.

But I do. I take off a big chunk of my lovely, precious hair and let it fall slowly to the floor. And so it begins. I relinquish the clippers and let the expert have at it. And in no time at all I'm left with just a floppy mohawk, a length of hair down the middle of my head that's all bunched up in a hair-band and sticking up. The sides are gone. The back is gone. I want to cut this last bit off myself, so I ask the hairdresser to hold it upright as I take a large pair of scissors to it.

Snip. It's gone.

It's all gone.

I run my hand over my head. It feels like a tennis ball. I'd dyed my hair before I left for New Zealand; I wanted to look my best for the documentary. Well that ship has sailed, hasn't it? All those different shoddily applied dyes and weird self-cuts have left what little hair I have now, my tennis ball head, looking like a leopard, a motley patchwork of reds, browns and bleached bits.

Actually, it feels quite nice. Weird, but nice.

I stand up and look down at the floor. It's a sea of hair. It looks like at least fifteen people have had their hair cut. I pick up a pile of my discarded locks and stroke them sadly for the camera, but actually I feel okay. I tell myself that nobody who knows me will give a monkey's if I have short hair, and anybody I meet that doesn't know me won't know that I used to have such magnificent hair. So who cares?

It really doesn't matter.

I'll just have to find girls who like short hair.

◆

Drew must have taken pity on me and my new hairdo. Either that or my suspicions – based on his facial hair and build – that he likes a beer or two were well founded. Either way, he's got the pints in and we're sitting 'bonding' outside a bar that backs onto the harbour. I suppose it was inevitable. We're stuck together for a few months here, so it was unrealistic to pretend we wouldn't have a conversation or two that doesn't involve a camera.

And it turns out we have something profound in common. Drew lost a brother a few years ago. Chris, who had cerebral palsy, had defiantly lived as active a life as his disability permitted. He'd undertaken voyages on tall ships and been hoisted up the mast in his wheelchair. He was gregarious, with a sharp sense of humour. Listening to Drew talk about him, I couldn't help think of Mike. Even though Chris had never enjoyed the breadth of physicality that Mike had before the MND set in, he clearly spent his whole life railing against expectations of what he could and couldn't do. Until what should have been a routine hip replacement operation when he was only thirty-seven led to an infection that proved virulently, and fatally, resistant to all the different antibiotics he was being given.

'I didn't want to say anything,' Drew tells me. 'I don't want to presume to know what you've been through, just because of that. But here we are.'

It's like seeing Drew for the first time. Previously I had decided that he was just part of the camera that was always on his shoulder. I didn't need to have these conversations. I didn't need him to be a friend. And yet, now, I see that he could easily be just that. I can see in his face a natural empathy. He gets it. He's experienced a similar tragedy to me, and now he's on this journey with me too.

I sip at my beer. Half a pint will probably do me. It's funny, I think when Drew next points the camera at me, I will talk to him rather than the lens.

The Rock and the Bottle

It's Mike's birthday. Or it would have been. It's hard. Anniversaries, birthdays, Christmas, those kind of days . . . they're always painful. Yesterday was tougher though, remembering the day we buried Mike two years ago.

I'm glad Story is here. I picked him up from the airport a couple of days ago and hugged him tight. He's a grown man now, but he's still my baby boy.

I was in my mid-twenties when I became a father. I'd never considered parenting as something I'd be any good at. I don't think I was particularly good around kids, but then who is at that age? I was too busy being young and free and vaguely wild. I was managing bands, living in a big shared house, a party house, and had started a clothing business with Mike.

There was a woman in Liverpool who made jeans by hand to any specification asked of her. Mike and I were both into rap in a big way, so we liked our jeans voluminous. After a while I realised that we could corner this market. We took orders for jeans, offering as much bagginess or crotch room as you could handle, and had T-shirts printed with cool designs done by a friend of ours, Jon. My favourite was a car full of teddy bears, mid-drive-by, one of them levelling a gun straight down the perspective line at the viewer.

For a while we called the business Hobbit – Truly Phat Rags, until we got a friendly version of a cease and desist letter from the estate lawyers, politely pointing out our copyright infringement and asking us what on Middle Earth we thought we were doing. We quickly changed the name to Fernandez – Stitches for Bitches, assumed alter-egos when we posed, rap style, for the brochure. Mike became 'Micky' and I became 'CitKat', a nickname I borrowed from a porn star. Ridiculous. But, for a while, business boomed.

But then, faced with imminent fatherhood, everything changed. I moved into a static caravan outside Dad's house. It was cold, draughty and somewhat wobbly in high winds, but it was free. I worked for him too, learning the ropes at the printing business that I would later take over. And when Story was born, everything changed again. The moment he appeared I felt an instantaneous and overwhelming love for him, like nothing I had ever felt in my life. It made no sense, yet it made perfect sense. I had a real person to love and care for, to protect, to provide for. For the rest of my life. I suppose I grew up. I matured. A bit. I phoned Dad from the hospital and I could hear the pride in his voice. I wasn't a kid anymore. I was a father. I'd done what he had done and we had something powerful in common.

Story's mum and I split up a couple of years later, but amicably shared custody. I threw myself into being a single dad, learning as I went, and I think I did a decent job of it. While Story was in the womb, Mike would tease me when I refused to indulge in the lifestyle of someone with no responsibilities. But he took to being an uncle. He would still rib me for not going out, for being boring, but he got it. He understood even better when, several years later, Edan came along. Mike joined the club. Like me, he doted on his son.

And of course we parented a little differently. Mike was Mike. He was happy for Edan to assert his independence, to be adventurous, to take risks, to scrape his knees or bump his head. I was the opposite. I wanted to wrap Story in cotton wool. I wouldn't let him ride his bike without a helmet. The idea of even the slightest injury to him was a source of anxiety to me.

I wanted Story to share a part of this journey with me. He's got a year's work visa so he'll go off at some point and make his own adventure. If I can bear to let him. He's like me in a lot of ways. He has an itch for travelling and loves to expand his horizons. When he was old enough, he spent six months hitchhiking around Europe. He spent another six months travelling and working in India, ending up promoting a bar in the Himalayas, of all things. Story isn't just my son; he's my best mate as well. We're huggy and extremely close. We always have been. Since the day he was born I couldn't let him go. Since Mike died my whole family has taken to hugging and kissing and saying 'I love you'.

Loss does that to a family.

Andy is here too. Andy's a good mate of mine, who was close to Mike as well. He used to play drums in a band that I managed back in the day. He's been to Norway with me and Mike, and he was there in Avoriaz, pointing a phone at my leopard-print thong. He even has a scarab beetle tattoo. As well as Story, I wanted someone else who knew Mike to be here.

So we're all here on Mike's birthday, sitting quietly and a little sadly outside a lovely little café in Ponsonby, a beautiful bohemian suburb of Auckland, and I've just had some slow-cooked eggs. To be honest, they tasted pretty much like eggs would if they were cooked at the normal speed, but what do I know?

'Right, Father,' Story announces quite formally. He's got the dreaded iPad in his hands. 'This is a message from Mike.'

I close my eyes and let my head fall forwards. This feels, especially today, such a private moment. I listen to my son. Reading his uncle's words.

'I wrote something on the TV for you. Remember that moment. It meant the world to me.'

I remember it well. Too well. Not even Story knows what this is referring to.

It was about nine in the evening. I'd been with Mike for what had been a long and exhausting day, and Laura was about to take over for the night. We didn't know at the time, but this was only a few days before he passed.

Mike wanted something.

For the briefest of nanoseconds I thought to myself, *I'm tired. I want to go home and recover.* Then I kicked myself and started to go through the checklist with Mike. I ascertained it wasn't an emergency, so out came the Apple TV. I started to enter the letters as Mike slowly and painfully blinked his big eyes at me. I was looking at him, not the television, but after a few blinks I glanced over at the screen. There in the search bar were the beginnings of a phrase, 'I lov—'

'No, no, no, no. Mike, I know. I know,' I told him, welling up. 'I love you too. You don't have to . . .' I didn't want him to go through the pain of blinking his way through the rest of the sentence. He didn't need to. But no, his eyes told me. That wasn't what he wanted to say.

So we continued. I finished off the word 'love', then studied Mike's face while he looked at the screen, blinking, determined to get his words out. I always knew when he was finished because his eyes would open slightly wider, as if to say 'take a look'.

His eyes opened a fraction. I turned to the TV.

I love hugs.

I melted.

And I gave him a massive hug, which wasn't as simple as you might imagine. Mike couldn't move a muscle, and he was constantly tender and in pain. When I hugged him I had to weave my arms through the sling and the harness and the tube from the breathing assist and various other things that were attached to him or used to prop him up, and be really careful not to hurt him in any way. I'd wrap my arms around him and nuzzle my face into his neck. I know Mike desperately wanted to be able to throw his arms around me in return, to embrace me and hug me back, but he did all that he could. He pushed his head against mine as firmly as he was able.

'I'll see you in the morning, bruv,' I told him. 'I love you.'

I love hugs.

Mike must have had Laura write that task barely days before he died.

'Write it on one of these flyers,' Story finishes, handing me a printed photograph. It's me and Mike, a school photo. It must be Mike's first year in primary school and my last, the only year we would have been in the same school together. There we are with our little uniforms and our laughable school photo haircuts. Unbearably cute.

I love hugs. I write it on the photo with a sharpie. I'm ragged inside, a whirling mess of remembering Mike in the days before he died, wishing he was here on his birthday, looking at his five-year-old face, and having my darling son, Story, beside me.

I do the only thing I can do. I hug Story, pushing my face into his shoulder. 'I love you,' I whisper. When we get in the car after breakfast I can't let go of Story. Sitting in the front passenger seat as we drive out of Auckland, I reach back behind my head and my hands find his. Nobody talks. There's just music playing and noisy thoughts in my head.

After some time I spot some landmarks that seem familiar.

I know where we're going.

◆

When Mike and I were in Auckland for the Air New Zealand safety video we hung out with a couple of friends of mine, Cliff and Larry, who had also been asked to be in the video. They worked for TheOneRing, a fan site that had initially sent spies to photograph the sets of *The Lord of the Rings* from hilltops, just to satisfy the hunger of the Tolkien fans. Having initially been escorted from the set, they were soon invited back and ended up being an integral part of creating the press and hype around the films as they were made.

The day before filming, Cliff suggested we drive out to a place he'd been to back in the day, a beach where the sand was volcanic black. He called it Black Sand Beach, but it probably has a proper name. So Mike and I hopped into a car with them and off we went.

It's a stunning bit of coastline. We made our way from the car park along a path that opened out to a huge expanse of black sand. And we spent the day there, walking, hanging out, taking some great photos and chatting with Cliff and Larry. The weather was perfect, sunny and warm, and the sand was flat, smooth and firm, making walking almost hazard-free for Mike.

Mike used his cane to write a word in the sand. It's not a nice word, but in the interest of being authentic . . .

CUNT.

I took a photo of Mike, the end of his cane still resting on the sand at the bottom of the 'T', wearing a cheeky smile. It was so incongruent with those beautiful surroundings, and it had precedent for us. Once, he'd splattered the word in blobs of paint from a paintball gun and sent me a photo. I'd pissed it in snow (no mean feat!) and sent him a photo. Another time, when I was pressure-washing Mum's patio, I managed to etch it in the mildew and moss and greenness. I sent Mike a photo, captioning it with 'Just washing Mum's house – this is as far as I got. Can't be arsed anymore, so leaving it like this.'

It was just a thing Mike and I did. We'd find amusing and original ways to affectionately call each other a . . . that word, and often at the most inappropriate moment. So when Mike called me over to see what he'd done with his walking stick it was a way of connecting, of marking the moment with a private joke that still makes me smile to this day.

Besides, the tide was going to come in. It's not like it was permanent.

Walking back to the car, I was chatting with Cliff and Larry. Mike had gone on ahead. As we rounded a corner, there he was in his long coat, perched on one of the huge rocks that circled the car park, thoughtfully holding his cane. He just looked really cool. Obviously I didn't tell him that. I didn't say, 'Hey Mike, don't move. I want to take a photo because you look cool as hell, man.' But I did want to capture the moment.

'Hang on, that's a nice picture,' I said, feigning a degree of apathy, and snapped a great shot of him sitting there doing his own thing. Being Mike.

◆

Black Sand Beach. I'm given a bottle to put the flyer in, the picture of me and Mike with 'I love hugs' written above our smiling faces. To be here on his birthday, with Story beside me, is just perfect.

I scout around the car park, Story by my side, with my phone in my hand and the picture of Mike on the screen. Cool Mike. Sitting on the rock. I tell Story all about that day while we look for the rock. And then I see it. I compare it to what's on my phone. That's the one. Vegetation has grown up around it and the light is different, but the shape is unmistakable. It's weird seeing it; it's just a rock. And Mike isn't sitting on it.

It's empty.

Mike wants me to throw this 'message in a bottle' into the sea, into the great bosom of the Pacific Ocean. Story and I walk across the black sand towards the foaming water. It's a big beach, and a long walk. But it's beautiful. I'm teary and overcome with emotion, and there's no one I'd rather have to hold on to than Story. We walk on, me remembering Mike here, smiling, writing a bad word in the sand, and Story seeing it all for the first time.

It's a blustery day and the waves are up. I try a few times to hurl the bottle into the surf as far as I can, but the tide keeps pushing it back onto the beach. It's not happening, Mike. I'm sorry. I pick up the bottle and slip it into the pocket of my hoodie. I'll commit it to the sea when the moment is right.

I promise.

Where Faith Lives

It's a lengthy crossing from Auckland to Coromandel by sail. But we've made it. The peninsula is beautiful. Lush green hills climb up out of the small harbour town, and that's where we're headed next. Up and into and over those hills. Beyond that, I've no idea. I'm just glad to get back on firm ground.

I was tasked, on the way over here, with learning to sail. I had plenty of time to pick up a few tips; I've hoisted the sail, steered the boat, added a few knots to my repertoire and have even been thrown overboard for a crucial lesson in maritime survival and 'man overboard' procedure (or so I was told). To be fair, I jumped. Apparently that's the most fun thing about a catamaran. You can throw yourself into the sea from the front of the boat and safely let it pass over the top of you, untouched by its twin hulls. I'm not a confident swimmer at the best of times, so I'm never overly thrilled about jumping into any bit of water if my feet can't touch the bottom. It's the not knowing what's down there that scares me. Like sharks.

But I did it. And I did it again. The second time, as per instructions, I didn't grab the safety rope at the stern and I allowed the boat to drift slowly away from me. I trod water for a while, watching the catamaran shrink into the blue. It was unnerving, but I was in good hands. Treading water next to me was one of the most ideal people to have around in such a situation, champion Kiwi oarsman Rob Hamill.

Rob's a legend. He won silver at the World Rowing Championships in 1994, and went on to be one of the winning pair in the first Atlantic Rowing Race in 1997. He rowed all the way across the Atlantic. Naked. If anyone can keep me safe at sea, Rob can. It's his catamaran, and it's thanks to him and his lovely family that I've made it here to Coromandel.

The crossing wasn't all hoisting and splashing and learning. I got to chat to Rob for a while too. We sat on the netting strung between the prows of the two hulls and traded tragedies. Back in 1978, when Rob was just fourteen, his older brother Kerry was sailing between Singapore and Bangkok when he got caught in a storm. His boat inadvertently strayed into Cambodian waters and he was captured by the Khmer Rouge, who tortured, interrogated and eventually killed him. As if that wasn't enough, his other older brother, John, killed himself after learning of Kerry's fate.

Rob talked openly about his experiences, about pursuing and testifying against the war criminals who had killed his brother, but he was as interested in hearing about Mike as I was in hearing about Kerry. As grim as the subject matter was, it was a joy to open up to someone so naturally empathic and generous. Rob and his partner Rachel often take to the sea with their three boys, Finn, Declan and Ivan, and have chosen to home-school them. And they're nailing it. Those boys are so kind, mature, sweet and intelligent. Sharing a small boat with them has been a special time, and one I know Mike would have loved as well.

◆

We're driven by a representative of the Coromandel Tourist Board up into the hills, where there was something of a gold rush in the nineteenth century. Mike's eyes would have lit up at hearing that. It's a stunning drive to the other side of the peninsula, where we arrive at a beach and I'm presented with a kayak.

Themes are already becoming apparent in the tasks Mike has set me. Some are meant to challenge me. Some are emotive throwbacks to times I spent with him. Some things are, bluntly, meant to make me look like a tit. And some are simply things that Mike really wanted to do.

Paddling over the clear water on the eastern coast of the Coromandel, around the rugged headlands, and pulling my kayak up onto the beautiful secluded beach of Cathedral Cove is definitely something Mike would have loved to have done. And something I wish I could be doing right now with him. I know, when he was making this list, that he googled places to go in New Zealand. I can imagine him looking at pictures of this place, finding it on a map, and being wowed by its beauty.

And it is breathtaking. Cathedral Cove is clearly best accessed by the sea. There is a path, one which Drew is hopefully currently making his way down, having passed filming duties to water resistant GoPros, but striding ashore from the Pacific Ocean, like some intrepid adventurer, is definitely the way to arrive. The soft sandy beach is dotted with boulders and framed by cliffs that rise up sharply at either end. There's a cave, a natural waterfall and a nice rock for me to sit on and look out at the sea, now glowing golden in the early evening sun.

'Thank you for loving me and looking after me the way you did,' Mike wrote as part of his brief for sending me here. 'I'm with you always.'

He gifted me this experience. As a way of saying thank you. I never wanted Mike's thanks. Not once. Every day, when he was ill, I would hug him and tell him I loved him, and he'd tell me he loved me. And he'd thank me. And I'd wave it off. I didn't want anything in return for loving and caring for him. Of course I didn't. People say to me that what I did, looking after Mike, was incredible. I can't see it. I can't see how anyone would have done anything different in that situation. But unless you're faced with it, you don't imagine yourself having to care for your brother, or any loved one. You don't consider what it involves. You can't train for it. You can't prepare yourself. But when it happens, you step up. Because it's important. Because that's what you do.

And still, 'thank you,' Mike would say in the evening, before I went home for the night.

'Shush,' I'd wave it away. 'What for? I've just been sitting watching TV with you! Shut up!'

Well, I have to accept his thanks now. I can't dismiss it. He's not here.

'Thank you for loving me.'

What do I say to that? Nothing. He's got me. He's finally managed to thank me and get the last word in.

My sweet brother.

I wish you were here, Mike. More than anything in the world.

I can picture him here. He would have felt so at home, so at peace. He'd be sitting here beside me, looking at the sea and the sunset, barely speaking except to marvel at the sheer glory of our surroundings. Absorbing the beauty. I let the peace wash over me, let it level out my emotions, my fear, my apprehension, my emptiness, my grief.

'Thank you for loving me.'

No, Mike. Thank you.

◆

The resourceful Kiwi kayaker, who led the way here, saunters over.

'You want a coffee, Royd?'

'Oh,' I say, surprised. 'I'd love a latte, please.'

'Right oh, mate. Sugar?'

What? I wasn't serious. Well, I was. I'd love a latte, but I was obviously being flippant. We're stuffed into slick wetsuits, on a beach in the middle of nowhere, having just got out of a kayak. There's nothing here but nature. Certainly not a café.

Bless the Kiwis, though. This guy knows how to enjoy his wilderness. He carefully unpacks a waterproof pack and assembles some kit, all he needs to make good on his promise, and in a few minutes I'm clutching a steaming, frothing, latte.

'You want a homemade shortbread cookie with that, mate?' He holds out a small Tupperware pot.

Uh . . . yes please.

Drew finally makes it to the beach, down that awful-looking path. He looks flustered and out of breath. He grumbles about how heavy the camera kit is and how far he's walked and how steep the three headlands are that he's just traversed. Despite that, it's good to see him. At one point back on Black Sand Beach he pointed the camera at me for a while and we talked. He put me in the frame and we chatted about Mike. I ignored the camera and talked to Drew. As I would to a friend.

'Yeah,' I faux empathise, 'kayaking is pretty physical stuff too.'

'Sure. You want to swap for the way back?'

I pretend to consider this. 'Nah, you're alright,' I smile as sweetly as I can. 'Have a cookie. It'll give you energy.'

Above the Clouds

I'd ridiculously believed we were just going for coffee.

I'm back in Auckland now, having sailed back from the Coromandel with Rob and his family. When we were motoring into the harbour, Rob suggested I have a go up the mast. I'm not one for heights, but sod it. I agreed. It's amazing how frighteningly small a boat can look when you're hanging from a wire sixty feet above it. I did get a good view of Sky Tower though, standing proud over the Auckland skyline.

And I've got a good view of it now, albeit extremely close-up. My coffee suddenly tastes more bitter than it should. Why? Because apparently I now have to go up that tower and jump off it. Why would anyone want to do such a stupid thing? It's madness. And I'm bricking it. Again.

We go into the tower and immediately down some stairs to the basement. I get weighed (what's a good weight for this kind of thing, anyway?), kitted up in a jump suit and strapped into harnesses, all the time looking around at photos on the wall of other people, similarly dressed, smiling and looking like they're having the time of their lives. I suppose they can hardly put pictures up of people like me, pasty white, wide-eyed and dry-mouthed with abject fear.

Now that I look like I'm about to be shot out of a cannon at a circus, trussed up in my multicolour jump suit, we get in the lift. It's the kind of lift that makes your ears pop. Halfway up I can see Auckland out of a window and, I must say, we're plenty high enough already. I don't know or care how high. Thousands of feet, I'd say.

Eventually we get to the top and follow a narrow corridor to a bright windowed room. Out of the window I see some lunatic throw him or herself off a walkway and disappear quickly in the direction of the crowded downtown pavement. There's a hideous screaming grinding sound and I look over to see a cable rapidly unwinding from some kind of pulley system, the other end mercifully remaining attached to the jumper.

'Has anyone ever died doing this?' I ask as someone double-checks the tightness of my straps.

'No. We wouldn't still be open if they had.'

But they could. Someone could. I could.

Drew gets to venture outside before me. He's dressed in a bright orange jump suit like some kind of convict which, judging by his rejected ESTA, maybe he should be. I can't see his face past the camera on his shoulder that he's pointing at me, but surely he's at least a little bit nervous? The pulley whines and screeches next to me as the wire is retracted.

It's my turn. I shuffle unsteadily out of the door into the wind and am subjected to a baffling sequence of being clipped and unclipped and clipped again to various bits of the metal walkway and side rail that jut out from the side of the tower. I look down. Why did I do that? The floor is mesh. I can see right through it. I'm instantly dizzy, and my knuckles whiten as I grip the rail for support. People do this for fun.

The poor woman who has to stand out here for a living, sending people to their self-imagined dooms, takes great delight in telling me just how many hundreds of thousands of feet up we are. Look at the lovely view of Auckland. Do I have to? She speaks to the (clean-up?) crew on the ground, and tells them I'm about to jump. Am I? Really? I shuffle reluctantly towards the edge. A sudden gust buffets me and I grip the rail even harder.

'Okay, Royd is coming down now.' She is starting to sound impatient.

I had planned to do some kind of superhero jump, to descend in some Karate Kid crane-like pose with one foot up and my hands outstretched, then land like Captain America. That was before I saw what it was like millions of feet up in the air.

'In three . . .'

No, wait.

'Two . . .'

Okay, I'll do it.

'One . . .'

I'm going to jump!

'Go!'

Sod that! I freeze. My hands absolutely refuse to let go. She looks at me with a mix of amusement and frustration. She's doubt-less seen every manifestation of fear up here. I'm just another blouse that's too scared to jump. Or too sensible. Or . . . oh, why didn't I just jump? Now it's even harder.

'Come on, Royd!' Again it's a subtle mix between 'get on with it' and an encouraging, 'you can do it, mate.'

I brace myself.

'In three . . .'

Please, no.

'Two . . .'

I really don't want to.

'One . . .'

You're a superhero, Royd. Do it.

'Go!'

I go. My crane pose lasts for all of a couple of seconds, and then I'm at the mercy of gravity and the wire that I can't even feel attached to me. It's weird. It's called an assisted fall, which means you only fall as fast as the wire wants you to, which is plenty fast enough by the way. I feel a slight resistance, something holding me back from complete free fall. Looking at the ground billions of feet below me, I can make out ant people and some toy cars. And for the briefest moment, with the wind and the screeching wire drowning out any scream I could emit, time stands still.

And then, out of nowhere, the concrete rushes up towards my face and the brakes kick in. My seemingly fatal fall is rapidly slowed and I'm pulled upright just before I come to a standstill and land perfectly, if a little shakily, on the ground. I cough, a ragged smile of relief on my face as I am unclipped from the wire. My mouth is a desert and my legs have turned to jelly. If I haven't actually soiled myself, I think I came very close. But it's done. Tick. Finished. Never again.

And then I remember that Story is due to come down after me. That's a whole other level of fear. Nobody has ever died doing this. I didn't die. He'll be fine. But what if he's not? My precious son! I wouldn't even let him go out on his bike in the village when he was young. It took months of him begging me before I eventually caved. And it's a really quiet village.

And now he's about to jump. It's safe, of course it is. I just did it. But what if it's not? Oh, is that him? I look up and see Story, arms outstretched, plummeting towards me. Towards the earth. I can barely watch.

He lands safely. Gracefully, even. 'That was easy,' he grins. 'Can I do it again?' He's not even remotely fazed.

Just how Mike would have been.

◆

I'd completely forgotten the second part of the task. But I've changed into an orange jump suit, along with Story and Andy. Drew's still got his on. And we've gone back up in the lift. It's time to do the sky walk. We're going to go out of the top (nearly) of the tower and walk around it. I forgot about it because it didn't seem like such a big deal. Not compared to jumping off the thing.

I take all that back. I'm out in the fresh air, clipped worryingly loosely to a wire above my head. The walkway around the tower is mesh, maybe a metre wide, and several away from the walls of the tower. There is nothing to hold on to or lean on, nothing to provide any kind of comfort or sense of security. And the so-called safety rope is slack; it's not supporting me in the slightest. I've been reliably informed that it will hold me if I fall. But I don't want to fall. Not even a little bit. And I've got Story behind me, so I'm doubly scared.

You'd think it would be easy to walk along a metre-wide path with a degree of confidence, but trillions of feet up in the gusting wind, it's hard enough to keep your balance, let alone walk. I'm convinced I'll trip over my own feet and fall, and the safety line will snap. I look over at the tower, into the windows of The Sugar Club, one of the restaurants belonging to award-winning chef Peter Gordon, and Drew is taking a break from filming. He's scurried into the safety of indoors and is sipping what I imagine is the best coffee in the world. Lucky bugger. He salutes me with his cup and smirks, clearly happy to let the GoPros he has attached to us do all his work for him.

Our guide (I still can't believe people do this for a job and come up here every day to casually stroll around the tower) tells us it's time to test our safety lines. Not test. Demonstrate. He wants me to put my feet on the edge of the walkway and lean back, out over the precipice. Madness. I don't care who's waiting to go next, I'm taking my time. I shuffle towards the edge. There is nowhere to look that isn't terrifying. I stare at my feet, because I'm determined to keep them attached to something, but I can see down through the mesh at the ants and toy cars below. It takes every ounce of effort and self-persuasion I possess, but I slowly lean back. My hands, slick with sweat, grip pointlessly onto my rope until I feel it tighten and take my weight.

'Let go of the rope, Royd,' our guide tells me. 'Stretch your arms out.'

I know that holding the rope makes bugger all difference, but the idea of letting go seems counter-intuitive. Oh well. I slowly relinquish my grip and push my arms out a little from my sides. For a second. Then I'm pulling myself back onto the meagre comfort of the walkway with my heart pounding out of my chest. I look to my left to see Story, casually leaning back with complete faith in his rope. His arms are perfectly splayed out, and his head is back. He's loving it and I almost faint seeing him flirt with danger so casually.

We carry on around the tower. At one point the wind picks up and any slight confidence I'd found dissipates quickly, but I can see the door now. We make the final few yards and I grab hold of the handrail as soon as I can reach it. And then we're indoors. Safe. For now.

Was there anything enlightening about the whole experience? Did I learn anything about myself during the jump or the walk? Was I grateful for it being on the list?

No. No. And no. All it really did for me was confirm what I already knew.

I'm a massive pussy.

The Need for Speed

I'm back in a jump suit again. Or maybe it's a boiler suit. I don't know. But there are no towers in sight today. No, today I'm at Hampton Downs racetrack in the Waikato. And I'm going to be showing off my driving skills. In a really fast car.

In the wet.

This should be fun.

◆

When Mike and I were young, we were keen amateur racers. Living in the middle of nowhere as kids, if where we wanted to go was too far to bike, we'd have to rely on our parents or a pretty useless and slow bus service that only ran every two hours and stopped running altogether at six in the evening.

I couldn't wait to learn to drive. When I was sixteen I got my first car for Christmas, a battered Mini Clubman. It was a knackered old thing, in need of a lot of restoration. The idea was I'd spend the next seven months or so, until I turned seventeen and could take my test, learning how it worked and doing it up. So I gutted it, leaving only the driver's seat intact, and did my utmost to turn it into a rally car.

In that time I taught myself to drive. And I learned stunt driving too. Or at least that's what I called it. Any time my parents weren't around I'd be out in the car, barrelling around the drive and the fields, smashing out handbrake turns and churning up the turf doing doughnuts. I was constantly being told off by my dad, but that didn't stop me.

Our drive went down a long hill to a cattle-grid at the bottom, then climbed up and around a corner towards the main road. A friend of mine, Justin, also had a Mini. We once watched a stage of the RAC Rally racing through woodland near us, and were inspired to do everything we could to jazz up our Minis. Roll cages, bucket seats, all that. One day, Mike wanted to get in for a ride.

He was maybe ten and a bit, and we were sixteen and stupid. So Mike got in the car. It didn't have seatbelts. It didn't have seats! It didn't even have doors! Off tore Justin, with Mike holding on for dear life, ragging it down the hill and over the cattle-grid then gunning it up the hill and around the corner towards the main road. It's not a busy main road, but it's still a road. There was a bit of grass opposite the top of our drive, just across that road. I would usually stop at the road, look left and right, then cross it, do a handbrake turn on the grass, then spin the wheels and roar back up the drive again. Relatively safe. I don't think Justin was aware of the normal procedure.

From the top of the drive I could see another car on the main road, heading our way. I could also see Justin speeding my Mini up the hill with no sign of slowing down. With my little brother on board. The cars looked like they were on a horribly perfect collision course, with no way of seeing each other through the trees. The other car was also coming from the left, so it was set to smash straight into the passenger side of my car. Where there was no door, no seat, no seatbelts and where ten-year-old Mike was holding on.

There was no sense in shouting. Even if there wasn't a roaring engine in his ear, I was too far away to be heard. Visions of Mike being sideswiped by that car flashed in front of my eyes. I would be in so much trouble with my parents too! I prayed that Justin would remember the junction and slow down. But he didn't.

He came out of our drive at speed, missing the other car by what must have been inches. Not feet. It was painfully close. He spun it around and tore back up the drive to where I waited. I was rattled, so vented at him for a while, but we were sixteen; it was soon forgotten. Nothing bad had happened in the end, so what the heck?

Mike got into cars as well when he was older, always fast ones. Even after his diagnosis he got himself a muscly Golf. It was squat and mean, super light, and had paddle shift gears because a clutch would have been too difficult for him to use. And it was lively. I drove it a few times with him. Normally he would assume I couldn't handle it and would constantly tell me to take it easy and not put my foot down, but not then.

'Go on, give it some,' he egged me on. 'Let it go.'

Holy hell, it was fast.

◆

I did a few laps of Hampton Downs with an instructor next to me. I'm sure they would have let me just take the car out on my own, whatever car it was. I thought of him more as a co-driver. Did I mention it was wet?

Well, I thought I was fast. I thought I must have done the fastest lap ever by a civilian, non-professional driver. When I pulled into the pits I was feeling pretty damn chuffed with myself. 'Did it look fast?' I asked, wanting validation. I was greeted with the shaking of heads. Well, it's wet. What was I supposed to do?

Anyway, I'm now strapped into the passenger seat of a Porsche. Don't ask me what kind of Porsche, I've no idea. Behind the wheel is Kiwi racing legend Greg Murphy. He's going to show me how it's done.

'I've never driven this car before.' I think he's grinning at me, but it's hard to tell when he's got a crash helmet on. 'Shall we see what she can do?'

I don't suppose he'll go much faster than I just did.

We eat up the tarmac in the pits and hit the track. Okay, this is fast. Proper fast. He's never driven this car before. Is this a good idea? We hit the first bend and it really doesn't feel like he's in complete control. I want to look over at him, but I'm fixated on the blurry road in front of the car.

'It's a bit slick, ay?' Greg shouts over the scream of the engine. 'I want to see how far I can push it, hold on.' Then he throws us round another bend, drifting perfectly like we're in a scene from *Fast & Furious*. The car seems to barely cling on to the wet tarmac. It's almost like he's trying to throw the back end out. I must be pulling at least a thousand Gs every time we take a corner. I actually feel nauseous. Nauseous and a bit scared, but absolutely thrilled.

Mike would be grinning from ear to ear if he was in my place right now. He'd be goading Greg to go even faster. I don't know if Greg can go any faster. He's pushing the car to the limits of control, if not his then certainly the car's. I'm witnessing a master at work. This is how it's done.

After several blindingly fast laps, we pull in and come to a standstill in the pits. My stomach is churning and my legs are trembling. I can barely get out of the car, and struggle to remove my helmet.

'Wow,' is all I can say.

◆

Mike probably only drove that Golf about ten times. His hands were getting weaker, but more importantly, his drop foot and weak legs meant that he couldn't be sure to operate the brakes safely. It was a real shame. He loved to drive. He loved that car. But he just couldn't use it. Not even at a sensible speed.

Later, when he needed a wheelchair and eventually started getting disability allowance, he got a bigger vehicle. Something his wheelchair would fit into. Something other people would drive, and he never would. It was a bit van-like, but it still had a decent engine for its size. For a while, with a little help, he could just about lift himself upright and get in. I'd drive him, often nowhere in particular, just because he loved being in a car. We'd cruise around, listening to music, trying to out-rap each other.

After a while it came to the point that Mike didn't want to go in the car at all. He didn't much like being a passenger, constantly being reminded of something he loved and would never do again. Driving had played a huge part in his life since he was seventeen, so to lose that, and to lose that independence, was utterly senseless. By the time he needed to be lifted into the car (no mean feat), he had all but completely lost interest in it.

I know exactly why he put that task on the list. It was for him. But I loved it.

Hobbits and Gummies

The Hobbiton set is nestled amidst rolling hills and farmland in the New Zealand countryside. It was spotted by an eagle-eyed location scout in a helicopter, who quite rightly thought the undulating hills and meadows would make the perfect representation of the shire. Mostly dismantled after *The Lord of the Rings*, it was permanently rebuilt for *The Hobbit*, with the view to turning it into the tourist destination it now is.

I'm happily milling around the gift shop with Story and Andy. We drove here from Auckland this morning, ahead of the crew. Yesterday was a 'day off' and today looks set to be the same, just a pleasant visit to this awesome place.

◆

Last time I was here, I was with Mike. I'd been before, years earlier, when I did some press for *The Hobbit*, but I wanted Mike to see it.

Numbers are limited in Hobbiton. You can't just turn up and expect to get on a tour. People tend to book months, sometimes years, in advance. When I knew Mike and I would be in New Zealand, I emailed a friend of mine, Seb, who also happened to be Peter's personal assistant, and asked him if he had any contacts for the Hobbiton set. Seb put me in touch with Russell, who co-owns Hobbiton with Peter. And we were in.

When we arrived at Hobbiton I was expecting us to pay our money, and quietly be allowed to tag along with an existing tour. That would have been favour enough. But when we got there, Russell came out to greet us and invited us to get into his jeep. Visitors normally get special buses down from the gift shop area into the unspoiled set, but instead we had the owner of the place give up a big portion of his day to give us a personal and very unhurried tour.

Although the sun was beaming, it had rained in the days before we got there, so Russell warned us that parts of the set were a bit moist.

'You want some gummies, mate?' he asked generously. We were in a shed near the entrance to the set, stacked with wellington boots. Wellies. Gummies, if you're a Kiwi.

'Oh, yes please. That would be great, thank you.' I was thrilled to be offered an alternative to messing my own shoes up, so I took a pair of size nines and slipped them on.

Russell turned to Mike. 'You want some gummies too, mate?'

Mike looked at me impishly and politely declined. I knew full well in that instant that he would soon be ridiculing me in my wellies. Nobody looks good in wellies. Mike, on the other hand, would look cool in his snazzy trainers. As long as he kept out of the mud.

Hobbiton is quite hilly, and Mike, as you know, was using a walking stick by this time. The stick in question had actually come all the way from America. One morning, while Mike was nursing a beast of a hangover, Marcus (my Camp America friend) and Dave and I played football with some Mexicans in the hot Chicago sun. I'd been out all night, ending up accompanying a pretty girl to a speakeasy bar, and had staggered home around first light to find that Mike had spent most of the night deep in conversation with a toilet. But despite Mike's incapacity and my own woolliness, despite me stumbling around uselessly, hungover and barely getting a foot to the ball, it was Marcus who ended up injured. He tweaked his back. Dave leant him a walking stick and it came back to England with him. And years later, Mike needed it. It's a small world.

Naturally, I was cautious around Mike on the slopes of Hobbiton, not wanting him to fall over or trip, and certainly not wanting to do anything too quickly. I was on constant alert, ready to catch or steady him if needed. Russell, straying from the path of the regular tour, didn't rush us. If we wanted to go and look in a hobbit hole, we'd go and look in a hobbit hole. We had the blessing of the man that owns the place. Some of the holes are facades built into the hillsides, with barely enough room behind the door for an actor to be able to appear to go in or out. But apart from that it looks exactly like it does in the films, a beautifully maintained working hobbit village. There's even a carefully tended garden, bursting with fruit and veg, that supplies the Green Dragon, the pub by the mill pond. If you let yourself, you can imagine all the hobbits taking an afternoon nap. They are all that's missing.

We took a proper look in Bilbo's home, not something you can normally do. It's not a facade; there's room in there for dwarves, a hobbit and Gandalf. Up above Bilbo's house, atop a hill with a stunning view over the rest of Hobbiton and the surrounding countryside, there's a big fake oak tree – in keeping with the books. Every single fabric leaf was handmade and individually tied to the tree, so that it would always look the same, so that it wouldn't lose its leaves in the autumn and winter. Mike and I spent a good hour foraging in the long grass for those that had somehow escaped their branches and settled on the ground, gathering up several that we could take home and give to family and friends.

At one point, down in the valley area, we stumbled across a tour.

'Oh man, those guys would freak if they knew who you were,' Russell beamed.

'Go ahead and tell them,' I volunteered. 'We don't mind at all.'

'Oh wow, really?' So Russell went over to the group. The guide perked up immediately and I heard him effusing about how lucky they were that the owner of this wonderful establishment, of Hobbiton, was there with them. And they started taking photos of Russell and squealing with delight.

'Hang on a minute, ay,' Russell interrupted them. 'You see those two guys over there?' He pointed at us, then proceeded to tell the group that we were great-grandsons of J. R. R. Tolkien, and a bit about us.

Hobbiton is a long way to go for a lot of people, and takes planning to visit, so most of the people who go there are already big fans. Soon we were knee-deep in selfies, photos and enthusiastic conversations about Middle Earth. Those fans had an unexpected extra thrill that day, but Mike and I thoroughly enjoyed the experience as well. And the thing about all those pictures, many of which I still have and love, is that they nearly all show me in wellies. When I look at them now I can still hear Mike laughing and shouting, 'make sure you get the wellies in'. Typical. And we hadn't even seen any mud at that point.

We did though. Shortly afterwards. There was a particularly steep bit of path that descended around a corner, which had become something of a swamp in the recent rain. It wasn't enough to trouble a physically adept young man in gummies, but it was a tricky bit of path for Mike to negotiate.

'There's a bit of mud here, mate,' Russell observed, clearly feeling the same concern as I did for Mike. 'Hop on my back, ay.'

Mike pulled his stick free from the muck with a wet plop. 'No, no, no, it's fine, thank you.' Mike was still fiercely independent and wanted to cling onto that for as long as he possibly could. He had just about got used to accepting little bits of help from people he knew, family and friends, but I think it took him back to have a stranger offer him assistance.

'Come on mate, hop on.' Russell insisted. I could see clearly that Russell wasn't taking pity on him or patronising him in any way. He saw Mike was struggling and he wanted to help. He would have done it for anyone. Kiwis are like that. They're bred differently to us. They're just big-hearted people who don't see any shame in offering or taking help. Russell owned Hobbiton, which occupies a tiny portion of the great swathes of farmland his family owns, but he's just so generous and down to earth. He's also an ex-rugby player so he could have probably picked us both up, one under each arm, and finished the tour that way if he wanted. 'It's just this corner, mate, then we'll have you back on the ground.'

He made it hard for Mike to refuse. So Mike got hoisted up onto Russell's back and off they went. My first instinct, probably born of revenge for the whole 'gummies' business – although I was pretty glad of them at that particular moment – was to whip out my phone and take a photo of Mike being emasculated, being carried by another man. Normally, at any time in our lives up to this point, that's exactly what I would have done. I would have saved that picture and relentlessly teased Mike with it. But within a heartbeat of seeing my dear sweet brother on this gentle and kind stranger's back I was overcome with a feeling of such warmth and love.

Russell barely thought anything of it, but for Mike and I it would become a moment of profound beauty. It made an enormous impression on both of us. Not only did it help Mike in that specific moment, but it opened the door to Mike being able to let people help him more, something that he would soon need to do more often.

◆

My phone rings. 'We're in the main car park. Come and find us.' Simple. They'll be in a vibrant green and purple Jucy van. For those of you who have ever been to New Zealand, you'll know exactly what I'm talking about. For those who haven't, let me explain. If you want a good value place to stay in New Zealand, you stay in a Jucy Snooze hotel. If you want a good value set of wheels, anything from an 'El Cheapo' small car, right up to a massive camper-van, you go to Jucy. They even offer cruises in Fiordland on the South Island. And everything is painted bright luminous green. And purple. And more often than not there's a picture somewhere on the vehicle of Miss Lucy, some filthy-looking green bikini-clad fifties pin-up redhead whose smiling face promises a good time. Anyway, Jucy are kindly sponsoring the vehicles and some accommodation in the documentary, so we're staying in their hotel and driving their vehicles, in this instance an eight-seater van with sliding side doors and a particularly naughty-looking Miss Lucy.

As expected, we find it easily. Drew's next to it with the camera on his shoulder already. I'm sure this was meant to be a day off. As I climb into the rear seat of the van, I'm handed an iPad (not product placement – other tablets are available) and some headphones. I settle apprehensively, and press play on the video that is open and waiting for me.

'Royd,' a voice fills my ears, oddly familiar. Only I'm looking at a pair of feet pointed up at the sky, in front of a beautiful landscape. This voice I can't place is coming from someone upside down on some odd back-stretching contraption that slowly begins to right itself. A face comes into view, smiling broadly.

'Ahhhh,' I squeal in delight. It's John Rhys-Davies. Sallah in the Indiana Jones films, Pushkin in *The Living Daylights* and Gimli in *The Lord of the Rings* films. Which is, of course, how I know him.

'Welcome to New Zealand,' John continues, fully upright now. 'This is my little place in the Waikato. I have for you some instructions. These are your brother's words.'

I feel a surge of emotion in my chest. Mike is about to talk to me. I can't help but smile.

'You are an artist. There should be an outfit waiting for you. Offer to paint Hobbiton visitors. I love this place, and our time here.' John looks straight into the camera, inhabiting Mike's words.

I feel my eyes wetting, filling with bittersweet tears.

'I am with you and I'm everywhere. I love you, bro.'

And I crumble.

◆

I rarely introduce myself as anything other than just 'Royd'. I don't usually say my surname. And more often than not, people I'm meeting for the first time think my name is Roy or Lloyd. But now I have to go up to people, in Hobbiton of all places, and blatantly introduce myself as the great-grandson of J. R. R. Tolkien. And I'm wearing a smock and a beret and carrying a sketch pad. Again, I feel like a prize tit.

Oh, and I can't draw for shit.

The weather is stunning. The hills of Hobbiton are lush and green with summer vegetation, the sky is a deep blue and the light is a warm gold. The water of the mill pond is sparkling and the mill wheel is gently churning on the other side. I spot my first victims, and introduce myself.

'Hi.'

'Hello,' a confused-looking couple greet me, clearly itching to get past me and into the Green Dragon for a few mugs of hobbit cider.

'I'm the great-grandson of J. R. R. Tolkien,' I rush, embarrassed, through my introduction. I explain why I'm here, making sure to blame Mike. I wouldn't be doing this of my own volition. They kindly allow me to draw them, so I do. And it's predictably awful. They politely thank me and go on their way. I spot a pair of attractive young females. I might as well offer to draw them, I suppose. Someone should. So I do.

They pose, giggling awkwardly, in front of the mill pond.

'I can't draw,' I announce, happy to see they look just as uncomfortable as I feel. 'Okay, a little bit of background there. Oh, let me get Bilbo's hobbit hole in.' I'll be honest, it's a squiggle with a circle in the middle of it, and a cartoon tree on top that looks like a small child drew it. I even sketch in an oddly flattering stick-figure rendition of Drew with his camera. Since he got in the way.

Off they beautifully go. That wasn't so bad. Then I hear a shriek and see that the wind has caught my masterpiece, wrenched it from their grasp and deposited it in the reeds on the edge of the mill pond. Story, blessed with his father's opportune sense of chivalry, rushes over and gallantly retrieves it.

I find a third pair of willing models, a sweet young couple who perhaps think I can actually draw. Not wanting to disappoint, I usher them onto the middle of the lovely stone bridge. If I'm going to be embarrassed, I decide, I'm taking this guy down with me.

'I'll catch you just as you propose,' I suggest. They laugh, awkwardly. I position the young man on one knee. He has quickly made a ring out of a small wild flower. Very sporting. 'Look,' I shout at anyone nearby who might pay attention, 'he's proposing, for real, in Hobbiton.'

That draws a small crowd.

'Will you marry me?' he asks quietly, holding out the makeshift ring as I finalise my stick-figure rendition.

'What's your answer?' I ask his intended, grinning.

'Yes!' she giggles.

'It's predicted.' I had already written 'yes' in the speech bubble on my awful caricature.

Engaged for real or not, these two are clearly in love. The sun is shining. And Hobbiton looks majestic.

◆

I remember Mike's words, in John Rhys-Davies' voice, as I wander slowly around Hobbiton with Story.

'I love this place, and our time here. I am with you and I'm everywhere.'

I love you too, bruv.

Story has never been here, so I show him around. I show him where Russell carried Mike over the mud, and we linger in the places Mike and I lingered. He's heard the tales countless times, so it means a lot to both of us that he can see this place for real. Story was close to Mike, and helped out loads when he was ill. It was so important to have familiar, loving faces around Mike, people who accepted things as they were for Mike's sake and made sure the sickness didn't get more attention than him, people he loved and trusted and could be open and honest with, and Story was just that. He has a natural empathy and such a warm, generous and caring soul.

The day is drawing to a close, and the darkening orange of the low sun casts long shadows over the shire. We climb slowly up the hill to the top of Hobbiton, to where Bilbo's home is. We look inside and, for a moment, I imagine I could turn round and see Mike standing there with his cane, in the round doorway, beaming. I hesitate, not wanting to leave.

'I'll go on ahead, Dad.' Story smiles at me gently. I nod. He knows.

I go around the side of Bilbo's house alone and scamper up the slope to sit above it, under that big fake oak tree. I lean back against its trunk and reach out my hands to touch some of the wild flowers that flourish among the tall grass here. Below me much of Hobbiton is now in shadow, and I can't see anyone. The sun, now touching the hilltops on the horizon, still just reaches Bilbo's tree and me. I close my eyes to its fading warmth and think back to the day I spent here with Mike. I remember sitting up here with him, gathering the cloth leaves as keepsakes. I remember him, in his long grey coat, with his cane, standing grinning outside Bilbo's house for a photo. I remember how we got so lost in the happiness of being here together that, for a moment, we put aside thoughts of the difficult path ahead.

I'm languishing in the memories of happiness, but I'm also sad. I want Mike to be here now. And in some way he is, if only in a memory. But the memory is so vivid, so real, I feel like if I stayed a little longer he might appear. I could stay up here all night. I could sleep here, under this tree, under the pure starlit sky. It's in moments like this, moments of clarity, that I remember why I'm doing what I'm doing. Mike's bucket list. Because every so often it brings me back closer to him, and closer to some vague, almost attainable sense of peace.

I wipe a little moisture from my cheek with my sleeve. It's getting dark. I stand up, resolute. I'm going to do this bucket list. I'm going to tick off all the tasks one by one. And I'm going to do them in a way that will make you proud, Mike.

◆

The Green Dragon is a hive of revelry. Guests from the last tour spill out onto the banks of the mill pond, sipping Hobbiton's own ale or cider from the lovely little porcelain hobbit mugs.

I find Story, and Russell finds us both. We're ushered into the pub where more guests are having a great time. Hobbit music, or what you'd imagine might be hobbit music, is playing, and the beer is flowing. Russell calls for the group's attention, then announces me and Story as guests of honour, as relatives of the man who created hobbits.

After the obligatory selfies, he asks us to draw back a pair of heavy curtains to reveal the most magnificent hobbit feast I've ever seen. Several tables are groaning with food: plates of meat, vegetables, fruit, bread. The crowd surges in, joyous, oohing and aahing at the bounty on show, and everyone finds a place at the tables. This sounds like I've slipped into some dream about hobbits feasting, but believe me, and those of you who have witnessed it will stand by me, every morsel is real.

Our little party shares a private table with Russell, who I cornered earlier in the day to quietly thank for what he did for Mike, and for having us here today. Someone foolishly thrusts a hobbit-sized flagon of beer into my hand.

And in two minutes I'm already light-headed.

And happy.

Icarus

Story is spreading his wings. Again. He's found a niche in a beautiful coastal town called Raglan. We've been here a few times on days off. Him, Andy and I. Last time we came here we were enjoying a coffee in a little café on the way to one of the top ten surf spots in the world, when Story overheard the manager and the chef talking about being short staffed. He leapt up, apologised for interrupting, and promptly offered his services. He's no mug at making coffee (pun intended), so when they asked him to jump behind the counter and rustle up a flat white and a latte he duly obliged. The manager offered him a job there and then.

So here we are. We've stocked up on supplies at the local supermarket and got him settled into his accommodation. Rustic would be a kind way of describing it, but Story is officially a Wwoofer now. WWOOF, or World Wide Opportunities on Organic Farms, enables people to stay in accommodation in exchange for a small amount of labour. Wwoofing. Yes, it's rustic – but it's secure, it's beautiful, and I'm not in the least worried for Story. Not really. He'll find other accommodation once he's settled. But for now . . . well, I couldn't do it. I'd be too scared of spiders.

They'll proudly tell you all over New Zealand that there's nothing dangerous in the country, nothing that will hurt you. It's not like Australia, where everything wants to eat you. There's nothing to be scared of at all: no snakes, no scorpions, no nasty plants and supposedly no scary spiders. Tell that to Andy.

Alarmingly, it was here in Raglan that Andy got bitten. We were having a coffee and there were a few bugs buzzing about as you'd expect, but since apparently nothing here is dangerous, we thought nothing of it. Andy had his arms and legs under the table when he felt a sharp pain near his wrist. Just a bug bite, we all assumed. He put a plaster on it and carried on. A couple of days later it started to annoy him, so he peeled back the plaster to reveal a pus-filled, angry, inflamed infection and probably necrotic flesh.

'That looks like a spider bite, ay,' said Chris, the friendly former All Blacks player we were staying with at the time. 'You should go to the hospital. Now.'

Within the hour Andy was hooked up to an intravenous drip and given a course of strong antibiotics. They reckoned the culprit was probably a white-tailed spider.

'I thought New Zealand didn't have any poisonous animals,' Andy remarked glibly to one of the doctors.

'It's an Australian spider. It's not native.'

Well it bloody is now.

Apparently this particular spider is quite dangerous. An extreme reaction to its venom, untreated, could lead to losing a hand. Fortunately for Andy, he got treatment just in time. He nearly had to delay his flight home while he waited for the swelling to go down.

So please, Story, be careful of the spiders.

I give him a big hug and a kiss and tell him I love him. He'll be okay. He's well travelled. He's savvy. He spent six months in India, though he was bitten by a dirty great rat there. He'll be fine.

Reluctantly I get back into the Jucy car with Drew and drive away.

◆

A few days later and it's me who gets to spread their wings. In a rather less metaphorical sense. There's no more hiding what my next task is. The cat is well and truly out of the bag. There's an enormous sign in front of me advertising . . . skydiving.

'I think I might need to put some jeans on for this,' I grimace at Drew as we get out of the Jucy van. He returns a smug look that tells me I'll be relying on GoPros again. While he gets to stay on terra firma, the slacker. 'And a nappy,' I add, already starting to perspire.

◆

It's not going to be my first time jumping out of a plane. Mike and I decided years ago, after watching *Point Break*, that we wanted to give it a go. Well, it was mostly Mike. Even though I thought Patrick Swayze and Keanu Reeves looked cool doing it on screen, I was less than certain I'd enjoy it. A friend of ours called Carl hooked the three of us up at a skydiving centre near Telford. It was a day-long course that was going to culminate in us doing a static line jump from three thousand feet.

The training took place in a hangar. We covered emergency procedures, which is always a recipe for upping my anxiety levels. If for some reason the wires on your main chute got twisted, you had a reserve. Simple enough concept, but the procedure for ejecting the botched main and toggling the back-up seemed to baffle the three of us. Granted, we were messing around, but still. The point of any training is, hopefully, to prevent panic in the event of an actual emergency. You know what you need to do and you do it. Panic kills. So we were told to look, locate, grab, then release. Look for the toggle, see it with your eyes (easier said than done when you're hurtling to the ground at a zillion miles an hour), grab it, then punch the Velcro strapping away from you in a firm movement that would both eject the main chute and pull the reserve. We dangled a few feet above some mats and practised.

'Look, punch . . . bollocks.' Even Mike got confused.

'Ha! You're dead.' Carl and I fell about laughing.

We all died a few times before we got it. And once we had, and once we knew how to tuck and roll and not break our legs on landing, we were ushered towards a waiting Cessna. It was a tiny plane with the side door missing, and as we were walking towards it I felt Mike's hand on the parachute on my back.

'There, that's better,' he grinned.

Panic gripped me. 'What did you touch? What have you done?' I demanded, but he just laughed.

Mike got on the plane first, followed by me, and Carl brought up the rear, and we'd be jumping in reverse order. We slid into the coffin-sized fuselage, slotting inside each other's legs until we were crammed in like a trio of anxious sardines. The instructor got on last and casually hung about by the door as he gave the pilot the thumbs up. Then we took off, like a rocket. There was no gentle ascent. The pilot had one mission: to get up to altitude as fast as he possibly could. It felt like we were pointed straight up, being pulled up into the firmament by a single angry propeller while the riveted panels of the small plane rattled perilously around us. Until we eventually levelled out.

'You don't have to jump if you don't want to,' the instructor reassured us, probably noting the three ashen faces that gawped back at him in terror. 'I should warn you, though, if you think the take-off was bad, the pilot will be in even more of a hurry to get back on the ground. It's not pleasant.'

At least I think that's what he said. We were roaring along at seventy odd miles an hour with half the side of the plane missing. Between the cacophonous roar of the engine and ear-splitting onslaught of wind, he could have said almost anything. Then he leant over to the open door and looked down. His face, buffeted by the hurricane blowing out there, turned into a rubber mask and folded back on itself, flapping around like a loose sail. We looked at him, unblinking and mute. He had a rolled-up length of sock or something, some material that would give him an insight into wind direction and so forth. When he dropped it out of the plane it shot backwards and immediately out of sight. Of course it did, we were flying at speed. But it just seemed so aggressive and violent. And it gave me an insight into what we had got ourselves into.

Carl had to go first. He slid over to the door and held onto the railing as he let his legs dangle over the side. Dry-mouthed, I laughed nervously, terrified for Carl but unable to tear my eyes from him.

'Let go,' the instructor shouted over the wind noise. But that was clearly not what Carl wanted to do. 'Let go now,' came another shout. And then the instructor was peeling Carl's fingers, one by one, from the rail, and practically giving him a good shove to send him on his way. Like the instructor's spare pair of socks, Carl disappeared, sucked backwards and away.

Then it was my turn.

I looked back at Mike, and for once he was barely grinning. There was no witty banter. Either he was scared too, or the look of abject terror on my face was enough to shut him up. Before I knew it, I was in the doorway, like Carl had been. The wind pushed me back towards the rear of the plane, up against the edge of the door. I tried to fight it, terrified I'd somehow get tangled up in it, and I heard the instructor shouting at me to jump. In a rare moment of blind obedience, I pushed myself out. The world spun around me, dizzying me, and I thought I might black out. I had no idea what was going on. Then the chute opened.

It was only a few seconds of free fall, but it was petrifying. And then, when the chute opened, it was serene. I floated earthward, able to see Carl beneath me and Mike above me, both specks but both safe. It was amazing. We had to pull over on the drive home to break the stunned silence. We all got out of the car and danced around whooping like rednecks at a rodeo.

You were supposed to do five of those static line jumps before graduating to the next level. We never got round to going again. Not for want of trying, but even the slightest aberration in the weather is enough to ground you. We were scuppered numerous times and then sort of forgot about it.

A few years later I was producing a film in Fiji and got the opportunity to a tandem jump there. I was all for it, figuring I'd already worked through the irrational fear of hurling myself out of a plane. I could just get up there, jump and enjoy it. And where better to do it than over the turquoise waters of a Pacific island? Plus it was a tandem dive. I didn't have to do anything, just hang off some other guy and enjoy the view.

I roped the film's director, Ez, and Dean, another producer, into it. They were nervous, but I had enough confidence for all three of us. They went up before me, one at a time, and I watched them drift gracefully down to the waiting sandy beach with big grins on their faces. This was going to be great, I thought to myself, and when it was my turn I was more than ready.

I went up, impatiently waiting for the plane to reach altitude. It took a while. We ended up at way more than three thousand feet. I was fine. Leaving the plane was fine. The free fall was fine. The chute opened, and it was magnificent. I was dangling, tethered to an experienced jumper, in just shorts and a T-shirt, being gently buffeted by the warm South Pacific air.

'Do you want to have a go at steering?' my guy asked me.

'Sure,' I replied confidently. I took the controls and soared like an eagle.

'Do you want to spin?'

'Hell, yeah,' I answered, not even knowing what he meant, but up for anything at that point. He took back the controls and tugged down hard on one side, collapsing that part of the chute and sending us into a sudden spiral. Within seconds I felt like I was in a tumble dryer. We spun faster and faster, to the point that our whole bodies were horizontal, perpendicular to the ground. The blood rushed out of my head and pooled in the soles of my feet. I started getting dizzy.

I get dizzy really easily. I can spin around a couple of times on my feet and need to sit down before I fall. So I've no idea why I leapt on his ridiculous suggestion with quite so much fervour. It was a bad idea. And yet it wasn't terrible. The adrenaline got me through it. Until we came out of the spin.

Vertical again, drifting slowly towards the crystal waters of the ocean, the blood jubilantly rushed back into my brain. I suddenly felt violently nauseous. I don't think I've ever felt such a ferocious urge to spew. And after a couple of involuntary gags that my partner was blissfully unaware of, I let rip. What would, in normal circumstances, have been an impressive display of projectile vomit became something else entirely. As it gushed forwards out of my mouth it was instantly hurled back by the wind, back around the side of my face and all over my partner. I was drenching him in puke.

'Sorry,' I tried to apologise in between retches, but I knew no amount of contrition was going to make his day any better. We were maybe only three hundred feet from the beach at that point, but I couldn't stop. I spotted Dean below, filming me. And when we finally touched down on the sand, I was a state. My hair, blown in every direction, was sticky with my breakfast. So was my chest. And so was the poor sod who'd been strapped to me. He was quietly furious. Dean and Ez ran over, tears in their eyes from laughing, and all I could do was continue dry retching. I still felt terrible, but there was nothing left to come out.

◆

Even despite the memories of Fiji, I'm surprised at how nervous I am at having to do another jump. I tell myself that it's because of my heightened emotional state, because of what I'm doing here, because of the bucket list. I also consider that I'm not a young man anymore, despite what I like to put on my Tinder profile. Fear comes easier as you get older. You're more aware of your mortality. And I have a son. I don't need to take risks. I shouldn't be putting my life on the line. Whatever the reason is, I'm scared.

Drew beetles off on the back of a quad bike towards the runway to get in position to film the plane taking off. That looks way more fun. What I wouldn't do to have a day messing around on quad bikes rather than jumping out of a plane from fifteen thousand feet.

Sorry, how many?

It's a bigger plane than the ones I've been on before. A big pink plane, I think; I'm starting to get tunnel vision. We take to the air and begin a painfully slow ascent. I have a little altimeter strapped to me and I glance down at it when I think we must be at altitude. It reads seven thousand feet. We're barely halfway there.

'Do you have any last words?' asks the jovial Kiwi who is strapped to me and waving a GoPro in my face. He could almost be Patrick Swayze in *Point Break*. If it wasn't for the accent.

'Yeah,' I say with as much facetious swagger as I can manage. 'Cheers, Mike.'

He laughs. And offers me an oxygen mask so I don't pass out from the altitude.

Eventually, unfortunately, it's time to jump. I'm suddenly pulled back tight against Kiwi Swayze and we slide forward to the open door. I'm not even sitting on the edge. He is. I'm already dangling in the ether, helpless and dry-mouthed, seriously considering emptying my bowels. And then he pushes forwards and we are falling.

Falling.

Falling.

For the longest sixty seconds or more of my life. I don't know how long it is, but for the whole time I have that feeling you get when you go over a humpback bridge at speed, that feeling where all your innards seem to leap into your throat for a fleeting moment. Only this isn't a fleeting moment.

And there's some dude casually filming beneath us. He's falling backwards, pointing his GoPro up at my face. Then he does some kind of flip and he's above us. And I forgot the one thing I had to do in my passenger fall. I failed to keep my mouth shut. As soon as the updraft hit my parted lips, my face ballooned into a flappy open maw and I get deprived of every drop of moisture I might have been lucky enough to still have in there.

And it's terrifyingly fast. The ground, a scale model of my reality, doesn't seem to be getting any closer. But that's little consolation. I know I'm falling like a stone. Until I feel a hand on my forehead and know that Swayze is about to pull the chute. Then I'm dangling, still several thousand feet up, desperately thirsty and shaken enough by the experience to know that I'm not really safe until I can feel the earth under my feet. It's still toy land down there, but it's starting to get closer. I can make out Drew pointing his camera up at me.

And then we're down. I could almost cry with joy at the feeling of the soft earth beneath my feet. Remember when I said there would be times I'd rather be sipping a cup of tea in my garden?

This is one of those times. I wriggle out of my chute and lie on the ground, stroking the grass.

'This is what I do at home.' I look up at Drew and his camera. I pick out a few individual blades of grass, rubbing them between finger and thumb, comforting myself. Calming myself. I don't like jumping out of planes. I like having my feet on the ground. I don't ever want to do that again. Ever. And, above all, I'm relieved Story isn't here now. He'd have wanted to jump too, and my heart wouldn't have coped.

Heroes and Monsters

Native to New Zealand, a Wētā is a massive flightless cricket type insect. It's also one of the world's leading film special effects and props companies, founded by Richard Taylor and Tania Rodger and based in Wellington, a company that really landed on the world stage after contributing all the sets, weapons, costumes, armour, creatures and other effects to, yes you guessed it, *The Lord of the Rings* films.

That's where I am, and I love it here! I love Wellington. I've got loads of friends here, and it's home to one of my favourite places in the world to get a coffee, Chocolate Fish Café. It's usually the first place I go to when I arrive in Wellington, and this trip was no exception. It was also the first place I took Mike when he came here with me. Back then we sat looking out over the sea, sipping our lattes, and we loved it. This time, without Mike, it was tinged with sadness, but I still loved it. I sat and remembered all the places around Wellington that I took Mike: driving around the peninsula and seeing seals, meeting friends and going to cafés, and showing him Weta Workshop.

I'd messaged Richard at Weta to let him know I was going to be in town, and he suggested I come along to the workshop for a bit of lunch. I leapt at the opportunity. I've had a few tours of Weta over the years, always lucky enough to have Richard show me around. You can go on official tours (after signing an NDA!) and get to peer through windows at people making weapons and monsters and whatever it is they're working on at the time, but you really can't beat a personal tour that takes in all the areas you wouldn't otherwise get to see.

It must be one of the best places in the world to work. It's filled with passionate people, world leading in their industry, always so happy to be there, to be making cool stuff. I've always been impressed with the passion of the people who worked on *The Lord of the Rings*. When I was here before, during filming, I went to what became a traditional Friday evening screening here at Weta. Peter used to get advance screenings of films and put them on for the cast and crew as a way to relax together at the end of the week. That particular evening, as I walked through the busy workshop before the screening, I saw a guy sitting at a computer, tweaking the CGI of one tiny phrase of Gollum's, adjusting his face in minute detail. And two and a half hours later, when I emerged from the screening, he was still tweaking that same exact phrase. Total dedication.

Another time, I was lucky enough to sit in with Peter during the recording of the score for *The Return of the King* at Abbey Road Studios in London. I sat in the control booth, watching in awe while Howard Shore conducted the London Philharmonic as they played live over a scene from the film. Peter sat back in his chair and clasped his hands behind his head as the music soared. I saw goosebumps rise on the skin of his arms, and the hairs stand on end. Even then, after all the years and years of work, Peter was as passionate, invested and driven as he was at the beginning of his journey.

Richard is the same, always brimming with enthusiasm, always bursting to show and explain new pieces and tell anecdotal stories about them. It's his domain, and he loves it. When Mike and I went, Richard was incredible. As busy as he was, he made plenty of time for us, and showed us everything. He picked up on the caution we were exercising around the staircases and corridors, always wary of Mike's walking. We took our time, and Mike and Richard had a real connection. So much so that Richard and Tania sent a beautiful email to me after Mike died, reminding me of how much they had enjoyed having us there, and how sad they were to hear that Mike had passed.

So I came to see Richard for lunch. And because of this whole bucket list thing, and my never knowing what the hell is going on until it's thrust upon me, I didn't dare try and arrange anything more than that. So I'm genuinely surprised and absolutely thrilled when Richard, sitting in the boardroom, surrounded by Oscars and other awards and props and so on, gives me a big grin, and says, 'Shall we have a little tour?'

'I'd love to.' I leap up, eager to see what's new. And off we go.

Some way into the tour, we come to a door I don't know. I'm ushered in and introduced to a couple of people I remember seeing around on previous occasions, Jason Docherty and his wife, Kim.

'So Royd, these guys are going to turn you into an orc,' grins Richard. 'How does that sound?'

'Wow,' is all I manage to say. And then 'Ahhhhh,' when I see Drew emerge from hiding behind a make-up bench, camera levelled at me. Deceived again. And I thought I was just here for lunch and a catch-up. And then the ruse of the 'tour' – just a way to surprise me with a new task. An orc! I mean, that's exciting stuff. I'm going to get a full orc prosthetic make-up and costume and I'll look the mutt's nuts. I've been a ranger, twice, but never an orc.

◆

The other time I played a ranger was in the second Hobbit film, *The Desolation of Smaug*. It was a bigger scene than the one I did in *The*

Return of the King. It was a whole day's filming. The scene involved several rangers carrying the body of the Witch King of Angmar, wrapped in chains, and laying it in a big stone sarcophagus in the depths of a fire-lit tomb. One of the other rangers had to throw the Witch King's sword onto his corpse.

'Cut,' said Peter. 'Actually, you know what, we'll get Royd to do this. He's the captain of the troop so . . . as the captain it would be him that comes forward and throws the sword, okay?'

'Okay,' I agreed. Yes! I get the cool shot, I thought triumphantly.

So the plan was I'd walk down this narrow corridor, past people holding burning torches alarmingly close to my face, go up some steps, then throw the sword onto the body in the sarcophagus and hope that it lands inches from the very expensive lens of the very expensive 3D movie camera.

'What if I miss?' I asked Andrew Lesnie, the director of photography, who has sadly since passed away. I had no idea, but I'd have guessed that just the lens was worth tens of thousands of pounds, lots of tens of thousands. And if it got broken, and filming got halted while they found another . . . well, I didn't want that on my conscience. The stone might have been fake, the set may have been a facade, but the sword was real. It was metal. It was heavy. And it had plenty of potential to mess up a nice camera.

'Yeah, good point,' agreed Andrew. And we waited while he had a Perspex screen placed in front of the lens. On the very first take I threw the sword onto the body of the Witch King and it dutifully bounced and smashed into the Perspex screen right in front of the lens. Close call. It took a few more takes to really nail it. But what a scene.

Some time later, I arranged a 'Welsh' charity premiere of the film in our local theatre, with permission from Warner Bros. Mike had been with me to the London premiere of the first Hobbit film, but by the time the second one was due to come out, he was in a wheelchair, so rather than him go to the premiere, I brought the premiere to him. It was my big moment, after all.

I sat next to Mike in his wheelchair to watch it. The cinema was packed. I was really buzzing to see my scene and to maybe brag a tiny (massive!) bit – me as the captain of the rangers, burying the Witch King, throwing a sword and looking badass – so when I knew it was coming up, I leant over to Mike. 'This is it. My part's coming.'

Mike leant over to Laura and told her. She leant over to Story. Story leant over . . . and so on. I watched the word spread down the row, through all the family. Everyone was on the edge of their seats. Waiting. Anticipating.

'Where is it?' Mike whispered to me after a few minutes.

'I got cut.' I was gutted.

And Mike bellowed with laughter. He absolutely pissed himself. I slumped into my seat, disappointed that I hadn't made the cut, but also painfully aware that Mike would dine out on this for ages. He had ammunition for multiple piss-takes. I'd never hear the end of it. But don't worry, you can actually see the scene. It might not have made the first theatrical cut, but it was included in the extended edition.

The third film, *The Battle of the Five Armies*, in which Story made a longer appearance (and wasn't cut!), was released a year later. Mike never got to see it.

◆

It turns out I'm getting the full 'hero' get-up. A 'hero' in this sense is someone who is intended to be right in front of the camera, so no detail is going to be spared. Not only that, the prosthetic they are going to fit to me was worn by Shane Rangi, a stuntman/actor friend of mine who was a front-line orc in the films, not that you'd ever recognise him hidden behind layers of prosthetics. This just gets better and better.

I sit down in front of a mirror and take a last look (for a while) at my own face before it disappears. Around me, covering the walls right up to the ceiling, are countless life casts of faces. A lot of them, as you'd expect, have been taken from the cast of *The Lord of the Rings* films and *The Hobbit* films. There's Ian McKellen, Elijah Wood, John Rhys-Davies and so on. But there's also other big names like Marlon Brando, Sigourney Weaver, Patrick Stewart and Peter Cushing. Richard collects life casts and has even managed to get hold of the likes of Napoleon, George Washington and Abraham Lincoln. That's a really odd mix of white plaster perfect likenesses of famous people to be sombrely looking over my imminent transformation.

Jason and Kim get to work. The prosthetic comes in several pieces, each lovingly stuck to my face. I bite down on a mould so I can be fitted with wonderfully disgusting orc teeth. Pretty soon there's nothing left of me in the mirror, just a gnarly bald horrible orc head. They stick pointy ears on the side of my new face and start air-brushing make-up onto the prosthetic, then touch it up with smaller brushes.

Fast forward an hour or two. Kim and Jason help me into a full costume and apply the hair to my head. The transformation is complete. I need a smoke, so I casually walk through the workshop and head outside. That's not something you'll see every day, an orc rolling and smoking a cigarette. I get Drew to take a picture of me with an eight-foot replica of King Kong. As you do.

◆

I thought that was it. I figured I'd dress up as an orc, look cool for a bit, then get back to loafing around Wellington and waiting for the next task. But it appears I'm not quite done yet. I'm led into the bowels of Weta Workshop, alarmingly close to a frighteningly large model of Shelob, the giant spider that snares poor Frodo. I loathe spiders. Absolutely despise them. More accurately, as I might have mentioned, I have something of a phobia. It's only a model. Walk on.

Round a corner, I am greeted by a familiar smiling face. It's Shane Rangi.

'Mate!' I rush up to hug him. 'I'm wearing your face!'

'Good to see you, man!'

We catch up briefly, but Shane has a schedule to keep to. 'Are you ready?' he asks after a while.

I'm not sure what I'm meant to be ready for but I tell him I am.

'Good, because we're going to put you through a bit of a regime.'

It turns out I'm going to do an audition of some kind. There's a few empty chairs nearby, soon to be filled with people who are going to judge my orc acting. Well, I'm halfway there, surely. I look the part. I've even started practising my growls. I can't help it. I'm already inhabiting my character. I just lower my voice and . . . who am I kidding? I probably sound like some pathetic weedy old man gargling through a load of rotten teeth. Especially next to Shane. He's a big bastard. He looks scarier out of costume than I do in it.

Shane spends an hour coaching me on how to move like an orc. I keep my knees bent a little, legs bowed, and trudge as menacingly as I can. I lift my horrible snub nose to the ceiling and sniff, imagining the sweet smell of human flesh. We get some curved orcish swords out and do some vigorous weapons training. And then, when Shane thinks I'm ready, we prepare a little scene for my audition.

◆

I'm standing up against the wall, facing away from the room, head down, one gloved hand placed on the wall in front of me. My laboured breaths rasp in my throat. I'm an orc. I AM AN ORC. I hear several sets of footsteps entering the room, the rustle of clothes as people sit on the waiting chairs. They are here. Shane clicks his fingers, my signal to begin. I AM AN ORC.

I sniff, smelling the air, still facing the wall. There's a familiar odour in here. I cock my head, trying to get a better sense of the scent. Man flesh. And I am hungry. I slowly turn around, into the room, to seek out this delicious morsel of living flesh. I AM AN ORC.

'Cut, cut, stop, stop, stop, no, hang on, hold on a minute,' a Kiwi voice rings out. It's only Peter bloody Jackson! Peter Jackson is sitting next to Richard, watching me. I'm auditioning for Peter Jackson! And I was in full flow. Sheesh! The nerve of the man. Oh wait, have I ballsed up already? Ten seconds in and I'm the worst possible orc that anyone has ever seen. And if anyone knows what an orc should be like, it's Peter Jackson.

'We need a hobbit. Have we got a hobbit? Can we get a hobbit please?'

I hear someone from around the corner, muttering an apology for being late. 'I was just having second breakfast,' comes the soft Scottish accent. I know exactly who it is. It's Billy Boyd, Pippin in *The Lord of the Rings*. I've known Billy for years, and instinct tells me to greet him as a friend, even if I am unrecognisable. But no, I am not his friend, not today. I AM AN ORC.

'Back to first position please,' Peter tells me, and I turn back to the wall, shoulders slumping a little.

Mmmm, hobbit flesh. There's the inner orc. Seriously, I'm not breaking character, not for anyone. I growl softly, and wait. I hear Shane's fingers click, and I begin again. I sniff the air slowly. I smell hobbit now. And I hate hobbits. But man, they are delicious. I want to eat this hobbit. I will eat this hobbit. My senses are tingling, screaming at me to find, kill and eat. My breathing is heavy, my stance is good. I'm inhabiting this role. Yes! I AM AN ORC.

'I . . . smell . . . fresh . . . meat . . .' I growl breathily. Nailed it. And then I see them, the men and the hobbit. Sitting there, looking all fleshy and yummy. I take several long quick strides towards them, towards the bearded one in the middle, and deliver an almighty roar right into his face.

Yep, I just roared at Peter Jackson, about six inches from his face. He pulled back a little, smiling slightly. Richard and Billy recoiled too. Well, you would, if you saw this face leering at you. I'd say I nailed it. I hold the pose for a second, then straighten up and take a step backwards. As the tension dissipates, I can't stop myself doing a funky little jazz hands shuffling dance. And they all laugh.

'That was very good,' Peter says.

'That was scary,' admits Billy.

'I was afraid you were going to have some kind of, you know, post-traumatic flashback,' Peter says to him drily.

'Yeah,' said Billy, 'and try and save my captain!'

'Ffffaaaaangggyyyyyyyyaaa,' I say, proud of myself.

I'd better take these teeth out.

Nature's Larder

I've been abandoned. Left to fend for myself in the wilderness around Otaki Gorge. Well, not entirely. I am in the care of a thoughtful and kindly man, Steve, and his family for a day and a night, and I'm going to learn more about foraging. I'm going to experience living off the land. Drew has given me the GoPros and made sure my phone is set up to film at a decent resolution, and I'm going to document myself. Oh, the responsibility.

Growing up around Halkyn, Mike and I were always around nature. We climbed trees and made little campfires. At one of the Summer Moots in my early teens some of the guests found a mass of horse mushrooms growing in one of the fields that adjoined ours. They gathered some and fried them up in butter and we ate them. I remember being amazed that you could just pick something from the wild and eat it.

Both Mike and I became fascinated with the notion of living off the land. We devoured episodes of *A Cook on the Wild Side*, where Hugh Fearnley-Whittingstall motored around canals and waterways in his narrowboat, The Bain Marie, gathering fruits and fungi and meeting other boating people who would trap rabbits, scramble around for wild nuts or scrape up roadkill to cook. Then, in another series, he was in his Land Rover, kitted out with a mini kitchen, and he'd be foraging and bartering, and cooking up free food in the countryside. Then came Ray Mears, living off the land, meeting indigenous peoples, and learning their culture and their bushcraft. We lapped it all up.

Carl, the reluctant skydiver, started dating a Norwegian girl, Grete. He showed me and Mike photos of the fiords in Norway he'd taken on a drive with her, and we were instantly hooked. We decided there and then that we needed to go there on a camping trip, and we'd catch fish and live off the land for a week or two.

When the time came, Mike couldn't go. He couldn't get time off work, so he backed out. But Carl and I, and Mark (who ran the printers that Mike ended up working for), set off on our adventure. Grete's cousin had a spare boat that he had been persuaded to lend us. We piled our weighty backpacks into the small vessel and clambered aboard. He asked us if we knew how to operate the motor and drive the boat.

'Yeah, yeah, no problem,' I said. I'd never been in a boat before then, let alone driven one. And I'm not sure he fully believed me, as he quickly explained how to go forwards and backwards and how to steer. 'Yeah, yeah, easy, got it!' I said.

I immediately slammed it into the side of the jetty.

'No, no, no, you must not do that,' exclaimed the rather annoyed cousin.

We figured it out.

Powering down the middle of the fiord, the landscape was breathtaking. I had to call Mike. 'You idiot,' I shouted down the phone over the roar of the outboard. 'Why didn't you come? This place is glorious.'

We took the boat to a little island; a place Carl had scoped out on that drive with Grete. We had no idea if we were allowed to camp there, but we pulled the boat up into the little bay and leapt ashore. I waded into the long grass in my shorts and flip-flops and nearly trod on a snake. This wasn't the English countryside, I realised, suddenly wondering what else was out there. Bears maybe?

We hadn't a clue what we were doing. We had fishing rods fit for children, the wrong kind of spinners, and the few fish we did manage to catch between us got thrown back in the fiord rather than cooked on an open fire. We didn't know what fish was what, and which fish was safe to eat or not. It was a ham-fisted expedition, but it was wonderful, and we resolved to go back the following year.

Back home, I enthused to Mike about it endlessly, to the point that he wasn't going to miss out a second time. We brushed up a little on our knowledge of knot tying and fire-lighting, and resolved to kit ourselves out in army gear. The plan was to travel in our civilian clothes and, once there, change into full camo as if we were some army unit on special ops out in the wilderness.

When we returned, we went to a different place. We flew into Stavanger and got a ferry up the fiords towards a place called Sand. We spent the first night there, in a log cabin belonging to this cool Norwegian guy called Bjorn. He plied us with his home brew beer (I was hammered after half a pint) and sorted us a boat for our camping trip. We discovered that you can camp anywhere in Norway for a couple of days without a permit, and you don't need a licence to fish.

So we got into our army kit and set off an hour or so down the fiord to find a place to camp. We were only slightly less clueless than before. We knew how to tie a couple of basic knots, but had no idea how to really lash something to a tree securely or how to build a decent shelter. We knew how to light a fire, but cooking on it was a whole other thing. We clumsily balanced our billy cans on rocks around the flames, but they kept falling over and putting the fire out.

After that year, we all decided we needed to be better prepared. We did a brief bushcraft survival course. We learned how to build a structure over a fire for cooking, how to tie more knots and how to erect a proper shelter that wouldn't collapse five minutes after constructing it. We spent the rest of the year building our kit up, arming ourselves with swanky knives, new cooking pots, proper fishing gear. And we learned to identify different fish. We were determined to be able to live off the land. We'd go back to Norway the next year and would drink water from the streams and eat only what we could catch in the fiords or forage from the forest.

I say we, but it was mostly Mike. He really went for it. Norway became a regular fixture. We went back every year with other friends who joined us and became regular amateur survivalists. I liked to take a few packets of food, rice and so on, to supplement what little I was likely to catch. While Mike would carefully maintain his kit and set up his hammock under the bivouac he'd built, the rest of us ended up sharing this gigantic comfortable tent that we could stand up in, that housed all our pointless gear spread out all over the place.

We used to take a big container that we'd fill with water for cooking with, and most days I'd secretly empty it out so that I had an excuse to take the boat back to Sand. Carl and I would motor up the fiord and go to the café for a slap-up breakfast binge, then scoff a load of cake from the shop. Once, Mike asked us to drop him off with his fishing gear on a rock that jutted out of the waters of the fiord a good fifty feet or so from the shore. He clambered out of the boat onto about ten square feet of bare rock and we left him there and buggered off for our illicit feast. He couldn't have cooked a fish if he'd caught one. He was stranded there for as long as it took us to eat our fill and browse the shop and mosey back down the fiord again. About three hours, as it happened.

When we picked him up he was all cool and macho. He said he'd caught a load of fish, but had let them go again. It had been a great few hours, he said. But he told me months later that he'd instantly regretted his decision. It was a baking hot day, and he'd gulped down all his water in the first few minutes, then tried to avoid the sun by lying in a few inches of half-shade on a narrow ledge until he heard the distant rumble of our engine.

Each year, in keeping with the army theme, we'd get new sets of dog tags with the year printed on them, along with our names and ranks. Whoever's turn it was to get them made got to choose everyone's rank. So when it was my turn, I was a General (obviously), and Mike was a Private (also obviously).

But, to be honest, when it came to living off the land, he definitely outranked me.

◆

Mike's love of nature and determination to be able to live off the land led to him compiling a journal that he called 'Nature's Larder.' It came about because . . . well, let me use Mike's words, scribbled on an early page:

> *There are many survival books out there on the market nowadays, but none of them tell you what you can eat in this country and how to cook these things over a fire . . . this book is being written and produced for people who would like to know more about the fruits of nature in this country.*

I still have it near me, the sleek black notebook that he wrote in over the years. On the inside cover is a list of books he clearly wanted to get hold of, along with their ISBN numbers. There's *Food for Free*, *The Hidden Harvest*, *Plants with a Purpose*, *Wild Flowers of Britain*. And then there's pages of lists, lists of wild vegetables, herbs and salad plants, with both common and Latin names. Then it goes into edible flowers and fruits. And there's recipes. One that sticks in my mind is clear instructions on how to make coffee from the roots of dandelions.

Mike started this book years ago, long before he was ill, and long before a lot of this information was widely available on the internet. If he was still here now, I suspect he would have tried to develop some kind of Nature's Larder app that could identify plants and tell you what you can do with them.

And if he was still here now he might well be living off grid, using his knowledge, or at least still working towards his dream of self-sufficiency. He got close, once, when he bought a house with his then wife on the side of a mountain in Wales. It was his dream home, in the middle of nowhere, near a little stream. There wasn't a shop for miles, and the nearest neighbour was across several fields. When his marriage ended, he had to move from that house, and he never quite found that lifestyle again.

Though we still had Norway.

◆

I waved goodbye to Drew and the Jucy van a little while ago, and have been telling Steve all about Mike and his love for nature. Our love for nature. Well I'm stuck in the middle of it now, so I need to at least try to show some appreciation. Steve and his partner Jen share a big round yurt with their children, Turtle and Dawa. They're maybe eight and six, and are running around barefoot in the long grass. I feel like I've just discovered them, untouched by the outside world.

Steve gives me a quick tour, shows me his beehives and his orchard. There's no mains water, no electricity. Mike would love it here. For some reason I'm apprehensive and decide I need to go for a 'number two'. Steve is happy to accommodate. He directs me towards a little cabin away from the yurt.

'There's toilet paper in there, mate,' he tells me. 'And sawdust. Once you've done your business, just grab a handful and sprinkle it down there.'

There is no door on the shed. A reed screen provides some privacy. That's okay. I'm no stranger to a hole in the ground. It doesn't smell and it looks clean. I can do this. And then I see the spider. It's a big bugger, just sitting on the wall of the shed looking mean, not two feet from where I need to sit. That's that then. I can't go. Not only that, I don't even need to any more. Even my poop is scared. So I stand outside the shed and pee up against a tree instead. That'll have to do.

I explain myself to Steve. I tell him about the spider. He smiles wryly, and offers me a cup of mint tea, an infusion from leaves freshly picked from his garden. I'll have to be careful where I pee. We saunter over to Steve's grove and gather hazelnuts from the ground. He offers to show me how to light a fire with a bow drill, something I've seen before but never tried. I make the base board first, chopping a small plank to size with a hatchet then cutting a small socket in it with a knife for the spindle to sit in. I tie cord between two ends of a stick to make a bow, wrap it around the spindle and get to work. Eventually, the friction generates enough heat that I am able to blow a flame onto a fistful of dried tinder. We roast the hazelnuts and drizzle them in honey harvested from Steve's beehives. Honestly, it's like the most delicious sweet I've ever eaten: warm, nutty and scrumptious, and it's all come from this little bit of land.

Steve points out a bush to me, peppered with small red 'fruits' that look a bit like chillis. He tells me they add a bit of spice to your cooking, and hands me one. He looks a tad surprised when I brazenly pop the whole thing in my mouth and bite down. My head explodes with fire. If it isn't a chilli, it sure tastes like one. Steve is looking at me, amused, as if to say, 'I wouldn't have done that myself, mate, but you go for it.' I keep chewing, not wanting to appear rude, though I desperately want to be rid of it. I don't do spicy food, so this is unbearable. Eventually, seeing my distress, Steve motions to me to spit it out. I turn to my side and empty my mouth, to the giggles of his kids.

Still hurting, I am ushered onto the next lesson in foraging. Cicadas. I'm not sure exactly what a cicada is, but Steve tells me to listen. Listen to the sound that is all around us. I cock my head and open my ears. It's like crickets. I realise that it's always been there, not just here, but all over New Zealand. I've tuned it out, like a white noise, the scratchy whine of millions of little legs being rubbed together by these insects. Cicadas. Our next snack.

Steve and I, with the kids, walk among the fruit trees of his orchard. Turtle and Dawa keep reaching out and grabbing the bugs from the foliage, then drop them into a little Tupperware box. How do they even see them? I can't. They show me one. It's big enough, maybe an inch or two long, lacy wings draped back behind its bright green patterned body, with long jagged and spiky back legs. I start staring at the leaves and branches of the trees all around me, and eventually my eyes become attuned to the task at hand and I can see them. I grab one, cupping my hand gingerly around it. It's lively. It probably doesn't want to be eaten. Its spidery legs tickle my palm, sharp feet seeming to dig into my soft flesh. Spidery! I try to hide the fact that I'm a little freaked out, and happily deposit my catch into the pot.

'You can eat them right off the tree,' Steve grins at me. Yeah, no thanks. And as if to prove her dad's point, barefoot little Dawa snatches a critter from a nearby leaf and, holding it by its wings, pops the whole thing in her mouth. She beams at me happily, like she's just picked chocolate from the tree.

They want me to try, but I just can't bring myself to do it. Not raw. Not alive. No thanks. Instead we take the Tupperware to an open-sided kitchenette and drop all the creepy crawlies we've collected into some hot oil. Steve fries them for a couple of minutes before adding a sprinkle of salt and a drizzle of honey. He offers me one. I'm naturally squeamish, but how bad can it be? I hold the now dead, warm, salty, honey-coated cicada in my fingers and look at it. Sod it, I'll give it a go. It doesn't pop in my mouth. It's not squishy and disgusting. In fact, it's delicious, crunchy, flavoursome. It's like eating really nice crisps. Who knew?

◆

It's mid-afternoon now, and Steve announces that we're going to do a bit of overnight camping in the bush. Are we not in the bush already? Apparently not. We load up our packs and pile into his jeep. He tells me that he has access to a big area of wilderness where nobody goes, not even the guy who owns the land, who he has an arrangement with.

We drive for about an hour over fields and through gates. There's no roads, not even dirt tracks. We're ploughing on, deeper into the middle of nowhere. And when we get there, we continue on foot for another hour. They know where they are going. They've been before. The bush is dense, the canopy overhead thick, blocking out most of the bright sunlight. We follow a dried-up creek and I become aware of smells and sounds I don't recognise. It's so untouched here. So natural and raw. However beautiful the bush is, remote and unsullied by humans, I have an underlying feeling of trepidation. Things buzz past me or scuttle noisily in the undergrowth nearby, and I have to remind myself that there is nothing dangerous in New Zealand. Nothing except the odd Australian spider. I need to trust Steve and his family. It's all perfectly safe.

'This is where you'll be sleeping, Royd.' Steve stops and points at a big pile of dried-up ferns. I would have walked right past it. At first glance it is just that, a load of brown ferns haphazardly leant together over branches in amongst the trees. I couldn't make any sense of it. Was I supposed to make a bed out of these bits of dead plants?

As if to answer my unvoiced question, the kids rush forwards and pull at the ferns, opening what one might call a 'door'. I thought it was a load of sticks covered in bird poo, but they knew how to open it. I peer into the darkness. There's a tunnel of sorts, a woody, ferny tunnel, barely big enough for a grown man to crawl inside. The forest floor is covered in more dead ferns that are probably meant to pass for some type of bedding. And I'm meant to be sleeping in there tonight. Not a chance.

First of all, I know for a fact (because Steve told me) that nobody has been here for months. This is their first excursion to this luxury home-from-home this season, and nobody else comes up here. And you know what that means? It means every little six- or (more worryingly) eight-legged monster in the area that fancied a bit of prime real estate will have moved into this shady opulent den and will now be lying in wait for me. Not a chance.

'Are there any spiders in there?' I ask as politely as I can. I can't really say what I want to say. Not in front of the children.

'Nah, nothing to worry about there,' Steve grins at me. Turtle and Dawa scramble into the hell-hole and start looking around with a torch their dad gives them.

'No, no spiders,' one of them chirrups, then, 'Oh wait, there's one.'

'It's a big one.'

'Yeah, there's a big spider in here.'

Nightmare.

They don't bother to get rid of it, or politely ask it to leave. They just calmly reappear and close the door on it.

Putting the pending horrors of bedtime to the back of my mind, I try to enjoy the rest of my evening with Steve and his family. We collect firewood and I put the bow drill to good use again. Steve has exchanged some of his honey for some organic beef from a local farm. We skewer chunks of it on sticks that we've whittled to points and cook it over the fire, along with vegetables from Steve's garden. The meat is outstanding, some of the best beef I've ever eaten. The whole meal is divine.

As night falls, Steve decides they are going to turn in.

'Where are you sleeping?' I ask him, and he points out some newly cut ferns strewn on the forest floor a little way up the hill. It looks distinctly fresher than where I'm heading.

After they go, I keep the fire burning for a couple more hours, trying to make myself so thoroughly exhausted that when I do crawl into that hole I'll be out like a light. But it's torture. All I'm thinking about is what's waiting for me. Eventually I pluck up the courage and go in search of my destiny. I need a torch now. Finding a specific load of ferns in a forest at night isn't straightforward.

After a while, I find it. I open the 'door' and look inside. Steve gave me a blanket, and I am wholeheartedly thankful for it now. I wrap myself in it, pull my hat down over my ears, trying to make as little skin available to little legs and fangs as possible, and somehow find the courage to shimmy my way into the shelter. I do it in the darkness. I don't want the torchlight to show me an army of angry arachnids ready to pounce on me. And I don't want it to attract them either. I'm so terrified I'm trembling. This is hideous.

Something just ran over my face. I must have drifted off to sleep somehow, and something has just woken me up by walking all over my face. I spit air and brush my face with my hand. Whatever it was, it felt massive. Definitely a spider. What else could it have been? Well I'm not putting a light on to check. That's the last thing I want to see: the many eyes of Shelob looking hungrily back at me.

◆

I wake up desperate for a pee. I shimmy feet first out of my den like a snake and empty my bladder against a tree. It's pitch black out here, and all I can hear are rustlings in the undergrowth and weird noises in the trees. Probably more giant spiders. I wriggle back into my hole.

◆

First light. Enough. I'm up. I escape the ferns and shake off what feels like millions of the sods crawling all over me, then head back to the barely warm embers of last night's fire. I get it going again and huddle by its sweet heat until Steve and his family appear a couple of hours later.

'How was your night's sleep?' he asks cheerily.

'Scary and not good.' I grimace. They know me well enough by now to tell that I'm not being rude. Just honest.

'Would you like some coffee?'

Oh! Yes, please.

He produces a little tin and opens it up to reveal coffee. Civilisation at last. It turns out it's dandelion root coffee, and I am immediately thinking of Mike and 'Nature's Larder'. And I'm thinking, Mike would have absolutely loved this. Of course, it would help that he wasn't afraid of spiders. He would have thrown himself into that pile of ferns and had a great night's sleep.

I dig Mike's old titanium mug out of my rucksack and savour every drop of that foraged coffee. I went through Mike's old Norway gear, all his camping stuff, a while ago. That was a painful experience, seeing so many things that reminded me of him, that still smelled of him, things that I could picture him using. He had a lot of titanium, always trying to lighten his pack with quality gear.

We pack up and make the journey back to Steve's place. Sitting outside the yurt there, I pull out 'Nature's Larder' and show Steve the page explaining how to make dandelion coffee. I tell him how, of all the things he could have offered me this morning, his dandelion coffee was the perfect connection back to Mike. I get out the mug again.

'I think this should stay here,' I tell him. 'I think Mike would have wanted you to have this.'

You're Having a Laugh

I'm outside Wellington Zoo. I didn't even know Wellington had a zoo. I've certainly never been here before. I've just blindly signed a load of forms. I didn't read them because I don't want to see anything that might give me a clue as to what I'm doing until I'm doing it. So I guess that means I'm waiving any right to sue them when I get mauled by a lion or bludgeoned to death by an angry silverback. Obviously I'm going to be doing something really dangerous, putting my life on the line again. Oh well.

After some time we're led through the zoo. We go through a gate and up a path that is for staff only. I knew it. No doubt this is the back entrance to the tiger enclosure or the bear pit. I'm going to feed some massive hungry carnivore with my bare hands. I'm certain of it. I'm let into a concrete-walled building, where apparently I'm going to 'get changed'. Someone let something slip there. So this is where I don the claw-proof vest or the chainmail or whatever serious safety gear I need for this task.

I'm presented with a giant cuddly penguin outfit.

Let me say that again. A giant cuddly penguin outfit. There's a body. And there's a head. And I have to put it on. Not what I was expecting at all. It's also not likely to offer a lot of protection against claws or teeth, so maybe that's off the cards too. I slip into the cosy outfit, not even wanting to know how silly I look, and off we go again through the zoo. Waddling up the path I giggle when I remember Cliff and Larry telling me about a convention they went to in America, called Dragon Con.

'They have furries there,' Cliff told me.

'What the hell is a furry?'

I had no idea that people liked dressing up in animal costumes and (allegedly) partaking in huge orgies, but that's how he described it to me.

And now I'm a furry.

Inappropriate to my more adult musings, I am actually here to entertain children. Not to partake in some fetishistic bacchanal. Most importantly, there's no sharp claws or slavering jaws in sight. Small mercies. It's actually a lot of fun. I'm anonymous, hidden behind a big soft penguin face, and the kids are delightful. I goof about for an hour or so and I'm done. What a sweet and fun task to do. Thanks Mike. That was easy.

◆

We're on our way out of the zoo. I'm back in normal clothes now, and pleasantly relaxed, despite a drizzle in the air. The zookeeper lady seems to be taking a vaguely circuitous route back to the entrance, but at least it gives me a chance to see some of the exhibits on the way. Oh, look at the wallabies. And there's a red panda. Cute lemurs. Awww . . . meerkats – they're funny. Spider monkeys. Horrible name.

We take a side path, which seems unnecessary as a detour and . . . hang on, Drew has the camera on his shoulder. That's odd. It's more than odd. It's a clear indication that something else is going to happen. Am I going to be fed to the lions after all? We're standing outside this octagonal building. I have no idea what's in there, but . . . oh . . . I've just noticed the murals painted around the walls.

Big. Bloody. Spiders.

I can't even begin to describe the dread that I am suddenly feeling. I know exactly what's coming now. Well, I don't know exactly, but it clearly involves eight legs, and I think we can all appreciate by now that these particular animals are my least favourite thing in the world.

Just last week, in Wales (I'll get back to New Zealand in a minute), I found a massive house spider in my bedroom before I went to bed. I do a spider check every night here. I have a pint glass and a piece of card in every room, ready to catch any spider I come across. I won't kill them, but they sure as hell aren't staying in the house. So there it was, sitting upside down on the bedroom ceiling. I have quite high ceilings so I couldn't properly reach it, and somehow it fell, or jumped, behind my chest of drawers. I pulled out all the drawers, breaking them as I hurled them out of the bedroom, trying to find that spider. You know what, I don't need drawers in my bedroom. I don't need any kind of furniture that can be a hiding place for a spider. I got rid of the whole thing. Still no spider. So I slept in a different room. It wasn't the first time and it won't be the last.

So I'm shaking with fear. I nervously mess about in front of the camera, offering to wipe the rain drops from Drew's lens, then pretend to do a runner. I really do want to run. The last thing in the world I want to do is go through that door. Go through that airlock. Airlock! The only possible reason to have an airlock on a building like this is that it's so utterly unthinkable that something in THERE could escape to out HERE. They're that monstrous and horrible and scary and hairy and venomous and . . . why on earth would I want to go in THERE? Surely nobody in their right mind would want to go in THERE! My spiralling fear tells me that they are loose, crawling around in that space, spinning webs and waiting for unwary travellers to venture into their lair. And when I go in they are all going to jump on my face and bite me.

Of course they aren't. And they don't. I shuffle uneasily from the airlock into the room. The spiders (I assume there are several of them) are all in their own little boxes, but I don't feel a particular wave of relief. I know I'm still going to be getting up close and personal. Dave, the spider wrangler, ushers me over to a table and chair by the counter that runs around the room. On the counter, in a glass terrarium, is a massive tarantula. MASSIVE. Just there, the size of a small plate, on the glass, defying gravity like they do.

'Does it bite?'

'Rarely.'

Rarely. But it does. It can. It will. I'll be the one person who gets bitten. Dave opens the door of the terrarium that it's stuck to, just waiting to attack me.

'Does she move quickly?' I ask nervously. Apparently it's a 'she'. Females are more aggressive, aren't they? Everyone knows that about spiders!

'She shouldn't do,' Dave tries to reassure me.

'She shouldn't, but she could?'

'Er . . . yes. She can if she wants to.'

I have visions of the monster scuttling up my arm and sinking its fangs into my face.

'If she does, I'll . . .'

I want to say I'll likely panic and smash through the door to escape.

'I'll rescue you.' Dave, my hero! Though, rightly, he's probably more concerned about saving his spider than me. Dave coaxes her onto his hand and brings her towards the table. I turn my body away, but I can't take my eyes off the spider. I put my clammy hand palm down on the table as instructed.

'I'll usher her onto your hand and put my hand the other side of yours so that she just walks over you.'

I have to do this. I can't pull out now. I mean, I could. But I'll have to do it eventually. It's on the list. That's all there is to it. If I bail on this, and on every other task that I really don't want to do, then I'll just have twenty or so horrible tasks to come back and do at the end of the journey. And that'll just give me a heart attack. I have to do this. Every fibre in my body is screaming at me that this is just wrong. But I have to do it.

Her legs touch the back of my hand. Her hairy legs are on me. I let out a pathetic fearful moan. I had really hoped that I wouldn't be as scared as I am. I'm okay with money spiders. They're so small that they barely even look like spiders. I tried to tell myself that tarantulas are so big, they're not like spiders either. Not like the big house spiders that I have in Wales. Too big to be scary. But no. I'm paralysed with fear.

She's on me. Sitting on my wrist. Heavier than I had imagined. Horribly heavy, and hairy. Every leg moves with its own precise and horrific intent. What's she thinking?

'Would you like me to take her off and try her on the flat of your hand?'

'Yeah, okay,' I say quickly with a nervous laugh. I don't want her on the flat of my hand, thank you. I just want her off me. This is insane. He cradles her while I anxiously turn my hands over, exposing my palms, then lets her walk her chunky legs back onto me. She sits in my cupped, open hands.

'Well done,' Dave says quietly. He's so calm. Weirdo. 'She's perfectly content,' he tells me. 'As far as she's concerned we're just logs, rocks, part of her habitat.'

'A shaking, sweating, log!' I try to make light of the situation, of my crippling phobia. She's bound to attack me any second. 'Oh,

I just had a cigarette,' I blurt out, terrified that some unfamiliar smell might provoke a vicious biting spree.

'That's okay,' Dave smiles.

'I had carrot cake as well. There's probably a crumb or two on my hand.'

'Ahhhh, carrot cake.'

What? What about carrot cake?

'It has been known to send them into a frenzy.'

I know he's joking, but it's still possible. And right now, nothing is funny to me. I can feel her weight, her strength, her hairiness. Her feet feel soft on me, and I can't stop looking at the great bulbous abdomen and imagining it bubbling with lethal venom. Venom that will dissolve my hands in an instant or paralyse me so that she can eat me at her leisure. I don't like it. I don't like it one bit.

Eventually she gets bored of scaring me and slowly and deliberately walks off my hands and onto the table. I pull my hands away as quickly as I dare so as not to startle her and breathe a long sigh of relief.

Dave does this kind of encounter to help people deal with phobias. Sorry, Dave. This one didn't work. I hurry out of the airlock into the beautiful fresh clean spider-free air outside, still afraid that some critter might have stowed away in my clothing, so happy to be away from that monster. I'm not changed in the slightest. I'm just glad it's over. Oh, Mike, you bugger – that wasn't nice of you!

Back at the Jucy van Drew chucks a cuddly spider toy at me that he bought in the shop. I jump and squeal and throw it off me. Not funny. Not funny at all. Although I do realise that if he'd done that a couple of hours ago I wouldn't have been affected. I'm still shaking from my 'encounter'. I can still almost feel the weight of that tarantula on my hand. Too soon, Drew. Too soon.

◆

I thought I was done with spiders, but no. I'm currently chain smoking outside a gay bar in downtown Wellington, preparing to do five minutes of stand-up comedy. My subject: spiders.

I got told I'd be doing this about an hour ago. And in that time I was supposed to have had the invaluable benefit of a comedian's expert advice. Unfortunately, the said comedian's bus was late, so it all got a bit rushed. We had a whole twenty minutes to plan my 'act'.

I didn't like the task when it was given to me, and I don't like it now. I can be quite funny, sure, but I'm no comedian. I've done Q&As, but standing up in a comedy club and trying to make people laugh with prepared material is something else. And anyway, surely most comedians get more than twenty minutes to work on their routines. This task has only one outcome. I will look like an utter dick. An idiot. I have been set up for a spectacularly humiliating fall. What's the point?

Spiders. But they aren't funny. What on earth am I going to say? It's going to be awful. The tardy funnyman, Alexander Sparrow (great name), was as helpful as he could have been. But, seriously, what can you do with twenty minutes? He was all animated and upbeat, and started by suggesting I play on my name for laughs.

'Hi, I'm Royd. Not Roy. Royd, like android.' Act like a robot.

Not funny.

'Royd, as in steroid.' Pull a muscle-man pose.

Not funny.

'Royd, like haemorrhoid.' Scratch your arse.

Still not funny.

It wasn't working.

He told me my routine needed a theme, some central idea that the jokes can be built around, something that had affected me recently, something funny or terrifying. It's only a couple of days since that traumatic experience at Wellington Zoo, so we settled on spiders. He suggested I play on the fears of the audience members, get them involved. But none of it was funny. And if I don't find it funny, what are the chances they will?

'What are you afraid of?' I could single someone out.

'Nothing.' What if that was their answer? It's too difficult. I don't want to rely on strangers. And yet what can I say about spiders that's remotely humorous? I don't find them funny. They scare the crap out of me. I put out my umpteenth cigarette. It's time. I head down the stairs to the basement bar, towards inevitable disaster, towards complete and utter embarrassment.

Sitting amongst the small crowd, I watch some of the other comedians have their go before me. It's an open mic night and there's maybe half a dozen of us ready to crash and burn. Well, they've probably been refining their routines for weeks. It's just me that will look like a prize tit.

I'm not laughing. I'll be honest, I'm not a big fan of stand-up comedy. I once went to a comedy gig in Chester and it seemed to me like people were trying too hard to laugh on cue, as if they wanted to let everyone around them know that they got the joke. I'm more a fan of observational comedy like Peter Kay or the various comedians on *Would I Lie To You?* Spur of the moment, off the cuff stuff, quick witted reactions from people who are naturally funny. Well-polished, scripted routines don't work for me. Nothing anyone says here is making me laugh. But then again, I'm way too busy trying to dampen my raging nerves. It's hard to laugh when you're bricking yourself, when you're trying to think of something (anything) rib-tickling about bloody spiders. I've got nothing. My head is rapidly emptying itself of anything useful. There's just a puddle of panic left sloshing around in my vacant brain.

It's nearly my turn. There's just one guy left before me. He gets up.

'So . . . spiders,' he announces. 'Man, I hate spiders. Who's afraid of spiders?'

You have got to be kidding. This has to be a set-up, and an unfair one at that. I look, slack-jawed, over at Drew. Behind his camera, he looks as surprised as me. Maybe it's not a set-up. But it's certainly a disaster. This guy has just stolen my thunder, such as it was. There's a few titters around the room, but I don't even listen to what this guy says. I'm frantic now. What do I do? If I thought I had nothing before, I've got less than that now.

Gulp. Now it's my turn.

When I'm up there, and the lights are on me, I just feel silly. I grin mawkishly, scowling into the glare and trying to make out faces. I put my hand up to my forehead and search the room for the spider-hating comedian. I can't see him.

'Has he gone?' I breathe heavily into the microphone. 'So, anyway, one of my biggest fears . . . is . . . spiders.'

There's a quiet ripple of sympathetic laughter. Pity, probably. I'm dying. Fast. I mumble on for a bit about my encounter with the tarantula, drily relating the event without the slightest comedic nuance. The crowd are quiet. I try and bring them in, get them to interact, ask if anyone else has a phobia. I get nothing. As predicted, it's a car crash.

I stumble my way towards the end of what has become a mind-numbingly dull story, and I'm done. 'Thank you, good night.' I'm ready to run outside and hopefully never see any of these people ever again.

'You've still got three minutes, Royd,' the emcee shouts up at me.

Oh, come on! My body wants to fold itself up and slither away into the shadows. I crumple on the stage, my hand still clutching

160

the microphone. How was that not five minutes? It feels like I've been up here, banging on, for ages.

I start talking. Burbling. I tell the audience how I've been travelling around New Zealand doing this documentary, sharing rooms and not even being able to have a wank. Where did that come from? It got a laugh. Smut always does. So I make lurid comments about covertly climaxing into Drew's beard while he was asleep. Crass, I know. Gross, definitely. But it gets another laugh. What now?

'How's the camera?' I ask Drew, grinning down his lens while willing it to stop working. 'Batteries okay?' Save me. Please. He gives me the thumbs up. Balls.

'Two minutes,' prompts the emcee.

Still?

'What can you do in two minutes?' he asks, mercifully feeding me a line.

'What can I do in two minutes?' I repeat, playing for a few seconds of time. 'I can have a conversation for a minute and a half . . . and then I can have sex.'

A proper laugh from the crowd.

'To completion,' I add, after a well-timed pause, and get a bigger laugh. This isn't so bad after all. All I had to do was not give a toss about what I say. Just be me.

I tell everyone how I'm rushing off on a Tinder date after this, the first date I've been on for ages. The audience are joining in now. Cue various interactive jokes about Tinder and Grindr (we're in a gay bar after all), and I finish with a laugh and a cheer from the room. I probably did just over five minutes in the end.

And it's true. I am meeting someone for a date. And I can't wait, if only because it means I won't be here. Although, saying that, it's turned out okay. What began as potentially one of the

161

worst and most humbling experiences of the journey so far ended up being quite fun. I enjoyed it. Sure I looked silly for a bit, but we all had a laugh.

And that's how it was with Mike. I would do silly things to make him laugh. Because I could. Because no matter how idiotic I look or feel, it's only fleeting. It's not the relentless decline that he experienced. If I can bring a little laughter, even if it's at my expense, I will.

The Official Diagnosis

When Mike and I got back from New Zealand there was a moment's calm before the storm. For a short while we revelled in our memories of the trip. But Mike was ill, and while we had a working diagnosis of motor neurone disease, there was still a hope, a faint belief, that it could be something else. Something less terrible.

Maybe it was wishful thinking, but there was a definite sense that not enough consideration had been given to other possibilities. Mike still had it in mind that it could be somehow related to the unusual fever he had suffered. There was still the possibility of Lyme disease, which at that time there was no test for in this country. The treatment for Lyme disease is an intensive course of high-dose antibiotics which again you apparently couldn't get in this country back then. I knew how to remove ticks from my stint in Camp America; there we used to have daily tick checks where we scoured each other's limbs and bodies for evidence. If Mike had contracted Lyme disease he would have had to go to America for treatment.

When he suggested the possibility of this to the medical profession here he was fobbed off. Instead of being listened to, or looked after, he was passed around for more tests. One of them involved being wired up and having electrical shocks sent through his body, his toes, his calves, his thighs, his knees, even his earlobes. It was intended to measure the electrical impulses as they passed through his muscles to see if his neurone pathways were carrying the current correctly. It wasn't pleasant, and it was never explained properly to him. Mike began to feel like he was part of some medical production line, jostled through a system and being experimented on with a notable absence of sympathy or any kind of bedside manner.

There was also a sense that, even if it was motor neurone disease, perhaps it had been detected early enough. His muscle twitching had died down by then, so surely it was possible that other symptoms could do the same? Perhaps there was some treatment that could halt or slow down the disease's progress. Mike was determined to remain strong-willed, hopeful. It was all he had. Hope. A refusal to give up. His snowboard that leant up against the wall was testament to that, even later on.

We wanted our questions answered but it wasn't happening. It seemed so vague, so unnecessarily complicated. Mike was burdened with a working diagnosis for months and months, to the point that he needed it to either be something else, or be made official. If you're diagnosed with a cold, you've got a cold. If you break your leg, you break your leg. If you've got cancer, you've got cancer. But with motor neurone disease it felt like a guessing game. It felt like 'we think you have this, but we can't be sure until we've finished all these tests on you.'

Mike was feeling the financial strain as well. He'd had to stop working just before we went to New Zealand. He was working as a printer, operating the heavy old-fashioned letterpress machinery. Printing was a trade our dad had spent his life working in, and something in which both Mike and I had effectively done apprenticeships when we were younger. An illustrator friend of ours, Mark, had started a business producing greeting cards. He began with a small treadle press in his garage but, as business boomed, he had to upgrade to a bigger, more automated letterpress machine, a Heidelberg. Mike and I helped him install the kit, and Mike ended up working with him, operating the press. It's a monster of a machine that can't be taken lightly. If you were to get your hand caught in it . . . well, you wouldn't have a hand for long. It's physical work, and it came to the point that Mike couldn't do it safely. He felt a powerful love and connection to printing, and it broke his heart to have to give it up. Hanging on the walls in my living room are Mike's most treasured fine art prints that he produced.

With only a working diagnosis, there was no financial assistance on offer. In order to access disability benefits and state support, Mike needed the diagnosis to be official. We'd tried jumping through hoops to get him help, but were constantly met with a complete lack of understanding. Even the prospect of signing on was bleak. Mike couldn't work, and even if there was a job he could do, a less physical job, the likelihood of an employer taking on someone with even a working diagnosis of a rapidly degenerative condition like motor neurone disease was slim at best. On top of the trauma of facing this death sentence, Mike felt degraded and belittled in his quest for support.

His doctor referred him to what was reportedly one of the country's leading facilities in neurological matters. And it was right on our doorstep; surely this was good news? It was there that we were told by the consultant that the final test in determining whether or not it was motor neurone disease, eliminating the possibility of it being some kind of viral infection, was a lumbar puncture. Sitting in the consultation room, I could feel Mike's fear. He had endured all manner of tests, but this one was terrifying. I remember his screams of pain when he was younger, in that cottage hospital, having the same procedure done as a test for viral meningitis. Mike remembered it even more keenly. When we walked out of the appointment, I knew Mike was broken. He didn't want it. He needed the official diagnosis, but the thought of another lumbar puncture was just too much. It felt cruel. It seemed they

165

had already decided that it was motor neurone disease, so why did they need to put him through this pain? I'd voiced the concern we all felt, and got the answer I expected; times had changed. That day in the cottage hospital was twenty plus years earlier, and this was a highly specialised facility with practitioners who do several lumbar punctures a day without incident. After a lot of discussion, and persuasion, Mike reluctantly agreed to proceed with the test.

When the day came I went with Mike. Dad, Laura and Mandy were there too. At every opportunity, while booking the test or talking to anyone there, I had reiterated Mike's fears and asked if there was any way of making the procedure more comfortable for him. Could they knock him out? I was told he had to be conscious, that there was more risk in administering a general anaesthetic than there was in performing the lumbar puncture. Walking in, we passed the consultant. She smiled at us and reassured Mike that everything would be just fine. Again I asked if he could be knocked out or sedated or something. No. He couldn't. She was pleasant but firm. We checked in at the reception desk. I pointlessly asked the receptionist the same question. A nurse took his blood. I asked her. I was starting to annoy people asking the same question, but I didn't care. I could see Mike was fretting, and I felt protective.

The doctor who was due to perform the procedure looked the part. He was in his early thirties, in full scrubs, and looked like he knew what he was doing. He was affable, confident and reassuring. He'd done dozens, if not hundreds, of lumbar punctures over the years and it had always gone smoothly. I could see Mike starting to feel more relaxed. He didn't seem to mind that the room we were shown into was little more than a store-room containing a bed and a curtain. People were coming and going, taking supplies from the shelves and so on. I wanted somewhere quiet, somewhere private, if only to make Mike as relaxed as possible.

Mike lay on his side on the bed, his gown open at the back, in a foetal position. He had to bring his knees up as far towards his chest as was comfortable in order to expose the spinal column to the doctor. The curvature of the spine in this position is meant to make it easier for the doctor to insert the thick six-inch needle into a specific place between the vertebrae. That needle then needs to pierce a membrane, before being inserted into the centre of the spinal column to draw out the necessary fluid for the test. It's a tough membrane, however, and it takes considerable force to penetrate it.

The doctor pushed the needle into Mike's skin. Mike was gripping my hand, palm to palm, thumbs intertwined. His grip tightened. I knew it was hurting him, but I was there for him. Something wasn't right. The doctor was pushing the needle in hard, presumably trying to get through that membrane, but it wasn't working. He had found bone instead. He was pushing that big needle hard into Mike's vertebrae. Several times. He pulled the needle out and felt again for the gap. He tried again. Same result. Mike was white as a sheet, swathed in sweat and gritting his teeth against the agonising pain that was being inflicted upon him. One of his nails bit deep into the fleshy part of my thumb and drew blood, but I wasn't letting go of him.

'Everything's okay, Mike,' I tried to reassure him, trying to keep my voice sounding calm.

The doctor looked confused. Concerned. 'Sorry about this. Let's have another look,' he said. 'Ah yes, there we are. I've got it now.' He pushed the needle in again. He didn't have it. He got the same result. It jabbed and scratched at bone. He couldn't find the gap or the membrane. Mike's nail dug deeper into my thumb. Eventually the doctor sat back, defeated, and apologised profusely. It had never happened to him before.

Mike got dressed. The excruciating pain of the needle was gone, but he was still in agony. As we walked out, he was bent double. And we had achieved absolutely nothing. Instead it had been everything Mike had feared it would be. On the way back to the car we bumped into the consultant, who cheerfully asked how it had gone. Mike, never one to be rude, couldn't bring himself to look at her. He hobbled off in the other direction, leaving me to vent our collective frustration.

She was apologetic, surprised and confused. But she also pointed out that Mike still needed to have the test done. He'd have to try again.

'Well he's not going to,' I told her firmly. 'And I don't blame him.'

Then she told me he could have the test in an operating theatre, under local anaesthetic, and the needle could be inserted under X-ray. I was absolutely livid. All the times we had told her and everyone we had ever spoken to about Mike's concerns and fears, and it turned out that he could have had the procedure done without any stress or pain. He could have avoided all of that.

Again, we had to persuade Mike that he needed the test. Nobody mentioned it for a day or so, but eventually we had to try. Mike took a lot of convincing. I didn't even believe the words I was saying to him. I just wanted him to have the test and be told that it wasn't motor neurone disease, and whatever it was could be treated and Mike would be okay. I was tied up in guilty knots, terrified for him but pretending that I was sure everything would be fine.

Because of the X-ray machine, I wasn't able to go in with Mike for the second attempt. He was given a local anaesthetic in his back and taken into the theatre. After a few minutes, it was all done. That easy. Why he couldn't have just had it done that way in the first place, I'll never understand.

A few days later, I showed Mike where his nail had cut into me during the first attempt. It was scabbed over by then, and starting to heal. His reaction wasn't 'oh, I'm sorry'; it was 'you should have put ink in it and made a tattoo out of it'.

The day Mike died, that's exactly what I did. I sat at home at the end of the long day, devastated, and took a blade out of a razor. I cut a line into the pale scar tissue at the base of my thumb, and another one across it, to form a small 'X'. A kiss. And I broke a pen apart and dribbled its ink into the bleeding kiss. Every time I need to feel close to Mike I kiss that little cross and it connects me right back to the day his nail drew my blood, and to the day he died. And to him.

◆

Whatever they were looking for in Mike's spinal fluid, they didn't find it. And that meant only one thing. It was motor neurone disease. It was official. Mike cried. He didn't sob or break down, but his tears came. That was the end of what little hope we had all clung to that it might have been something else.

Of course we had questions. We had a lot of questions. And we bombarded the consultant with them. We wanted to know what we could do. Nothing. There had to be something we could do that might slow the disease down, something that could buy Mike some time, buy us more time with Mike. No. Nothing. It's motor neurone disease. There's nothing you can do. That's what we were told. The single piece of advice that she had to share was this: 'get your affairs in order.'

Get your affairs in order? She might as well have said, 'You're fucked. Make a will and say your goodbyes, because you're going to die, you're off, you're gone, and it'll be sooner rather than later.'

There have been plenty of times in my life I have missed the opportunity to say what I really wanted to say, the times you realise too late what you should have said. And right then, shell-shocked, angry and sad, I said nothing effectual. It just didn't register at the time. I realised shortly afterwards that I should have said, 'How dare you? How dare you tell us that?!' I should have challenged that cold and horrible dismissal of Mike's bleak future. I don't want to paint the consultant in a bad light as she was a lovely woman, generally sympathetic and pleasant, but that was absolutely the worst, most callous thing that anyone could have said at that moment.

And any suggestion we had for ways to alleviate Mike's suffering were pretty much brushed aside as pointless. I asked about diet. What effect could nutrition have on the progress of the disease? Mike had always had a healthy diet. He was a vegetarian, and conscientious about what he ate. I mean, I didn't think a balanced input of vitamins and minerals would cure him, but surely the right foods could at least provide something of a boost to his energy and alertness and his ability to deal with the worsening conditions. But no, we were told it wouldn't make a difference. Mike could eat whatever he wanted. He had motor neurone disease. That was that.

We went straight from that appointment to talk to a physiotherapist. We were hoping for advice as to how Mike could strengthen his muscles as they began to waste, perhaps a course of treatment, something. Anything. But the verdict was the same. There was no point in physiotherapy. It wouldn't help. He had motor neurone disease. That was that. The physio we saw had suffered a stroke or something similar. One side of her body was weak from it, one side of her face drooping. When we asked what kind of physio would help Mike she almost laughed. She pointed at her face and stated that she couldn't do anything about what had happened to her. She had accepted it. And, not to put words in her mouth, Mike had to do the same. She may as well have said, 'You've got motor neurone disease. Your muscles are going to atrophy. There's no point falsely trying to keep them working, because they won't. You're fucked. Get your affairs in order.'

Instead, Mike was given a photocopied sheet of paper that detailed a few exercises he could do at home, and was then measured up for a device that would mitigate the effect of his foot drop. It was two solid uncomfortable pieces of plastic, one to fit around his foot and the other around his ankle and calf. However, they only had one of the two pieces available, and it was going to take three months for the second part to arrive. In the meantime, he'd just have to trip over! Over time, we were referred to about ten physiotherapists through the NHS, all with similar attitudes, all unwilling to 'waste' time on someone with motor neurone disease, until Mandy eventually found one privately. Claire had a physiotherapy company in Chester. She was unbelievable, and as shocked as we had been at the reluctance to try to help Mike. She came once a week to work with him, and showed us ways to massage and manipulate his body to relieve his discomfort and pain. She was kind, never rushed and was a great help and support to Mike.

Frustrated with the lack of help and support and practical advice for someone diagnosed with MND, Mike set about building a website he called NeuroHub. It was based on the shared experiences of those going through MND, rather than the conventional advice given (or notable by its absence) by the medical establishment. It would be a resource, a place of inspiration and hope on subjects such as diet, physiotherapy and equipment. Mike wanted any alternative therapies and treatments that benefited him to be explained to others, to offer them similar beacons of hope. He was frustrated with the 'wait and see' and 'nothing can be done' attitudes from the 'establishment', a crushing negativity that he wasn't used to. Mike's attitude was far more fighting.

◆

With the diagnosis official, Mike was finally able to access financial support. And yet this too was a protracted and painful process. After weeks of jumping through hoops and talking to idiots on the phone, Mike was awarded the full package of benefits, which amounted to a kingly £20.33 a week! I furiously called up the helpline and asked some kid, who was struggling to keep up with his 'script', who he knew who could live on that amount of money. Mike was terminally ill. He couldn't work. He was in pain. His condition was going to worsen dramatically. What on earth was £20.33 a week going to do for him? The kid referred to his script and told me that the money was to go towards getting a carer to come and cook Mike a meal once a day. That money wouldn't even cover the food, let alone pay someone to come in and cook it every day. Eventually Mike got a better package, and Laura was given just over sixty pounds a week as a nominated full-time carer, but it was an unnecessarily painful effort to get even that. Not to mention the fact that Mike needed more than one carer. And that's before we got into the costs of private physiotherapy and all the specialist equipment Mike would need.

It just felt like the system was letting Mike down, letting us all down. The way the diagnosis had been handled, and the prognosis delivered, and with the paltry help on offer from the state, we decided we wanted a second opinion. Mandy did some research and got Mike a private appointment with Professor Shaw at King's College in London. He was everything that the other doctors we'd seen hadn't been: compassionate, tactful and gentle. We desperately wanted his expert opinion to discredit the previous verdict. But it wasn't to be. Professor Shaw sadly confirmed the diagnosis. And to demonstrate how wonderful Professor Shaw was, he waived his fee. A rare gem.

◆

I don't remember the journey back from London to North Wales. I just remember being in the lift after that appointment, and Mike crying. We were all so deflated and upset. But Mike still wasn't about to merely 'put his affairs in order'. He still had fight in him. We all did. None of us were ready to accept the fatalism we'd been met with. We resolved to stand firm, together, and dig our heels in. We were going to fight it. We were going to fight it with physiotherapy, with diet, with alternative remedies, with anything we could find, from anywhere in the world.

We needed a plan. Dad became the fixer. If Mike needed something practical like the correct springs for his foot drop device, Dad would get them. If he needed a bit of kit adapting, like the hand grip of his electric wheelchair, Dad would sort it. A self-cleaning toilet would be researched, sourced and fitted. Nothing was ever too difficult. Mandy became the behind-the-scenes organiser. She could absorb the headaches and the torrents of paperwork, and make things happen. And, as I lived close to Mike, I was able to be with him every day. Together with Laura, Story and everyone else who helped, we made a great team.

Lost World – New World

I'm leaving the North Island. We have traded in our Jucy people carrier for a massive Jucy RV that's currently stowed in the bowels of the ferry I'm on. We chug slowly from the port into the big natural bay and pass the headland where Weta is, and onwards past the suburb of Miramar where I was staying. Heading for the sea. Next stop, Picton. The South Island.

A couple of days ago I was driven north from Wellington to Waitomo, where I rappelled into the Lost World. If you think that sounds cool, it is. The particulars of the task weren't all that surprising once I'd been waiting in the visitor centre for a few minutes. There were pictures everywhere of people hanging from ropes and clambering through caves, so I felt prepared by the time we had walked, all harnessed up and wearing 'gummies', to the cave mouth.

The drop itself took my breath away. We emerged from the woods onto a metal grille platform that hung precipitously over a misty dark sinkhole. I couldn't even see the bottom. It's about a hundred metres, which may not sound a lot, but it's significantly higher than the Statue of Liberty, or a whisker less than the top of the dome of St Paul's Cathedral in London, if you want some perspective. As I was clipped on and leant back over the abyss, I was scared. My damp hands clung to the thin rope that was supposed to see me to terra firma beneath the clouds of mist below. Drew looked a little nervous too. He asked how safe the rope was, and if it would hold his weight. He's heavier than (*cough*) average, especially with the camera as well, but our guides, Luke and Brad, reassured him this rope was designed to lift the weight of a tank . . . which got a giggle from me.

Once you've stepped off the edge, there's little point being scared. The rope takes your weight, and you can control your descent. And if I did screw up and let out too much cord, I was attached to one of the guides by a secondary line, so I couldn't go down too fast. I just had to try not to look down.

The descent was peaceful, leisurely and jaw-droppingly mystical. The landscape that opened up beneath us was extraordinary, verdant moss over great sleek black rocks that occasionally glistened in the few sharp beams of sunlight that penetrated the mist. If it hadn't been frequented by who knows how many tourists, you'd have the sense that you were discovering it for the first time. It's a magical, otherworldly place full of secrets and mystery. I half expected to see the head of a brontosaurus lift up from behind one of the great boulders, its mouth full of greenery.

We unhitched from the rope and set off into the cave system. Once properly underground we had to rely on head torches. We clambered over rock formations and squeezed through gaps, stopping for coffee and a biscuit (another show of the unexpected coffee-producing brilliance of the locals) at one point. Near an underground river, we turned off our lights and marvelled at the luminescent bodies of glow-worms twinkling like stars in the inky blackness all around us.

Apparently, the only way out of there was a rusting, rickety, slippery long metal ladder that was bolted (apart from where a few bolts seemed to have come free) vertically to the cave wall. It was a tough climb. I had a safety line, and Brad had gone up first to belay me, but it was exhausting, and a somewhat nervy end to proceedings. Back at the visitor centre, I thanked our guides and wished them a good life, assuming I'd probably never see them again. As you do.

The next day, back in the Jucy van, I started recognising landmarks from the day before. Had we forgotten something? We pulled into the same visitor centre, and there were Brad and Luke again, grins all over their faces. No, we hadn't come back for a misplaced lens cap or a lost wallet. I was going to go black-water tubing. I went into a cave, a different part of the same system, where the tunnels were significantly smaller. Tighter, and half-filled with freezing, dark water. Fortunately, I had a wet suit.

Only half concerned about the constant potential New Zealand has for earthquakes, and pondering what it would be like to be crushed by all this rock if the seismic plates decided to have a wobble at that particular moment, I spent a couple of hours squeezing through gaps and drifting down the underwater river on an inflatable ring. Again, we turned off our torches and watched the light show from the glow-worms. Lying back in the pitch darkness and unearthly quiet, floating on the gentle current, it was easy to imagine they were swirling galaxies millions of light-years away, unreachable above us in a night sky. Somehow, in the confined bowels of New Zealand, at its core, I had a glimpse of the universe and beyond.

Even if I was only looking at maggots' luminescent poo a few feet above my face.

Mike would have loved both of those adventures. And he would have loved to have been with me on this ferry, heading for all the rugged wildness and extreme sports of the South Island.

Leaving the North Island, I can't help feeling that I'm leaving Mike behind. Wellington was as far south as we came together, as far south as he ever went. I think of all the places I've just been in the city, places that I went with Mike, and I feel painfully aware that nowhere in the South Island will I feel that immediate connection to a memory of him. I feel like I'm being forced to do the second half of this journey without Mike, without those threads back to him. I'm having to let him go a little bit.

And that feeling of loss makes me sad. I stand on deck, leaning on the railing, sucking back a cigarette and watching the land disappear slowly from view. I feel alone.

I am literally, and figuratively, at sea.

The Nevis Bungy

Mike, me and Mandy

Me and Mike on a fiord in Norway

Mike and Edan

Mike at Black Sands Beach

Me and Mike in Hobbiton

Mandy, Mike and me at Center Parcs

'I love hugs'

PART THREE

ACROSS THE WATER

Random Acts

The approach to Picton on the South Island is magnificent. The ferry wends its way for an age between small islets and undulating tree-covered headlands, before anything more than an occasional remote homestead comes into view. Picton itself is a small town, uncluttered and quiet, a far cry from the vibrant variety of Wellington. As our camper-van rolls ashore, there is a sense of having arrived in some frontier town. The roads are wide and the traffic sparse. It feels alien and, dare I say it, far less welcoming than the places I know well on the North Island.

I've spent the crossing in a reflective state, absorbed by the passing of the (thankfully) calm waters. Cook Strait separates the two large islands of New Zealand, but I'm aware that due east from here lie thousands of miles of ocean, the South Pacific, that eventually reach the shores of Chile and Peru. North of New Zealand, barring the tiny islands of Tonga and Fiji and so on, it's ocean all the way up past Japan and China to the eastern reaches of Russia. And to the south lies the huge icy landmass of Antarctica. It's little wonder that I am feeling isolated and far from anywhere.

One comfort to me is the common ground Drew and I share. His feeling of being alone has followed him since landing in this alien country. His girlfriend is back home. She had a miscarriage shortly before he started this 'job' and I know how much he wants to be back there with her, rather than traipsing around New Zealand with me. For some reason he's also decided this is a good time to give up smoking. Probably wise given the prices here, but still. In his effort to slow the habit, he keeps buying these weird flavoured little cigarillos that are sold individually, and he's taken up vaping. I noticed him on the deck of the ferry, looking out at the still waters like I was, no doubt enjoying a camera-free moment, and offered to roll him a real cigarette. We smoked without talking, hypnotised by the gentle wake left by the ferry, and perhaps both felt a little less alone for a moment.

Mike has tasked me with performing 'random acts of kindness'. In his words, 'find people to help, even in the smallest way. Give flowers to people, hug strangers, buy lunch for the homeless, leave positive messages on sticky notes, go and talk to the old person on the bench, smile at people and brighten their day.'

I don't particularly feel like smiling. And the biggest issue with this task is that it doesn't lend itself easily to being captured on camera. It needs to be spontaneous. And I used the word 'performing' because I'm afraid that is what it will feel like. I absolutely understand the philosophy behind it, but I'm struggling with the timing. I've left the comforting familiarity of Wellington behind and am facing an onward journey across the South Island, a place with no immediate connection to memories of Mike. Story is working in Raglan on the North Island. Andy is long gone.

I've already, in many ways, done several of the things detailed in Mike's task. In a park in Hamilton, on his instruction, I dressed as a hippie and handed out free hugs. For a couple of hours, festooned in tie-dye and CND paraphernalia, I lurked near an imminent outdoor performance of a Shakespeare play, offering to wrap my arms around strangers and spread a little love. I handed out copies of that picture of Mike and me as kids, the one I decorated with Mike's words, 'I love hugs', the one I still have scrolled up in a bottle waiting to find a watery home, the one that refused to launch from Black Sand Beach.

In Wellington, a day or so before we left, I had to persuade passers-by on the street to give me a kiss. The catch? I wasn't allowed to talk. Like some kind of degenerate mime artist, armed with nothing more than what charm I could muster, I had to break down the barriers between strangers and convince them of the merits of fleeting physical contact. It seemed fun and silly at the time, but again I get Mike's sentiment. He was horribly isolated, trapped in his failing physicality, eventually almost wordlessly reliant on those around him to provide him with love and affection, with freely given hugs and kisses and touch. Touch was important to Mike, whether through massage, us holding his hand, or just sitting next to him in his wheelchair with a hand on his knee or shoulder. Unable to say all that he wanted to say, Mike saw what many of us fail to see; complacently marching through life and happily keeping other people at arms' length, it's so easy to not appreciate the comfort of strangers, to not reach out and make a difference to other people, to not revel in our mutual humanity.

I'm not naturally gregarious, and I find engaging with strangers sometimes awkward. It's not a switch that's constantly on. That made another of Mike's tasks undertaken in Wellington especially testing. I got kitted out with a radio mic and let loose in a bustling, be-fountained, grassy square called Pigeon Park, the naming of which is testament either to Wellingtonians' talent for on-the-nose description, or to the unusual literacy of the local birds. The eponymous birds, alongside plenty of menacing looking gulls, strutted with a well-fed arrogance amongst their human co-habitants, many of whom were just trying to enjoy a sandwich on their lunch break. My mission? To convince someone, anyone, that we had met before; effectively, to duplicitously embarrass someone into lying about knowing me.

The first few attempts didn't go at all well.

'Tom,' I called out to a Kiwi chaining his bike to a railing. Nothing. 'Tom? It is Tom, isn't it?'

He looked up. 'No, mate.'

'Oh,' I tried to look as friendly as possible. 'I'm sure I met you . . .' I waved my arm in the direction of Wellington in general. 'I met you in a bar at the weekend?'

'No, mate. Not me.' He was having none of it.

'Oh, okay, sorry.' I started to walk off, then turned back to him. 'Mate,' I muttered apologetically, 'there's a camera over there.' I pointed at Drew, who was being as discreet as he knows how to be, casually sitting twenty yards or so away with the camera on his lap aimed at us. I explained my mission and told him about Mike's list as briefly as I could. Even more awkward than trying to dupe people, I also had to get them to agree to being on camera.

'Good luck.' He laughed pitifully as he walked away from me.

The next 'mark' was even less rewarding. Not a glimmer of false recognition. He was built like an athlete, so probably didn't drink, probably remembered every second of his life with an unerring clarity. 'There's a camera over there,' I admitted again. 'I've got to go up to random strangers and convince them that we know each other.'

'It didn't really work, did it?'

No. It didn't.

'Sarah?' I spotted a young woman chowing down on a baguette and decided she might be more impressionable. Wrong. She seemed almost belligerently offended at the suggestion that I might have met her in a bar. Absolutely not. I apologised and made my escape. But I had to go back and get her permission to use the footage. Not awkward at all.

'There's a camera over there.' I waved at Drew. Bless him, he waved back. 'I'm basically in New Zealand doing my brother's bucket list . . .'

'Are you Royd?' she asked suddenly.

I'm sorry, what?

'I am . . .' I answered, utterly bamboozled.

'I've got you on Facebook,' she guffawed. 'That's how I know you!'

I mean, what are the chances? I looked over at Drew and saw his camera shaking as he clearly chortled away.

Typical me, accepting friend requests from any female that shows an ounce of interest.

I tried one more. A silver-haired man was sitting near a lurking seagull on a low wall. I pulled out all the stops, asking if he put on events (the logo on his T-shirt was a helpful clue!), and after a moment or two of me waffling on and pointing vaguely in the direction of Cuba Street and half of Wellington, he let slip that he organised a karaoke night at one of the local bars.

'That was it,' I pounced. 'Sorry, what's your name? I don't remember from the other night.'

'Steve,' he answered. 'I'm DJ Steve.'

'Ah yeah! Of course. Sorry, I was really hammered. I think I sang. Was I any good?'

'Yeah, you were pretty good.'

Result!

'So you do remember me?'

'Yeah, I remember faces, but names . . .' he shook his head.

Good enough.

◆

This whole 'random acts of kindness' task just isn't working. I'm waiting outside a retirement home somewhere near Nelson, and I'm dreading how forced and stupid this whole thing is.

I'm not blaming anyone, but the first attempt at doing something for this task was anything but random. At the behest of production, who had organised it all, we pitched up at a small shelter for homeless men on a quiet street in Picton, armed with a load of groceries and ready to cook some dinner. I had to put my foot down and say that we couldn't possibly take a camera in, which rendered the whole thing redundant in terms of the documentary. But far worse than that, just being there felt like some horrible touristic, faux philanthropic gesture that was almost insulting to the men who were trying to find a quiet refuge from the world. It felt like I was there to court gratitude for generously giving an hour of my time, without making a scrap of difference to their lives. It was too late to just walk away, so I did my level best. I cooked a meal and tried to find the balance between talking too much and too little to people who probably didn't want to talk at all. It was just awful. It was crass, uncomfortable, unhelpful and decidedly un-random. I know it wasn't what Mike intended at all.

And this? This is more of the same. No, it's even worse. This time, a journalist from a local newspaper has got wind of my visit and wants to interview me here. It's cringeworthy. I don't want some article on how the great-grandson of J. R. R. Tolkien deigned to take time out of his busy schedule to spend ten minutes gracing a load of pensioners with his presence. That's certainly not what I'm about. And again, I certainly don't want it to be filmed. Thankfully Drew understands and agrees. He's off for a Vera Lynn singalong in the common room while I get shown around. Let's get through this.

I spend ten minutes giving interview bumf to the journalist. She's respectful and professional, and I try to give her the courtesy of answering her questions properly, but she hasn't got me on my best day. After that I help put some biscuits on a plate, cut some cake, and sit and chat with some of the residents over a board-game. It's pleasant enough, but I'm still quietly seething that I've been press-ganged into this charade of do-gooding. I might as well be bellowing out 'We'll meet again' with Drew and the others, for all the difference this is making to anyone's life. No offence, Drew. Or Dame Vera.

Debbie, who runs the place, interrupts and asks if I'd like to see the part of the home reserved for those who are less independent. She rightly assumes that I have some knowledge of hoists and how to lift people safely. On our way to somewhere that we never reach, she suggests introducing me to someone called Alan. Apparently, he loves meeting people. I don't suppose he has the faintest idea who I am, but sure, why not. I imagine some polite old timer being merrily cajoled into a pointless conversation with me, while privately yearning to get back to his jigsaw.

As soon as I see Alan I know that I want to spend time with him. He's sitting in his chair in his little room, not looking particularly comfortable and looking at me with eyes that remind me of Mike. I'm not sure if he's had a stroke, or what condition he might have, but he can't speak any more and his mobility is limited to one arm. And his eyes are expressive, wide, emotive: like Mike's became. Debbie leans in towards his face and introduces me loudly and slowly, though I'm certain he isn't deaf. I saw a lot of that with Mike and it bothers me.

Alan seems keen to communicate with me somehow, so after a few minutes of quietly ignoring Debbie, I ask if I can stay and have a chat with him. She leaves us to it and continues on her rounds. I lapse immediately into how I looked after Mike. I go through a list of questions. Are you hungry? Are you thirsty? Do you need the toilet? He gives the slightest shake of his head to all these. Are you uncomfortable? A flicker of acknowledgement.

He isn't able to manoeuvre himself in his chair. I should have seen that. He is slumped forward a bit, not only making him uncomfortable, but also probably making it harder for him to communicate. A passing nurse helps me lift him more upright in his chair, and I can see the relief immediately in his eyes. I sit where he can easily see me and tell him a little about myself, and about Mike. I maintain eye contact. That was crucial with Mike, and I'm well practised, if a little rusty. Mike could speak volumes with just his eyes, and Alan is the same.

He has an iPad and a pen that he uses to indicate letters on a keypad, but even that is a struggle. His hand, limited in its movement, is shaking. He gets the wrong letter, and his frustration is palpable. So I offer to take the iPad from him and go through the letters, asking him which ones he wants, allowing him to spell out his words. It takes me right back to Mike and the Apple TV.

As his words gradually emerge on the tablet I discover that he wants me to read a document he wrote about himself and his life before he became ill. He wants to share it with me, as I have shared a little about me with him. It's somewhere on his laptop. Under his direction I try to find it, but it doesn't appear to be where he thinks it should be. He's adamant that he wants me to read it though, and asks me to get a message to his wife via Debbie to dig a copy of it out of a filing cabinet at home and send it to me.

I don't know how long I've been here. A couple of hours at least. At any rate, I feel like it's appropriate for me to go. I ask Alan if there's anything else he wants to say, and if he's happy with me leaving. His head is leant over to one side, but he lifts his thumb and there's a smile in his eyes. The minute I resolve to leave I begin to feel sadness and anger and frustration welling up inside me. I desperately want Alan to get this level of attention every day. I know, from experience, how much it means to him. Don't get me wrong, it's a wonderful nursing home and the staff are caring and professional, but there are dozens of other residents, all with physical and medical needs. Nobody there has time to spend all day talking to Alan, one letter at a time.

And that breaks my heart.

My eyes are wet with tears as I scurry through the corridors and outside to the camper-van. I want to drive. I want to get away from here. I don't want anyone here to see me like this. A mile or two down the road, feeling like I might burst, there's a bit of a park. Some greenery. I pull over and run away from the camper-van. I find a tree and slump to the ground beneath its boughs. Alone.

And I cry.

I'm a maelstrom of emotion. I'm sad that Alan really wants to be able to talk like that to someone every day, but can't. I'm angry that he can't. I'm frustrated that I can't do more for him, that I was just here on some poorly conceived attempt to fulfil a task of random acts of kindness, even if it somehow became just that. I made a difference to Alan for a couple of hours. But now I'm gone and don't know who will sit with him every day and pay him the attention he needs.

But above it all, Mike. I am right back there with him, remembering the Apple TV, remembering how it felt to see my sweet brother desperate to talk but unable to. No matter how patient you try to be, and how much time you dedicate to waiting for the words to come, there are always more words. There was always more Mike would have said, if he'd been able. Communication became more about what was essential. It wasn't the banter we had shared since childhood. Mike was a chatty, sociable guy all his life. And it came to a point where he couldn't just blurt out something funny, or rude, or casual. He couldn't tell stories or make flippant remarks. Every letter of every word became an ordeal. So of course there was so much he didn't get to say. Maybe I failed him. Maybe I should have found a way for him to say more. But how do you balance encouraging someone to say more with the knowledge that every word is a gargantuan effort?

I feel like I've been dumped here on the South Island. With no Mike. He was never here. And he never will be here. But he sent me here. I'd do anything to have him alive and well, of course, but spending time with Alan, reliving that way of communicating, has reminded me of Mike in his later months, and I miss that Mike too. I miss the way his big eyes looked at me, how they spoke to me, how they almost rolled in impatience at me being an idiot, how they softened with love, how they shone with humour, how they asked for help, or how they thanked me for giving it.

Kindness is painful. That's why we are sometimes happy to keep other people at arms' length, why we might shun the comfort of strangers, why we don't reach out and try to make a difference to other people often enough.

It's just too painful.

And I'm sure there's a lesson in here. I'm sure I should be resolving to do things differently in my life. I'm sure I should find more Alans, and perform more random acts of kindness. Actual random ones. If they didn't take me right back to Mike. Ill Mike. Dying Mike.

Right now I just feel a gaping hole in my heart. An emptiness I have no clue how to fill.

Hope

Motor neurone disease is a death sentence. The prognosis is beyond bleak. It's a progressive degenerative condition that has no cure. After diagnosis, life expectancy is between one and three years. As cruel as the advice about putting affairs in order is, or seems to be, there is a cold statistical sense to it. And yet there can always be hope. A small number of sufferers have lived with it for many years.

Mike took some inspiration from a book by an American man called Eric Edney. Having enjoyed a life of outdoor pursuits such as dirt biking, water-skiing, dune buggy racing and golf, Eric was diagnosed with motor neurone disease, or ALS as it is known in America. His book promoted positive mental attitude and promised to offer an alternative to the advice presented by the medical profession, that of 'go home and die'. 'Do nothing and die, or TRY' was his mantra.

And we were absolutely prepared to try everything.

◆

The first step we took beyond the doom-mongering of the NHS was Mandy securing Mike a private physiotherapist. I mentioned Claire earlier, but she deserves way more than a passing comment. We knew from the moment we met her that she was the perfect person to help Mike. Mike and I both connected with her, which is to say she's the kind of person that can take a bit of banter. And give it back even harder. She immediately saw the relationship Mike and I had and quickly became a good friend as well as a valued professional. She didn't object to the childish raising of eyebrows that I sometimes gave Mike when she had her hands on him.

We all knew that physiotherapy wasn't going to cure Mike. The other professionals we'd seen had made that quite clear. But Claire was a godsend, and Mike trusted her. He saw her once a week for months. She taught him how to manoeuvre from his wheelchair into his bed, or onto a seat, and to position himself comfortably in his wheelchair, and much more. When it became difficult for him to get to her, she travelled to see him. When Mike's hands started to curl up into claws as his muscles weakened and his tendons tightened and he needed relief, we didn't have the first clue how to safely help him. But Claire did. She came in once a week for a couple of hours and treated him. And she showed us how to massage him as well. I learned to place my hand on Mike's, palm to palm, and ever so slowly spread my fingers so that his spread as well. I'd massage his forearms and his biceps, all under Claire's instruction, all to give him brief respite from the tension that gripped his body.

When Mike's shoulder became excruciatingly painful later on, he couldn't even lift his arm. As his muscles wasted away, his joints, unprotected, became inflamed. At that point he couldn't swallow the usual anti-inflammatory pills like ibuprofen, and the only liquid version of that was for kids which is full of sugar and aggravated his throat. We tried ibuprofen rubs on the skin, but they didn't do anything. Claire gently massaged him and by the end of the session he could lift his arm up above his head without it being too painful.

Claire's expertise went way beyond massage. Her knowledge of anatomy was extensive. As Mike's breathing became weaker and he started having difficulty swallowing or coughing to clear his throat, she showed us how to give him gentle chest compressions to clear his airways. She put one hand on his back and the other on his chest. Mike took a breath in, and she applied a slight pressure to his chest when he went to cough out. It helped expel a bit more air, that's all. Simple enough.

My turn.

I've always fancied that I possess a superlative sense of rhythm and timing. I'd been given a drum set for Christmas when I was a kid, and I really took to it. I mean, I didn't stay at it for long; I didn't play in a band or anything. But I was still pretty sure my timing was metronomic.

I put my hands on his back and chest as instructed, and Mike took a breath in.

'Go on then, cough,' I told him. And he did. And I pushed at his chest.

Mike shook his head.

'You're a bit early,' Claire told me. 'Try again.'

Second attempt. Still wrong. I was sure Mike was doing something to mess me up.

'You're doing it wrong, Royd,' Laura told me. She, of course, had nailed it first time.

'Try again,' Claire encouraged me. I could feel Mike smirking at me. He breathed in and gave a little cough. I pushed into his chest. Too late. My timing was off again. Mike pushed my hands away with a laugh. Maybe I should have stuck with the drums.

Claire had also suggested Mike go to a facility with a warm high-salt pool. With the help of a couple of physios there he could float around weightlessly in the water and take pressure off his limbs. It helped, but we only went a few times. The effort of it, due to his growing lack of mobility, rendered its benefits a little insubstantial. It was undoubtedly pleasant in the water, but I imagine the return to dry land and the discomfort of resurfacing made it feel too difficult.

Claire played such an important role. Her influence went way beyond the physical. Her attitude and positivity, and her friendliness, gave such a tremendous boost to Mike's mental well-being as well.

◆

We all did our own bits of research into what options for treatment were out there. Mike and Laura scoured the internet and found a facility in Poland, run by a Russian guy, that promised it could cure everything. Their blurb mentioned cancer, MS and Parkinson's, but also motor neurone disease.

Mike had a few Skype calls with the guy. He never actually confirmed that anyone had walked into his facility with MND and then walked out free of it, but he did say he could cure it. He tried to explain the various treatments, and suggested Mike go and stay there for three months. At that point we considered anything that had the slightest chance of making even the smallest difference to the official prognosis, so I offered to go over to Poland and see the facility in person before Mike committed himself to spending three valuable months there.

I flew into Warszawa, or Warsaw as we call it, expecting Poland to be grey and miserable. I was pleasantly surprised to find it is the complete opposite. As I journeyed out of the city towards the facility, I passed through rolling green hills and immaculate postcard villages and towns that reminded me of Wales. The facility itself was spotless, a huge five-storey refurbished factory building nestled amongst a small Polish village. The guy who ran it didn't speak much English so had his daughter act as an interpreter, and we got straight into discussing the various treatments.

The first was a form of massage using an avocado-sized smooth flat pebble with horribly jagged edges. He rolled my sleeve up and pushed the stone hard into my flesh before scraping it viciously up my arm muscle. His daughter didn't translate my inevitable expletive reaction, but I doubt the sense was lost on him. Regardless, he did it again, and then applied it to my shin. That was more than enough. I immediately realised there was no way Mike could do this. It was explained to me that the scraping helps draw blood into the muscles, and so preserves them, slowing atrophy. As valid as that might be, Mike was already too weakened to be able to withstand such a rigorous treatment. It was far too aggressive, and his muscles were already too far gone. Maybe if we'd found this place earlier . . .

We moved on to another treatment. A ferociously hot sauna followed by a bitingly cold plunge pool. Horrible. And again, I knew this wasn't something Mike could cope with. The shock to his system would have been too much. Motor neurone disease is greatly exacerbated by extreme temperatures.

I phoned Mike and told him I didn't think this place was right for him. I described the treatments I'd seen. The idea of spending three months here, not speaking Polish or Russian, cloistered away from the world and being subjected to something not dissimilar to medieval torture didn't seem like the best course of action.

'Well you're there overnight. You might as well see what the other treatments are,' he told me. 'I'm sure you'll enjoy it,' he chuckled.

I was taken into another room. Earlier, in the fifth-floor office, I'd looked out of the window and seen what appeared to be a bees' nest under the eaves of the roof. But here, a glass tube appeared through the external wall and into the room.

'This is where we do our bee sting therapy,' the daughter translated for me. With exquisite timing, an elderly patient with Parkinson's was wheeled in by her daughter, just in time for her treatment. The Russian doctor (I assume he was a doctor!) coaxed a bee into the tube and into the airlock at the end of it. He plucked it out carefully and pressed its abdomen against the woman's arm. The bee dutifully sank its stinger into her. He gave it a press and a slap to push as much venom into her as possible, then threw the carcass into a bin that was overflowing with other dead bees. The woman, who clearly didn't speak a word of English, smiled charmingly as about twenty bees were nonchalantly sacrificed, their venom having been pumped into her neck, spine, legs and arms.

The theory behind this genocide was again that blood flow would be heightened, allowing the muscle to survive or heal. I'm not sure why the treatment couldn't be done with needles or some other method, anything that doesn't involve bees dying by the actual bucket load, but I was again certain that it wasn't suitable for Mike.

'Would you like to try?' He held up a seemingly eager bee.

Apart from the fact that I was in no mood for the pain that even one sting would give me, I'd never been stung by a bee before, and for all I knew I could have a massive allergic reaction to it. I doubted, given the naturalness of the remedies on offer, that they had a massive needle full of steroids ready to stab into my heart, *Pulp Fiction*-style, if I went into anaphylactic shock. So I politely declined.

Instead I had a natural wrap applied to my arm. A sticky ointment containing I have no idea what – chillies, honey and all sorts – was applied liberally to my skin and then tied tightly in bandages. Again, this is supposed to encourage blood flow, draw out toxins and keep the muscles working. In actuality it felt like my arm was on fire. I started sweating profusely. I lasted two minutes before I pulled the bandages off, and the burning sensation stayed with me for a good half an hour after that.

As archaic and 'traditional' as all these treatments seemed, they all made sense. There's plenty of discussion of the benefits of bee venom, for example, although I'm sure there's more politically correct ways of administering it. If it weren't for the sad fact that all the treatments I saw in Poland were just too aggressive for Mike to endure, we would have gone. We were still determined to try anything and everything.

Mike tried a kind of electroacupuncture device called a Vega machine. He tried a wet cell battery, an energy device developed by a group in the 1920s and 1930s working with guidance from Edgar Cayce, which is meant to help restore function to the nervous system. Using that became harder when it was less comfortable for him to lie down. He tried something called a Rife machine, which is claimed to use electromagnetic frequencies to kill or disable diseased cells.

Most of these things were dismissed by the medical profession, but that didn't surprise me. From my experience, it is plain that the governing bodies of the medical profession are driven more by money than anything else. The money is in pharmaceuticals. In treatment. Not in cure. The negativity we were met with by health professionals was entirely counter to our philosophy, to Mike's beliefs. He was constantly researching every possible angle, and if he thought something might work there was always the chance that the placebo effect would come into play as well. Staying positive and hopeful was often the best and only thing that Mike could do. I didn't fully buy into some of the contraptions he tried, although I never dismissed them and, if I'd been in his position, I can absolutely guarantee I'd have tried them all too. If I'd read somewhere that there was a health benefit to rubbing feline faeces in my eyes I'd have been down to the cat shelter faster than you could say 'meow'.

◆

A big help to Mike was marijuana. The medicinal benefits of this herb are now widely acknowledged, but were less so when Mike was ill. I'd seen these benefits first-hand when I was with Keith, who died of MS ten years or so before Mike got ill. I watched Keith, white knuckled and on crutches, take several laboured minutes to get up a narrow flight of stairs. He pulled out a joint and sparked it up. A short conversation later Keith jumped up and carried his crutches in one hand and bounded down the stairs with the sure-footed agility of a mountain goat. The transformation was phenomenal.

As much as Keith was an inspiration in terms of understanding how medical marijuana could be of help to Mike, he also ended up being the reason I don't smoke the stuff. Before Story was born, I used to dabble in the odd bit of hash at gigs or festivals and the like, and it was Keith who alerted me to the fact that it was filthy. There was no way of knowing what rubbish was mixed in with resin, and the high was vastly inferior to weed, or so he told me. Then one day he actually sent me, in the post (!), a big fat joint that he had rolled. He told me that it would be far more enjoyable than the dreadful stuff I'd tried. He gave clear instructions that I should take it into the middle of the forest on a nice day, and smoke it really slowly over a period of several hours. Just be at one with nature, he said. The idea sounded amazing.

That weekend, I ended up at Marcus's house. A few beers later and I was predictably squiffy. And that's when I remembered the joint. I promptly forgot all of Keith's instructions, and we lit that bad boy up. More used to the quicker, muddy high of hash, I was surprised at what little effect the marijuana had on me. We chugged it right down to the root and tossed the roach aside, feeling nothing. Just a bit drunk still. Maybe Keith had been winding me up, I thought. Maybe I'd just smoked a load of oregano. We shrugged and carried on watching TV.

Five minutes later I realised I didn't know where I was. I felt amazing, tingly, floaty, embraced by invisible arms and aware of every little noise. It was more than beer. I looked over at Marcus. He appeared perfectly normal. Maybe I was imagining it. A while later, around midnight, my girlfriend at the time came to pick me up. Before I said goodbye to Marcus, I asked him if he felt weird as well. It turned out that he did, and that he'd looked at me and thought I was perfectly normal too. So we giggled. We were both insanely high. And it was hilarious. Until I was just about to leave.

'Does your chest feel a bit tight?' Marcus asked me, probably with genuine concern.

'No,' I answered, still grinning. 'I feel great.'

We had barely pulled away before the doubt crept into my brain. Was my chest tight? Yes, maybe a bit. Definitely, actually. It was suddenly feeling really tight. Painfully tight. My heart was beating like a runaway train. River Phoenix had just collapsed and died outside the Viper Room in LA, so the news had said a day or two earlier. Maybe he'd smoked a joint too quickly as well. I wondered if that was how his chest had felt.

'Pull over,' I begged my girlfriend, who seemed oblivious to what I was going through. I stumbled out of the parked car, clutching my chest, and threw up. I recovered enough to get back into the car. Or so I thought. A few minutes later in full grip of 'the fear', my heart trying to break out of my ribcage, we pulled over to the side of the road again while I prepared to meet my maker. And River Phoenix, hopefully. My girlfriend called an ambulance (I don't suppose I gave her much choice) and I wound up in intensive care.

Kind of.

I imagine I floated into the hospital, jabbering on about how I'd smoked a joint and my heart was about to explode, and got dismissively dumped into a dark side room and told to go to sleep. And that's where I woke up a few hours later, feeling perfectly fine. As far as I actually came from dying, I decided that was the end of my joint smoking days, such as they were.

◆

It wasn't really Keith's fault, I know, but despite my inability to follow the simplest of instructions, I still carried with me the memory of him dancing down those stairs after smoking a little weed. It made perfect sense then, when Mike became ill, that it could have a positive impact on his condition and lifestyle. We sourced some medical grade marijuana from America. In the earlier stages, before his lungs weakened, he would have a little sprinkled in a joint, without tobacco, and sometimes in a pipe. Mike didn't smoke. He never had, but a joint gave him an instant relief, as it had done for Keith years before. He would have a tiny bit before bed. It just calmed everything down and helped relax him, allowing him a decent night's sleep.

As breathing became a little harder for Mike, he moved to vaping it instead of smoking. He used a contraption called a 'volcano' in which you'd sprinkle a little leaf and crank up the heat until it vaporised, then moved on to handheld vaping devices that he used for a while. They gave him the same instant relief as smoking, but without the effect of smoke in the lungs. But eventually even that was too much, so Story helped me make cannabis oil. It's now readily available as CBD oil, but back then we had to refine it ourselves. We had to soak the plant in organic alcohol, which drew out the medicinal properties, then patiently reduce the liquid until it was a sticky brown sludge. I'd mix it with coconut oil and add a tiny amount to his meals every day.

The effect of the oil is far more subtle. The relief is undeniable, without the high. At one point I had a bit of a tension headache. I was knackered and run down, and had a whopping great cold sore making an unwelcome and ugly appearance as well. I dabbed a bit of the oil on my temple and rubbed a little into the sore. In less than ten minutes my headache was history, and the next day so was the unsightly blemish. It's great stuff. I would use it when I needed to, wherever I knew the nerve receptors were, wherever needed quick and quiet relief.

When Mike was ill I spent a lot of time playing Candy Crush. I'd pop out for a cigarette and keep an eye on him through the window while I played. When one hand started aching, I just used the other one. I have a pot of CBD cream in the house that I rub onto my thumbs and wrist, morning and night, and I absolutely swear it helps. Whether it's a placebo or genuine, I don't know. And I don't care. I'd rather use this all-natural product than some chemical-laden ibuprofen gel.

Mike was militant about everything being as natural as possible. He may have been influenced by Eric Edney, who expounded the virtues of eliminating any kind of toxins from the body. Mike was already vegetarian, and quickly embraced going fully vegan and organic, to limit the amount of toxins he might absorb through foods treated with pesticides and so on. Every morning I would make him an organic paleo shake. It would have variations of everything and anything healthy in it: several cloves of raw garlic, a load of stem ginger, kale, wheat-grass, orange juice, turmeric, you name it. Well, Mike named it as I always followed his carefully concocted recipes depending on what part of his system needed a boost. Added to that would be a great long list of vitamin and mineral supplements. And if they didn't come in powder form, I'd have to empty the capsules into the shake before whizzing it all up in a blender.

It was the most disgusting thing I've ever tasted. But Mike swore by it. And if he thought it helped, then it did. When you consider that the only licensed medication for MND available on the NHS at the time was a pill (riluzole) made from who-knew-what chemicals, that vaguely purported (on the back of a fairly small trial) to maybe extend life expectancy by up to three months, with a long list of side effects, it was a no brainer for Mike to look elsewhere. To look to natural remedies and to rely on positivity, hope and mental well-being.

The Pious Bird of Good Omen

Of all the places to come in my current mindset, here probably isn't ideal. Only a few months ago Kaikoura was devastated by an earthquake. It hit at midnight, when most people were at home, and reached 7.8 on the Richter scale. The area suffered a volley of tsunamis after the two-minute long quake. Kaikoura shifted nearly a metre north-east and rose about the same amount. The main road into town, down the eastern coast of the South Island, is closed due to landslides and further risk of rock falls. We had to venture inland to get here, taking to smaller, hillier and much, much slower roads.

I'm still reeling from my brief time with Alan, still missing Mike, and still feeling detached and insular. I feel like Kaikoura. And being here isn't helping. There's an eerie quiet to the small town that stretches mostly along the coastal road. A few bars are open, but the streets are all but empty of tourists, who I guess would normally be here in their throngs. The setting is stunning, the broad bay overlooked by mountains, but I can't help think of that night and the thousands of tourists and residents who were dramatically stranded here, cut off from the rest of the island as roads and railways were ripped apart. It feels like a ghost town now.

This morning I swam with some of the local fur seals, fearing all the time that they might get a bit belligerent and take a chunk out of my leg. And yesterday I swam with a pod of dolphins. You can see them sometimes from the beach here, bounding out of the water in the near distance, feeding close to the shore. There're whales here too. Drew, who went for a six-hour hike around the headland (he too finds the atmosphere here a little oppressive), read that Kaikoura was a major whaling hub back in the day. There're high cliffs and hills with commanding views over the Pacific. Whale spotters would have sat up there, waiting for a spume in the distance before alerting the fleet. The sea bed falls away quickly into a deep undersea canyon not far from the shore and provides a rich feeding ground for whales, dolphins and seabirds. Drew saw an albatross on his walk. That's good luck, right?

I don't think Mike knew this, but my favourite animal when I was a kid was the dolphin. I was enchanted by these beautiful, mysterious and intelligent creatures. So you'd think I would have loved being in the water with them, all up close and personal. You'd have thought that would be serene. Life changing. Well I'm sorry to report it wasn't. Not at all.

I suppose everyone needs to survive, and one of the key elements of the now ailing tourist industry in Kaikoura is its marine life. A short boat ride, still within easy sight of the shore, can yield sightings of sperm whales and several species of dolphins. I was among a small group of tourists. So that made me a tourist: a tourist dressed in a wetsuit, flippers, mask and snorkel. I'd have preferred to watch them quietly from the boat. But instead, once our guides had located a large feeding pod, we were ushered into the water by a hideous klaxon and fervent shouts of encouragement.

And we (they) splashed around like hollering goons. The air was filled with whoops of delight as the multitude of sleek grey beasts slid through the water around us, probably rightfully aggrieved that we'd scared off the fish they were trying to catch. And when the pod moved on a bit we were summoned hastily onto the boat and ferried back amongst them. I felt sickened and appalled. This was clearly disruptive. The poor dolphins. Imagine sitting down to your dinner, drooling with hungry anticipation, only to have some screaming lunatic suddenly knock your plate away and gleefully squawk in your face. I stayed on the boat after that, thinking that if I was one of those lunch-deprived cetaceans I would happily grab a babbling tourist or two by their stupid legs and drag them down to the sea bed. Anyone who tells you that it's a big sea and that dolphins don't need to swim right up to you (ergo it's their choice, not yours!) is an unmitigated muppet.

That wasn't what Mike wanted. It's not his fault. It's not even really production's fault. Kaikoura is on its knees and desperate to generate revenue again after the earthquake. It's still half cut off from the rest of the country and needs everything it can get. I'm sure there's a better way of getting some kind of spiritual boost from being near dolphins, but it's not here. Not now.

It upsets me, but I suppose it is too much to expect that every task on Mike's list can be executed in the way it should be. It was the same up on the island of Waiheke, where we stopped on the way to the Coromandel, and where I went for some 'spiritual healing'. I sat one evening in a quickly darkening cabin in the woods with a sweet woman called Leila, hoping to find some connection with Mike. Rob Hamill was there, and so was Drew. Both, like me, have lost brothers. Even in the face of my habitual scepticism it could have been an inspirational moment. But again, apart from the fear of spiders appearing out of the woodwork in the failing light and attacking me, I wasn't remotely in the right place mentally. I needed a clear and empty mind. Rob and Drew weren't in any way invasive on the situation, but it was still hard to ignore their presence and the fact that there was a camera pointed at me.

But here, now, I feel fragile, barely held together. And guess where we are going next? Queenstown: the epicentre of extreme sports, adventure capital of the world. So I have a pretty good idea of the kind of things I'll be called upon to do there. And I don't feel ready. Not at all. Not long before we left the North Island, I had to go white-water rafting. That was more than physical enough for me. Barely believing that anyone had any control or influence over the inflatable boat as it bounced maniacally, threatening to fold in on itself, on its way down the river and over cascades, I paddled continuously. Just as I'd been told to. At one point, after a sharp and sudden plummet over a waterfall, the raft ended up upside down, an orange lid on what could have been a watery coffin, and I had to swim to the sheer rock sides of the gorge we were trapped in.

And as if that wasn't enough, my next task was to carry on downriver from there holding onto an insubstantial-looking purple sledge, little more than a sporty-looking flotation device, while I kicked my tired legs uselessly through the churning rapids, often perilously close to the dark and very hard-looking rocks that loomed over us on either side. In a slightly quieter interlude, my instructor paused to forewarn me about the next stretch of river.

'Coming up next is our biggest rapid of the day,' he shouted over the noise of the water. 'It's known as the abyss.' Typical Kiwis.

'Okay,' I said breathlessly. 'I'm not feeling super confident about that.'

'Do you want to pause for a minute and relax or do you want to go?'

Relax? Knowing I was about to hurtle headlong into the abyss? What would have been the point in that?

'No,' I sighed inaudibly in the watery din. 'No, I'll go, but just . . . drag me out if . . .' I trailed off, not wanting to put my fears into words.

And off we went.

He wasn't kidding. It was a fearsome stretch of rapids. I almost emerged from it, barely holding on, having been tossed around like I was in a washing machine, and then an underwater current caught me and pulled me under. He'd already warned me that, once under, it can be hard to know which way to swim to get back to the surface again. My lifeline was the sledge. I had to hold on to it. To trust it. To pull myself back up and on to it.

I did. Just. But not before I'd half come to terms with the belief that I might quite easily drown right there and then. I sucked in the clean New Zealand air the moment I could, then let the current pull me on downstream, exhausted and far more scared than exhilarated. In those few seconds, I'd had a terrifying glimpse of my own flimsy mortality.

The adrenaline, the journey, the landscape, the absence of Mike – it's all conspiring against me; I feel emotionally, physically and mentally frail. I'm leaving Kaikoura. But I'm nervy as hell about the challenges that undoubtedly await me in Queenstown.

Take a Seat!

The pay-off of starting a book with a literal cliffhanger is that at some point you get to return to that particular moment. This is that point. Remember that horrific zip wire, The Fox, over that revolting canyon? Remember how I had to run and jump off that platform and drop dramatically from one line to another? Well, that's where we are now.

After the drop, which was every bit as hideous as it sounds, the view from the zip line high above the canyon was glorious. The turquoise river sparkled far beneath me as I hurtled across the ravine to a small hut that was somehow attached to the opposite cliff. There were another couple of mad Kiwis there, waiting to catch me. Drew was there too. Oh yeah – I neglected to mention that he had to zip across before me so he could film me from the other side. Nobody considers the poor camera guy! With the tool of his trade double strapped to him, he had bumbled on gruffly about how there should surely be another, less 'thrilling', way across. But no, for the guys who worked on the other side of the canyon, this was their daily commute. And of course the only way off that other cliff face was a return zip wire. Mercifully it was a straightforward one, with no inhumane drop that threatened to hurl you into the abyss: a piece of cake after the first one. Even Drew enjoyed it.

We're in Shotover Canyon, near Queenstown, a vibrant alpine town built around extreme outdoor activities, a mecca for daring thrill-seekers, a clean and prosperous (and very expensive) hub nestled among usually snow-capped peaks and lapped at by the benign waters of the enormous Lake Wakatipu. We took a scenic route from Kaikoura, crossing the mountains that form a spine down the eastern side of the South Island. Instead of approaching from the larger main road like sensible people, we emerged from the narrow passes and dizzying heights in our cumbersome and somehow unscathed camper-van to look down in wonder on Queenstown. Faced with a dramatic series of hairpin bends, we nervously crawled our way down towards civilisation in first gear, all the time wondering if the next bend would prove too sharp for our huge vehicle.

After the thrills of The Fox, for a reason that will quickly become apparent, we don't walk back down the canyon-side to the small gravelled car park and the minibus that had shuttled us up to this beauty spot. We walk the other way. I'm not done yet.

A little way along, another daunting structure is bolted on to the craggy rocks. We walk through a small wooden shack that houses a tiny café, and down some steps to a metal platform that clings to the cliff. What now? More gravity defying stunts, that's what.

The Shotover Canyon Swing isn't like any swing you'd find in a playground. 'Play' suggests fun, and there's (hopefully) little or (preferably) no ground involved at all. You get attached to the usual array of harnesses and lines and safety lines, all of which arc away towards the middle of a great cable that spans the canyon. I can see immediately what is supposed to happen here. Unlike a bungy, that elastically catches you and hurls you back up into the air, when you reach the end of your free fall, here you are going to swing along the canyon like some mad human trebuchet. More grinning, mad

Kiwis delight in telling me all the different ways that I can launch myself into thin air. Forwards, backwards, or . . .

'What's the worst one?' I ask stupidly. 'What's the scariest?'

'I reckon you should give the chair a go, ay,' one of them pipes up.

I've still got a bit of adrenaline pumping through me from The Fox, so I foolishly agree to the outlandish proposal.

And instantly regret it.

Let's drop some stats here. The cliff I'm on stands well over a hundred metres above the rocky gorge bottom. I'm about to free fall for about sixty metres, and then swing for two hundred. Sitting on a chair.

I'm strapped into the plastic chair, the kind normal people usually relax on in a garden, with an old-fashioned lap seatbelt. My back is to the drop. The rear legs are right on the edge of the platform. Everyone is attached to something, trusty carabiners locked onto metal railings everywhere. Even Drew, sporting a new camouflage multi-pocketed gilet perfect for lens caps and other camera bits, is tethered. As his camera is to him. It's clear that nobody wants anything or anybody falling into this ravine. Except me. I'm going to. Am I? The adrenaline kicks up a notch and I can feel my heart fluttering.

I'm encouraged to lean back on the chair, like you do as a kid in school, daring gravity to do its worst. A strong Kiwi hand grips a safety line, the only thing stopping me from toppling backwards into nothing. Just as I feel like I'm about to go, I am pulled nearly upright again.

'False alarm,' someone says. 'This time . . .'

They're playing with me.

'I've got a weak heart. This isn't good for my health,' I laugh nervously, the words catching in my dry throat. The anticipation is torturing me. I rock back again. Waiting for that horrible tipping point. And I'm pulled forward again.

'That's the worst possible . . .' I exhale noisily, not even knowing what I'm saying, then turn to Drew's camera. 'It's not really,' I lie. 'It's no big deal.' That's part bravado and part not wanting to give these Kiwis the satisfaction of winding me up. They're clearly revelling in my fear. I know what's coming, but these false starts are only going to make my heart beat faster and my language get worse.

I tip back. Here we go again.

And back. He's going to pull me upright again. I know it.

And back.

Wrong.

That strong hand releases me. Gravity wins, and I'm falling. My first instinct is to shout at the top of my panicking lungs, to call those sadistic Kiwis the worst possible name I can think of in the heat of the moment. The hard 'T' at the end of it is almost certainly lost in the fall. Did I mention I was falling? Tumbling. Turning. In the rush of wind I can hear laughter from above, at me, at my feeble expletive. And I see a blurred flurry of landmarks rotating through my field of vision; cliff, sky, distant river, cliff, sky, river, cliff, sky, RIVER! And then, suddenly, I'm not falling. I'm swinging, soaring up and along the canyon in a huge whooshing trajectory. And back again. And I breathe. I laugh. In the privacy of the canyon's embrace, I kiss the tattooed 'X' on my palm and think of Mike as the swing eventually slows and the winch kicks in to bring me back up.

'Is that it?' I ask cockily as my head emerges over the lip of the platform. 'Is that all you've got?' And then I immediately backtrack, well aware that I am still dangling in space, ripe for further abuse. 'You guys are amazing,' I grin facetiously. A hand reaches out and unclips my seatbelt. The chair drops away suddenly, and blind panic surges through me for a split second. But of course, like me, it's tied on somewhere else. I'm pulled to relative safety.

Back on the platform I get away from the edge.

'Anyone else want a go?' someone asks.

Drew hides behind his camera.

'You know what,' I begin, not even sure I'd finished whatever thought process was going through my head, 'I'll go again.'

I imagine Mike being here. I almost feel like he is. He'd definitely have gone again. Even if I haven't worked out the details yet, I feel like I want, for once, to do more than the bare minimum. I want to be more than a puppet at the mercy of the list and Mike and my fear. I want to go a little further. To prove to myself that I can. To do what Mike would have done.

Moments later, harnessed and on the edge of the abyss again, I question that reasoning. If Mike was here, there would be absolutely no point in me putting myself through this hell more than once. He'd outdo me each and every time. What on earth am I doing? I've inexplicably elected to jump backwards this time, with hands clasped behind my head in faux nonchalance. Hanging over the drop, I can barely keep my sweat-slick fingers intertwined.

'Say something for posterity,' Drew mumbles from behind his camera, and my first instinct is to tell him exactly where to go.

'Hello, and welcome . . .' I start instead, then realise I don't have a lot to say, except this: 'Seriously, if you've got a bucket list, rip it up, because it's stuff like this. And this isn't good to do. And so . . .'

I glance down at the river below me. Why am I doing this a second time?

'I'm just rambling now,' I admit. 'I might as well just go.'

And I do.

I jump. And this time I am nauseatingly terrified by how quickly the lovely safe platform shrinks into a barely discernible dot above me. I had thought that not seeing the ground rush up to meet me would be a blessing, but the sense of falling is exaggerated even more by the diminishing launch pad.

That's enough. No more. I'm done for the day. On the drive back down to Queenstown the adrenaline fades and I can readily admit to being utterly exhausted. All I want now is a nice coffee and a pie. New Zealand is surprisingly famous for its scrumptious pies. They are hand-sized, usually minced beef and gravy or steak and cheese (that's a good one!), some with a potato topping but most with pastry, and they make for a perfect snack. They are everywhere and they are delicious.

So that's what I want. And a coffee. And to do absolutely nothing else for the rest of the day.

If Music Be . . .

Fat chance. No pie for me yet. I've been given another task for today. While in no way dangerous, it's no less scary. The task purports to be in the spirit of spreading love and happiness, but was actually more likely designed to make me feel as awkward as possible. I am supposed to set up an amp in the centre of town and, in Mike's words, 'offer to dance with people to make them happy'.

I'm not sure dancing with me is likely to make anyone happy.

There's more. 'You need to get at least ten people to interact and dance with you, no matter how long it takes.'

That pie is looking a long way off.

◆

This isn't my first musical task on this journey. Nearly two months ago, in Auckland, I was handed a ukulele by Rachel, Rob Hamill's partner, and told I had less than a week to learn how to play and sing a song that I would then have to perform to her family. The song in question, chosen for me, was *I'll See You In My Dreams*, a traditional song previously recorded and performed by the likes of Louis Armstrong, Bing Crosby, Doris Day, Ella Fitzgerald, Andy Williams and Pat Boone. No pressure there, then. The version I was given to listen to was by Joe Brown, who happened to perform it on the ukulele as the finale to the George Harrison tribute concert.

I'm not musical. Not in the slightest. You already know how I hugely overestimated my talent on the drums, although I still believe I was pretty good. For a kid. Mum used to have her hippie friends over for CND meetings at our house when I was young, and they'd sit around singing Simon and Garfunkel songs and all the other usual folk tunes. And Mum would strum a guitar. Whilst the style of music didn't itself move me, I started thinking that it might be quite cool to play the guitar. I had a handful of lessons, but my now almost legendary capacity to not stick with something was, despite my tender age at the time, already well developed. So they petered out quickly.

I did, however, write one song. It took me several weeks. It was called *Mandy's Got Chickenpox*, and I can still remember the heartfelt and poetic lyrics all these years later.

'Mandy's got chickenpox, Mandy's got chickenpox, Mandy's got chickenpox, oooh oooh oooh.' That was the first verse. By the time I had half mastered the two or three chords needed for the song, Mandy had nearly recovered. The change in her circumstances did at least inspire the second, and final, verse. 'Mandy's getting better now, Mandy's getting better now, Mandy's getting better now, oooh oooh oooh.' I guess I just thought songs were meant to be written in real time. When I played it to Mandy she just looked at me in slack-jawed incredulity at just how moronic I was.

If it wasn't for the fact that the world was being spared my innate lack of musical flair, I could have probably done with a bit more encouragement. Miraculously, at school, I outguessed the other kids at some rudimentary music assessment (we had to identify which of two notes was higher), and my reward was to be the lucky recipient of one of the princely total of three violins owned by the school. I had some lessons, and was allowed to take my instrument home to practise. One evening, happily engrossed in scratching out some ragged scales with my bow, I happened to look out of my window, only to see Mum and Mandy in fits of giggles at the noise I was producing.

That ended any ambition I had to play the violin (I didn't pick it up again after that), but it wasn't quite the end of my musical career. As an adult, I moved into management instead and looked after a few bands on the local circuit. I left the musicianship to those who knew what they were doing, to those who had managed to stick with the learning process and become accomplished. I love music, as did Mike, but neither of us could play a thing. I've often wished I could play something, at least one song on the guitar or the piano. I can't count the number of times I've wanted to be the guy sitting around a campfire with a load of beautiful girls who, when someone purrs sexily 'does anyone know a song?', quietly picks up the guitar and proceeds to make everyone fall in love with him.

Here's a less fatuous example. When I was lucky enough to be invited to Abbey Road Studios in London to sit in with Peter while the score for *The Return of the King* was being recorded by Howard Shore and the London Philharmonic, we were given a tour of the studios. In one of the rooms was a knackered old upright piano.

'That's the piano the Beatles used for all their classics,' our guide told us. 'Does anyone want to play anything?'

If there was ever a time to bust out a song on the keys, that was surely it. But none of us played. Peter shook his head. Elijah Wood was there. He shook his head. I shook my head. Gutted. Instead we all walked past it and took turns to plonk a single key, our heads hung in a group sense of self-disappointment.

The ukulele task felt destined to be a humiliating disaster. Rachel, who apparently knew a thing or two about playing the funny little four-stringed instrument, tried her best to tutor me in the chords, showing me which fingers to put where and how to read the chord chart she had given me. It looked simple enough.

But it wasn't. While one finger clumsily tried to fret the right note, another finger would get in the way. And it hurt. I wasn't used to pressing down strings on fretboards. I sat in a café, my latte getting cold, trying to master the first few chords. I just about got them, but it took me ages to change between them. Did it matter if I played the song really, really slowly? I stopped for a sip of cold coffee and Drew picked up the ukulele, effortlessly played through the whole song, barely even looking at the sheet music, then handed it back to me.

'I play guitar professionally,' he muttered in explanation. 'Sometimes.' Of course he does. As annoying as that revelation was, he did offer to help me learn the song.

I spent ages cradling that ukulele. I practised in my room, in the park near the Jucy Snooze, anywhere I could. I had the Joe Brown version of the song on my phone and listened to it over and over, trying to learn the lyrics and quietly singing along. It wasn't enough to learn to play the damn thing, I had to sing it as well. I'm not a performer. Notwithstanding my five minutes of comedy, which I was yet to do at this point, the extent of my experience of standing up in front of people is doing Q&As, where I have a captive audience. They want to be there. They want to know what I have to say. It's easy. Nobody wants to hear me butcher a song while my fingers contort around the fretboard of what looks like a small child's toy guitar. Nobody. And I was going to have to stand up in front of Rachel and Rob and their kids and look like a complete amateur. It was going to be awful. And it was going to be on camera.

So I practised. And I practised. And my fingers hurt. I thought I might have time to perfect it, but on this trip my time is rarely my own. There's always another task waiting in the wings, clamouring to be delivered to me.

◆

Another musical task. Pulled away from my ukulele, I found myself clambering out of the Jucy van, again approached by a smirking Rachel. We'd travelled down from Auckland and were staying in Hamilton, where she lives, and where I'd soon be called upon to sing. She read out Mike's next demand. I had to learn a dance sequence, and I'd be doing it as part of Rachel's son's dance group. And we'd be performing it at the end of the day.

'Can I smoke here?' I asked flippantly as we walked towards a red brick building.

'No,' replied Rachel with, I think, the slightest hint of irony. 'It's a school.' I huffed as I pocketed my freshly-rolled cigarette and followed her inside.

I wasn't remotely intimidated. I can dance. I have great rhythm. Mum and Dad used to dance to rock and roll when I was young. I'd watch Dad twirling Mum around like a pro as the music blared out of the stereo. And Mandy and I would copy them. I'd be first on the dance floor at a school disco when Elvis came on. It's all in the hips. I'd be out there, in the middle, the crazy hip-shaking kid strutting my stuff. I was going to nail this task. End of the day? Pfft, let's get it done and go home early, I thought.

I'm used to relying on natural talent. I like to wing it. If I'm dancing, I want to feel the music and let the rhythm take me, let my body go where it wants to go. What I'm not good at, it turns out (to nobody's surprise), is having to learn something. Or more accurately, remember it. These kids had been dancing together every weekend for ages and had frequently competed in dance competitions.

'Five, six, seven, eight,' went the soon-to-be painfully familiar cry of the instructor, and the room was suddenly full of ten-year-olds pulling off a newly learned set of moves in perfect unison. And there I was, standing gawkily in their midst, still trying to remember what the third step was, facing a different way from everyone else, feeling increasingly self-conscious. There was no way I'd learn all this in one day.

Not only that, it was knackering. I was sweating and aching and guzzling water by the gallon. I didn't even stop to eat the sushi that Rachel had kindly made for us. I spotted Drew taking a break from filming to shove some maki roll into his bearded face, but since I'd just suggested he probably had enough footage of me repeatedly messing up, I didn't pass judgement. I didn't even know why it was so tiring. The moves were simple enough, if I could ever remember what order they went in. It wasn't like I was doing back flips or breakdancing. I began to think that I must resemble a real newborn giraffe, all wobbly on its gangly legs, struggling to find its feet in the middle of a perfectly synchronised chorus line from *The Lion King*.

When it finally came to the performance, I wasn't ready for anything except bed. The audience was mostly made up of parents of my co-dancers, who must have wondered who this lanky idiot was, ruining their beloved progenies' routine. It's not like I could hide in the back line. I towered over them all, ridiculously garbed (as per instructions) in a backwards baseball cap and some wannabe hip hop three-quarter length trousers, trying to compensate for my clear inability to remember a damned thing by grinning haplessly and letting out an occasional 'whoop' while I basically free-styled through the second half of the routine. A routine which, it turned out, actually lasted a measly twenty seconds. Twenty! I'd spent an entire day, morning and afternoon, comprehensively failing to get to grips with twenty whole seconds of a dance routine. It felt longer at the time. It felt like at least a few minutes. But no, I watched the footage back with Drew later in some masochistic drive to see just how stupid I had looked, and it was embarrassingly brief.

But it was fun. I enjoyed it. At least that's what I told myself once I'd got my breath back over a cigarette and a hard-earned coffee. It gave me a new appreciation for dancers who learn hours of this stuff for big shows. Although they do likely have more than a day to master it.

◆

A day or so later we went with Rob and Rachel and their family to a country fair on an airfield out in the countryside. I absolutely love a country fair. I love the stalls, the animals, the farming machinery, the pulled pork burgers. Heaven. As well as the usual homespun crafts and delicious foods, this one had a great static display of vintage cars and aeroplanes, and there was a steady stream of microlights and small planes taking to the sky from the grass strip that ran the length of the fair. The sun was beating down from a cloudless sky and there wasn't a single thrill-seeking adrenaline junkie to be seen. Perfect.

'Shouldn't you be practising your ukulele?' asked Drew smugly, like a black cloud wanting to blot out the sun. Tonight was the night. After this Arcadian afternoon, which I had been thus far enjoying, my evening was destined to be ruined by a shoddy plodding rendition of that song I had been trying to learn. I waved Drew and his camera away and wandered off with as much nonchalance as I could muster.

There was a large gazebo set up at one end of the fair, where a decent crowd had gathered. A band was playing. And not just any band; it was Rachel's band. It turned out that she really did know a thing or two about ukuleles, and so did the other nine women who were playing and singing beside her. The Apron Strings, who have since changed their name to Sylvia's Toaster, are a ten-piece ukulele band. And they sounded incredible. All my preconceptions about what I thought was some kind of joke guitar, an instrument I had only really heard in the hands of George Formby while he sang comedy songs about cleaning windows, leaning on lamp-posts and Chinese laundries, were blown out of the water. Rachel and her bandmates were amazing. The ukuleles sounded beautiful. Dressed in long skirts and waistcoats, wearing hats with feathers, and looking like a cool cohort of steampunk land girls, the women took turns taking lead vocals and flawlessly harmonising around each other. I was captivated.

Then Rachel stepped up to the microphone between songs.

'You may have noticed there's a camera filming here today,' she began. I cringed. 'It's for a documentary. Royd Tolkien is here and his brother died from motor neurone disease two years ago.' She welled up, and fanned her misty eyes with her hand. 'Royd is fulfilling his bucket list.'

I had no idea where she was going with this.

'Royd had to learn a song in two days, and what he doesn't know is he's singing the next song.'

I wanted the earth to open up and swallow me. Theoretically, this being New Zealand, such a thing isn't impossible. But it didn't happen. Instead, I made my way, leaden footed, towards the 'stage', and was given a vintage flying helmet to wear so that I at least looked the part, even if I didn't sound it. I walked up to the microphone in the centre, my head whirling and my heart pumping.

'I can't sing. And I've got a bit of a cold,' I muttered my first pre-emptive excuse. 'I'm so sorry that I'm about to spoil your enjoyment of this lovely day.' I didn't know all the chords, much less was I able to string them together in time. I hadn't even managed to learn all the words.

Rachel held up a piece of paper with the words on in front of me. At least she was going to stand next to me while I humiliated myself. It took an age for my shaking hands to find the fingering for the first chord. I wanted to at least get the beginning vaguely right. The sooner I got on with it, the sooner it would all be over. I looked out over the sea of people (at least a hundred) and then ever so cautiously launched into the intro.

A couple of bars in, a wave of music hit me from behind. The rest of the band had joined in. There was a guy on an upright who counted them in, then began slapping away a jaunty rhythmic bass line as the gentle strums of all the other ukuleles folded generously around me. My shredded nerves were replaced with a warm sense of elation. We sounded great. We!

I started singing. I wasn't great, but I wasn't terrible. The band behind shored me up, and I found myself loving the experience.

The tempo was a bit much for my fingers, but it didn't matter to the overall sound if I missed out a chord or ten. I hit the ones I knew, and kept singing. I understood then why Rachel had sneakily planted in my head the need to be confident playing the beginning and end of the song. Turns out the rest was taken care of.

And when we reached the end, when I had to play the little riff that I had practised a hundred times . . . I nailed it. The crowd cheered and applauded and I was exhilarated.

◆

That was then. This is now. I've just zip lined across a canyon. Twice. And done the swing. Twice. I'm on a massive adrenaline come down, mentally and physically drained, in dire need of a pie and a coffee, and I now have to somehow persuade ten people to dance with me right in the middle of Queenstown.

Me despondently lugging a speaker and stand, and Drew carrying his camera, we make our way towards the waterfront.

'What are you guys doing?' A pair of brazenly friendly females accost us. Out of character for me, my instinct is to ignore them as best as possible and keep walking. I don't want to tell anyone what I'm about to do. I'm tired and embarrassed. But Drew decides to let the cat out of the bag.

They are Australian, it turns out, and ridiculously unreserved. 'That sounds amazing. We'll be there. Where are we doing it?' 'The square by the waterfront. We?'

'Yeah, we'll help. It'll be fun!'

Fun? Are they mad? It will be humiliating, awful, awkward. Almost the exact opposite of 'fun'. And it's inconceivable that I'll actually manage to get ten people to dance with me.

'See you soon,' they chime, then walk off in the wrong direction. Drew shrugs, and we carry on towards the lakeside.

I'm rigged up with a radio mic since the camera will be nowhere near me to pick up what I say. It also means I can communicate with Drew, who stops short of the square and waves me on. We're going all covert on this one. I walk down near to the quay and slowly start setting up the speaker. Much as I want this to be over I'm in no hurry for it to begin.

'Drew if you can hear me it's like you're right next to me,' I lie, feeling alone and abandoned. I look for him. There he is, trying to look like he's not filming. He's got his headphones on, and gives me a wave and a grin. He can hear me. 'Do you reckon I should set up right smack in the centre here?'

Thumbs up.

I had hoped there'd be some other street performers peddling their trades here, some jugglers or cartoon artists perhaps, maybe a human statue or two. But no. It's just me. There's an almost tangible feeling radiating from the tourists who meander past me, already giving me a wider berth than necessary, a feeling of dread that I am preparing to be, at best, a noisy annoyance. I slip my sunglasses on, and talk into my lapel, briefly comforting myself with some childish pretence at being a secret agent.

'This is even more terrible and terrifying than I thought it would be,' I tell Drew discreetly. 'I'm getting strange looks, like what's this guy doing?'

The speaker is up on its stand now, and I'm fiddling with my phone, procrastinating while I try to link it up to the speaker.

'You know, Drew, I've got to try and think that this is not unusual, that people do this all the time. Me setting up a speaker is no big deal.'

Who am I trying to convince?

'But talking to myself is a little bit stupid.'

I realise I've no idea how this speaker thing works. 'I should have got a lesson on this. Where's the volume?'

I think I have it. Now all I need to do is press play. I've got a good upbeat song primed to play on loop for as long as it takes me to complete my task. I kneel beside the stand, trying to make myself smaller.

'I'm getting some very suspicious looks,' I tell Drew. I don't know why I'm babbling on to him. All I get is the odd thumbs up or a nod of the head. I suppose it makes me feel a tiny bit less out on a limb. But I'm still trapped. My brain is screaming at me to run. Can I get a pass on this one? There's no point waffling on to Drew. He isn't going to let me off it. Mike, if he was here, wouldn't let me off it. I have to do it. Even the thought of actually pressing play, of putting the music on and shaking my stuff, is making me more than a little nauseous.

'This is so awkward,' I laugh to myself. 'Oh Mike,' I say into the ether, and kiss the tattoo on my palm. I have no choice but to do his bidding.

I press play.

I pretend I'm a brash American, outlandishly forthcoming and exuberant, filled with a primal enjoyment of the music, blissfully unaware of any kind of indignity. I start to dance. In my head, in a cod American accent, I tell myself, 'I love this. Let's rock out. Yeah, man!'

In reality I'm stiffly jerking my arms and legs around like a rusty marionette. I realise I haven't even managed a smile yet, so quickly plaster a goofy grin on my face and start approaching passers-by.

'Would you dance with me?' I ask a relatively sprightly looking elderly woman, hoping I come across as sincere. I take her hand gently and walk along beside her.

She laughs at me.

'Just a little bit?' I beg.

She laughs some more, and walks on.

'Will you dance with me?' I ask a younger woman in sportswear.

'What's it for?' she asks me with smiling suspicion, not even breaking her stride. As if naming her favourite charity is likely to convince her!

'It's for nothing,' I beam, trying to keep my energy up, trying to sound infectiously positive. 'It's for love and happiness.'

She scarpers. I can't say I blame her. This is terrible. The song finishes and immediately restarts. And not one person has even stopped to talk to me, let alone wiggled their hips with me. I look around for Drew, but he must have moved, must have felt the need to change angle. I can't see him. But then I see two other familiar faces. The Australian girls are here. They run up to me, all effervescent and shouting happily in my face, and just start dancing madly around me.

Well that's two people. A start.

But suddenly the atmosphere changes. No longer is there just some nearly fifty-year-old guy awkwardly shaking his hips and trying to manhandle strangers into dancing with him. There's young blood here. There's unadulterated Australian enthusiasm. Contagious fun. People start looking at the three of us, their curiosity piqued. Maybe this is something to be a part of. And my feisty new friends start cajoling people into joining in. Who can refuse them? I just smile and keep dancing.

In moments there's six of us. Then seven. Then eight. I ask a couple more people to dance, and they run for the hills. But I don't need to do anything other than dance. The Antipodeans work their magic, and before long we're easily past the required ten dancers. We cheer ourselves and I sigh heavily with relief. I did it. Well, they did it. Arguably, I cheated. But nobody said how I had to get ten people. Nobody said I couldn't recruit two aggressively happy optimists to do my dirty work for me.

Drew saunters up to me. His camera hangs idle in his hands, a sure sign that we have what we needed. 'Shall we go and get a pie?' he asks.

Yes. Please.

The Great Pretender

Queenstown isn't all adrenaline. Clearly. I'm wearing Lycra leggings and a mercifully long T-shirt, and I've just learned a couple of essential technical terms to help get me through my next task. I now have a rudimentary understanding of the cow, the cat and the downward dog. That's right, I'm about to do some yoga. Well, a bit more than that; I am masquerading as a yoga teacher and I am about to lead the class.

◆

It's not the first time on this trip I've been pushed into impersonating a trusted educator. In Hamilton I was introduced to a class of primary school kids as a famous potter, there to teach them some tricks on the wheel.

Before Story was born I would have been awkward and uncomfortable around kids. I didn't have any idea how to relate to them. But fatherhood is the one thing in my life that I have taken to like a natural. As someone who's prone to getting bored quickly and not sticking to things, any fears I had about my ability to be a father evaporated the moment I first held Story in my arms. Fatherhood was the one thing I gladly had no choice about committing to, and for the first time in my life everything made perfect sense. It seemed obvious. The great gulfs in my knowledge, the lack of experience in looking after another human being: they didn't matter. You just do it. It's instinctual.

It's funny how these key life events change your perspective. Before having Story I'd have been physically unable to witness the inner to outer workings of a baby. Confronted with a soiled nappy I'd have doubtless been horribly contorted in paroxysms while trying to find any way possible to not throw up in my mouth. But my natural squeamishness never got in the way of changing Story's nappy. I didn't even gag. Not once.

Before Mike got sick, I wouldn't have had a clue how to administer the kind of care he needed. I wouldn't have even considered having to look after another adult in that way. Again, you just do it. And doing it changed me.

So pottery was easy. I didn't have to contend with any of that. And because I don't feel the discomfort of a non-parent around kids, I positively revelled in messing about with the clay on that potter's wheel. It was a sweet, lovely task, ending in me being covered in wet grey clay and surrounded by laughing, happy children. I didn't have the first clue how to even operate the pedal-driven wheel, much less construct a pot. Instead I made it an hour of messy play that I probably enjoyed as much as my unsuspecting pupils.

◆

But the crowd of people here for their weekly yoga session are adults. The children neither cared about nor questioned my clay credentials, but how am I supposed to convince a roomful of regular yoga practitioners that I have the faintest idea what I'm talking about?

'This is Royd. Royd has a yoga retreat back home in Wales.' I am introduced by Sandi, the regular yoga instructor here. She is lithe and undoubtedly limber and, unlike me, wears her Lycra well. And that's the back story I fed her to build the conceit here. I'm some kind of yoga Jedi master, travelling around New Zealand to see how they do it here. This room full of thirty or more people, seasoned practitioners, who I've fooled into thinking they are honoured to have me here. They are privileged to have me lead the warm-up session. Gulp.

I slip into character. This is all performance. I've done yoga before, maybe twice. That's what I told Drew as we walked over here, as I lit a cigarette, as I utterly failed to epitomise healthy living. I'm not limber. My knees are shot and I sweat. But I don't have to do yoga here (not yet, anyway). I just have to supervise.

'Hi.' I make sure my voice is quiet, and its tone a little lower, a little treacly. The class is nearly all female. They're all looking at me in earnest expectation and admiration. 'So I have a retreat centre in North Wales. I don't know if any of you have ever been there?'

Thankfully nobody has. It's a placid sea of attentive devotion in front of me. The women beam peacefully and watch with bright, wide eyes. They are hungry to learn from this guru from Wales. This is like taking candy from a baby.

'It's kind of based on nature, and being at one with the ground and everything around you.'

In unison they nod and smile back at me. So I start by getting them into a resting pose. Like a troop of synchronised swimmers they slide forwards and down from all fours until they are sitting on their ankles and stretching forward, their heads resting lightly on their mats and their arms reaching in almost worshipful unison towards me.

'We're going to centre on our breathing for a moment. Breathe in, and nice and slowly out.' I walk, almost prowl, amongst them, feeling my voice wash over their upturned backs. I gently instruct them to let all their worries flow out of their bodies, down their arms and through their fingertips, to let them drift all the way out of the window and away. Drew is filming from a corner of the room, carefully motionless. I catch his eye accidentally and suddenly feel that awful bubbling of a naughty giggle trying to escape from my chest. I look away quickly and somehow suppress the instinct to just burst into laughter at the ridiculousness of my situation.

I take a cue from the main instructor, the legitimate one, who pads gracefully between the participants and rests her hands on the smalls of their backs as I talk. I do the same. There's a scene in the film *Couples Retreat*, where every time the toned budgie-smuggler-wearing yoga instructor places his hands (vaguely inappropriately) on someone in his class he quietly utters the word 'boom'. I can't get the scene out of my head, which may be why I'm barely stifling my amusement. Somehow I resist the overwhelming temptation to say 'boom'. I must not look at Drew. I must not laugh.

Instead I focus. I copy the instructor and calmly rest the palms of my hands on a few backs. I lead them through the cow and the cat and a few other poses that I feel like I'm making up, before ending the warm-up session and finding a space and a mat at the back of the room. Sandi takes over the class and I am now among her students. Within minutes I am sweating like a pig and barely able to maintain my balance. Thankfully, being at the back, no one can see me for the charlatan I am.

When the class ends I walk to the front again, humbled, and begin my apology.

'I can't teach yoga. I've only done it twice. Three times now. I'm so sorry.' I am sincerely repentant.

I'm met with cries of disbelief. 'But you were amazing,' someone calls out. They genuinely believed me. Some even came up to me and told me they had wanted to ask where my retreat was so they could visit if they were ever in Wales. Nobody expressed any offence at my deceit. They were all warm and lovely, forgiving and generous.

So there's something to be said for yoga.

I don't remember Mike ever doing yoga. This task wasn't intended to provide me with enlightenment or spiritual growth. Mike just wanted to stitch me up. But I smashed it out of the park. I may even open a yoga retreat in Wales!

Psycho Pimp

As kids, Mike and I used to play in the forest near Halkyn whenever we could. And it was there that we later tried out paintball for the first time at a site that opened there. The aim of the game was to work your way through the woods without getting shot, then grab the other team's flag and get it safely back to your home base. Mike and I ended up on opposing teams, feeding the competitiveness that raged between us. I was convinced I was naturally brilliant at playing army so I decided I'd treat the game like a serious exercise. I'd imagine that the guns were loaded with real bullets, not silly globs of brightly-coloured paint. And I'd be a total badass commando ninja and wouldn't even get shot once.

When the game started, everyone began creeping tentatively through the trees in different directions. With the imaginary threat of real bullets, I was overly cautious. There was no way of telling where the enemy might appear, and I didn't really know where I was going. I don't remember there being much of a team plan, so I resolved to be the sole hero. I'd win the game single-handed if need be.

I found a dried-up stream bed that ran up the hill towards where the enemy flag had to be. It had steep banks, ten-feet high or so, topped with trees. It offered perfect cover. Nobody would even see me coming. I got down on my belly and started wriggling my way up the hill. There was no rush. Stealth was the key. Nobody could see me, so I had to make sure that nobody would hear me either. Inch by inch I crawled my way, like action man, towards a victory that would be talked about on the recreational paintball circuit for days, if not weeks, to come.

PHUT.

What was that? I saw a puff of dirt next to me, and wondered what could have caused it. Had I sprung some kind of booby trap? If I had, then it didn't achieve a lot. The forest was quiet. I was safe. I just needed to press on.

The next 'PHUT' hit me right on the back of my skull. And it hurt. It really hurt. Suddenly there was paint everywhere and I was shot. Out of the game. How was it even possible?

While I experienced a humiliating defeat, Mike had enjoyed a wholly different experience of the game. He began by heading out from his base and scouring through the trees near the perimeter of the playing area. He found himself at the top of a steep bank. Looking down, he happened to see some muppet obliviously crawling up a dried-up stream bed. In plain sight. Acting like nobody could see him. He deserved what was coming.

Mike raised his gun and casually pointed it down the slope towards the sitting duck. He held it gangster style, one handed, befitting a nonchalant execution. His first shot missed. Just. It spat into the dirt next to the wannabe commando who, for some bizarre and ill-considered reason, took no evasive action, just stared, confused, at the spot of disturbed dirt next to him and continued to lie nice and still. So Mike fired again, and the paintball slammed into the poor sod's head and exploded its colourful innards all around him. It looked like his brains had been sprayed all over the forest floor.

'That was me,' I told Mike bitterly when he had finished relating his heroics. He of course roared with laughter that continued for years. And that was that. From then on I had a healthy respect for the surprisingly painful balls. The few more times I played I wore so many layers of clothing, regardless of the weather, that I resembled the Michelin Man. Sweating like a cow in a slaughterhouse, I'd wear a hat with a protective flap at the back. None of that stopped me getting shot, but it helped lessen the impact. All in all, after my chastening baptism of paint, I decided it wasn't really for me.

Mike, on the other hand, was hooked.

Paintball became one of Mike's most enduring passions. He turned semi-professional with his team, Psycho Pimps, which also included Ali and Slick, who I've mentioned before. It's a whole different ball game, so to speak. It's savage. They wear flimsy vests; there's no protective clothing, no padding, no sign of the Michelin Man anywhere, so the paintballs don't bounce off, which would be considered cheating. And the guns are in a different league from the recreational weapons. They shoot harder and faster. The triggers are so light that you can shoot constant streams of paintballs, each one with enough force to really hurt. They can raise a welt, sometimes even break the skin. But competitive paintballers don't care. They're hardened to it.

In these games, two teams face off on a rectangular field of play, dotted with inflatable obstacles that provide much-needed cover. A fairly standard tactic at the beginning of a game is to have a team member in each home corner fire a volley of balls diagonally across each other. They are effectively laying down covering fire, and anyone running into that paint stream is likely to be hit twenty times over. Mike's usual role was to charge the opposition, to safely advance under that covering fire and take up an aggressive position nearer the enemy. Mike and his team used to train in Wrexham, and ended up being victorious at a number of tournaments.

I was persuaded to join a night game in which Mike and his team would go up against maybe thirty of us civilians. The rules were simple. If one of us got shot, we were out. But we could shoot the handful of semi-pros as many times as we wanted. No matter how hardened they were to being hit, surely thirty of us could raise a welt or two. We found ourselves near a graveyard, a perfect place to ambush Mike and his cohorts. Some of us crouched down behind gravestones or cars. We were going to drench them in so much paint that they'd have no choice but to retreat. Victory would be ours.

Obviously that didn't happen. Mike's little posse sauntered out of the darkness, casually waving around torches while they chatted and laughed. They didn't have a care in the world. And they walked right into our trap. As we all unloaded our weapons with an unreasonable degree of inaccuracy, Mike and his mates just stood there and ruthlessly picked us off one at a time. In the space of about two minutes we were all shot.

Another time, Story, filled with the confidence of youth, decided that all his expertise gained from playing *Call of Duty* would give him a head start in competitive paintball. He wanted to go up against Mike. He was convinced it was going to be a chastening experience for Mike. I stood on the sidelines and watched, not wanting to get peppered by a laughing Mike. As soon as the game started Story had to take cover. Endless streams of paintballs were zipping through the air. Almost immediately pinned down behind a barricade, he could do nothing except listen to the fearsome barrage. Any time he even thought about moving, a volley of paintballs would thunder into the air-filled wall that was providing him with cover. He raised the barrel of his gun above the parapet for an instant, and it was instantly showered with about ten paintballs. And then Mike appeared, his gun levelled at Story at point-blank range. He spared him the pain of being shot, but proved his supremacy in no uncertain terms.

Watching him compete officially was a tense experience. It was like standing on the sideline of a war zone: noisy, aggressive, and fast. Psycho Pimps were good at it. Mike was good at it. If he was still here now, I'm sure he would have made good on his ambition to turn fully professional. I had no idea you could actually make money from paintball, and back then it wasn't a huge thing in this country. It's bigger in America, with the usual television rights, endorsements and sponsorships and what have you, but it's starting to catch on here now as well. And Mike would have been right at the forefront of it.

◆

I still have Mike's mountain bike in my garage. Gathering dust. My knees are rubbish, so I don't use it. It's a serious bike too, with full-on rear and front suspension and all manner of customised gizmos. Biking was another huge passion for Mike. He loved the extreme nature of dangerous downhill runs, on ridges flanked by precipitous slopes, where he'd throw himself into all the jumps and drops he could muster. At insane speed. He tried several times to get me to go with him, but it's just way too scary for me.

He loved snowboarding. And when he wasn't near a snowy slope, he loved wakeboarding. He bought a kayak too. He just wanted to be out in nature, doing adrenaline-fuelled activities. When he moved into his house in the middle of nowhere he also bought a stupidly powerful dirt bike. I remember Ali telling me about Mike's first go on it. He watched him struggling to control it as he bounced across the field in some kind of snarling high octane rodeo.

That was the main difference between us. I am passionate about remaining in control. I like things the way they should be. I want to stay safe. I don't enjoy being scared. I'm not drawn to all these insane activities. But Mike . . . Mike's fear response, if he had one, was different to mine. Mine is a constantly dripping tap that gushes forth at the vaguest suggestion of danger. Whether he even had a tap or not, I don't really know. I don't think he was opposite to me; I don't think he luxuriated in losing control. I think he revelled in being right on the very edge of control, just taming the beast, applying some level of control to the uncontrollable. That was his art.

Thick and Squat

It wouldn't be a bucket list, or a trip to New Zealand, without a bungy jump. What could be more natural than diving head first from a great height with nothing but a big rubber band attached to your feet? I'm waiting near the Kawarau Gorge Suspension Bridge, site of the first ever commercial bungy, opened in the late eighties by the thrill-seeking entrepreneur AJ Hackett. It's him I have to thank for today's nightmare. He made all this possible.

Hackett made bungy jumping a booming commercial enterprise, but he wasn't the first to do it. In 1979 a couple of mad students, members of the Oxford University Dangerous Sports Club, hurled themselves from the Clifton Suspension Bridge in Bristol. Here it was called a 'bungee' rather than a 'bungy' but the process was the same. 'Bungee' derives from West Country dialect for anything 'thick and squat', which sounds about right. This intrepid pair of pioneers, who survived but were immediately arrested after their jumps, took inspiration for their insanity from a tradition observed on Pentecost Island in the South Pacific nation of Vanuatu.

The legend on Pentecost is that a woman, trying to escape her husband, threw herself from a banyan tree after tying vines to her ankles. When he followed her, not realising how helpful the organic safety line might be, he plummeted to his death. What became known as 'land diving' emerged from the myth, and involves the painstaking construction of wooden towers from which men, tethered to vines, hurl themselves into oblivion so as not to be tricked by their own wives. The practice grew into a ritual believed to improve the impending yam harvest, and is said to enhance the health and strength of the divers. Most obviously it seems like unrelenting machismo. Boys undertake it as a rite of passage after circumcision. A successful young diver removes a cloth protecting his modesty and reveals to the elders, in no uncertain terms, that he has become a man.

The most striking difference between land diving and bungy jumping is that land divers actually intend to hit the ground. They tuck their heads in before impact and allow their shoulders to touch the earth, relying solely on the stopping power of a carefully selected length of vine to not break their necks. At least nobody is asking me to do that! With no immediate threat to my man parts, and the promise of a rope designed carefully not to let me hit the ground, I clamber aboard a minibus. Because, no, I'm not doing this one. I'm not here for a history lesson. It might be the first, but it's not the biggest. We leave Kawarau Gorge and its historic bungy behind and head up into the mountains.

To the Nevis Bungy (dramatic music goes here).

◆

Mike never did a bungy jump, but had he ever managed to complete his own bucket list, he wouldn't have left New Zealand until he'd leapt from every bridge, platform and cliff on offer. I've already done one here. In the middle of a pleasant, safe-feeling walk up and over the huge Auckland Bridge, I stopped for a surprise jump from its belly. Back then I was oddly less afraid. I was nervous, a little dry in the mouth, but also stupidly cocky.

'Can I just run off and jump?' I asked.

'Sure, mate. You can do what you want.'

So accommodating, these Kiwis.

Reassuringly surrounded by massive steel girders, I was standing on a robust metal platform that hung beneath the heart of the bridge. I couldn't really see what was directly beneath me, though I knew it was water. I could see the bay stretching out in front of me. Somewhere down there, on Rob Hamill's catamaran, Drew was pointing a camera up at me. When it was time to go, I ran as many steps as I could then threw myself backwards into the air.

I had misjudged just how scary that jump was. I had no perception of how high we were. As I plunged in free fall towards the wet blue of the bay I caught a glimpse of Rob's boat. I'd been up to the top of his mast on the return journey from the Coromandel, so I knew how horribly vertiginous that was. The boat looked like a toy beneath me. I screamed. My heart leapt in my chest, and very nearly out of my open, ululating mouth. I'd made a mistake. It was terrifying.

◆

I survived. I'm here, in the Southern Alps near Queenstown, on a dirt track ascending towards the highest jump in New Zealand, the third highest in the world, three and a half times higher than Auckland Bridge. And I'm not feeling remotely cocky. They always tell you nobody's ever died doing a bungy. That's not true for a start. And sure, nobody has died on this one, or it would probably be closed, but someone has to be first. Let's unload a little scary research here . . .

Assuming the rope and safety line don't fail, in which case you're basically dead, there's all kinds of possible injuries you can sustain. The abrupt rise in upper body intravascular pressure experienced during the elastic recoil, or whiplash for short, can cause retinal haemorrhages and potential long-term vision impairment. One person remained quadriplegic after their neck broke from the whiplash. If you get somehow entangled in the cord, as one unfortunate person discovered, you can damage the carotid artery and end up having a stroke. And, get this – these injuries have occurred in fit and healthy people in their twenties and thirties. I'm nearly fifty. It's a good job I didn't google all this before the jump. Bungy jumping has also been shown to increase stress and decrease immune function. So why am I doing this? Why would anyone do this?

It doesn't hurt that the marketing representative from AJ Hackett, currently driving our minibus, is drop dead gorgeous. But I'm still trembling with fear. We spit dust up behind us as we climb the single track dirt road that clings precariously and unguarded by any safety rail to the side of one of the Remarkables. That's what this mountain range is called, and it's easy to see why. The jagged alpine peaks rear up hungrily all around us, conjuring up images of, well . . . *The Lord of the Rings* films, if I'm honest. And, just to be clear as to why I'm here, if I somehow survive this perilous minibus journey at the hands of this beautiful but mad Kiwi woman, I am to be rewarded with the chance to hurl myself face first into one of these dreadful abysses. Thanks, AJ Hackett. And thanks, Mike.

The track curls up and round and arrives at a plateau among the peaks. There's a large building here, and an actual tarmac car park. It's significantly less rustic than the approach might have suggested. Inside is positively civilised. There's a shop and a café and a wide desk where I am weighed and checked in. Outside again, I get kitted out in the usual extreme activity paraphernalia. Mike has also stipulated that I wear a pink tutu and carry a sparkly wand. Whatever; that's the least of my worries. I haven't seen the jump yet, but I know the stats and I'm showing them the requisite level of respect (fear). A coach load of people arrive behind me (I wouldn't want to do that track in a coach!) and make predictable macho noises at the pink tutu I am stepping into. I don't have any capacity left for embarrassment; every cell in my brain is screaming in terrified anticipation.

I'm taken out of the other side of the building and get my first glimpse of the jump. There's a convenient viewing platform jutting out from the top of this plateau. Off in the distance, midway between this mountain and another, the two peaks separated by a steep-sided valley, a small enclosed platform is suspended from cables that appear (thankfully) as thick as my arm.

'How do we get there?' I ask, not even wanting to know the answer. I'm led towards a wire-frame bucket, for want of a better word. It must be the world's smallest cable car, a coffin-sized sieve that is slung from a cable that runs out to the jump platform. I am clipped on with a trusty carabiner and we lurch and sway our way out into nothingness. Looking down, the cliff recedes and I am treated to a bird's-eye view of the valley below. Nothing looks real. My mind is whirring with all the possible ways of dying. There are so many factors in play here. The platform could fall, this wire basket could fall, any of these cables could decide to snap. And then where would we be? How often do they actually check all these wires for wear and tear? I haven't even started panicking about the actual bungy yet. I cling onto the side of the sieve just to stop my hands from shaking.

When we get to the jump platform I clamber through the small door as if somehow this next structure is safer than the last. I get more safety equipment attached to me.

'Have you done a bungy before, mate?' I am asked.

'Yeah.' I can barely talk; my mouth is so dry. 'I did the Auckland Bridge one.'

'Tiny,' comes the reply. 'The secondary drop here is bigger than that.'

'Right.'

I'm moved to a chair perilously close to the edge of the platform and strapped in. The chair reclines with a jolt, filling my head with visions of being tipped into the abyss before I'm properly attached. The platform creaks in the breeze, a grinding metallic noise that reminds me of prison cell doors clanging closed, or some ominous sound design in a disaster movie that heralds the shearing of metal girders and cables, a horrible metaphoric ticking clock, a countdown to calamity. I don't even try to hide my fear. How can I? I don't think I could even if Mike was here. I imagine him watching me in fits of giggles.

I'm given the thumbs up after my leg straps and bungy cord is attached, and I try to stand. My legs feel like jelly. They are shaking. Grabbing on to anything I can, I shuffle towards the edge. Strong fingers grip my harness behind me, and I see the pink sparkly fairy wand in my hand. I'd completely forgotten I was even holding it. I know that the bungy cord is attached to my feet somehow, but I can't feel it. I have no sense whatsoever of being strapped in to anything. As far as I'm concerned I'm about to hurl myself to my death.

'Okay, mate, I'll give you a countdown. Go on three, okay?'

I shake my head, trying not to look down as I twist my neck to look back. 'No, no, I don't want a countdown please,' I stutter. 'I'll just go.'

'Sure. Go when you're ready.'

There are other people waiting to go, I assume. I don't imagine 'when you're ready' means I can milk it for half an hour. They want me to get on with it. Time is money. Besides, I don't think I'll ever be ready. I just have to do it. Because Mike has told me to.

I look down.

Why?

What I imagine, up close, is a great wide river carving through the bottom of the valley is a twitching hair to me, a glittering gossamer strand of a spider's web, a pale blue vein threading its rocky wet way between these mountains. I jerk forwards, then stop myself. I can't do it. I wobble for a second. My heart screams at me like a whistling train about to career off its tracks. I twist my neck again and hysterically address anyone that might be listening.

'Don't do that,' I issue a surprisingly altruistic warning. 'Don't start to go and then bail. It makes it so much worse. Just go.'

A leap of faith.

For Mike.

I jump.

The Nevis Bungy gives you a generous eight and half seconds of free fall before the elastic kicks in. For the first couple of seconds I am screaming an obscenity. Then I am deafened by the wind rushing past my ears. In free fall, at a significant enough height, you don't get a sense of your velocity. The ground only rushes up to meet you in the last terrifying second. And just as I feel like I'm about to plunge straight into that huge foaming river I feel the resistance in the cord attached to my feet and then I am arcing back up into the ether.

And then I'm falling again, for several seconds. Then up. Down. Up. Down. Some part of my brain remembers being told to pull a release cord so that I don't end up dangling by my feet. I do it instinctively and, after an unnerving moment as my feet are freed, I find myself sitting upright, clinging for dear life to the rope.

I kiss the tattoo on my palm, laughing and smiling. I did it. I'm still alive.

And no, I don't ever want to do this again.

Immortal Bird

Mike was getting weaker. He needed a wheelchair, and he needed help transferring in and out of it. He needed help getting in and out of bed. He still had enough strength to not be a dead weight when we lifted him, and he could still grip a cup and lift it to his mouth to drink. He was still eating solids, though he ate slower and in smaller mouthfuls, chewing each one with added care so as to avoid the risk of choking.

He was living at Laura's house, 'Number 34'. They had a special bed put in. It had separate controls for each side, controls that could lift or lower the top or bottom. It had a massage function that he would use in the morning to stimulate the blood flow around his body. But he still had trouble sleeping. He was in pain. Unlike me, Mike wasn't prone to reaching for painkillers. If I get the slightest headache, just a tiny throb behind the eyes, I slam a couple of paracetamol.

'What are you doing?' Mike would ask me. 'Just drink water.' But for me it was all about the quick fix. Pop a couple of pills and there you go, sorted.

Mike was clearly becoming anxious about his worsening condition, so we needed to see a doctor. Getting Mike anywhere was a protracted business. We'd been using something called a kidney board, a thin but sturdy piece of wood shaped like the eponymous internal organ that we could wedge underneath him. Using a sleeve of material on the board, we could then safely transfer him, slowly and carefully, from one surface to another. Even that was becoming demanding.

His GP came out to see him and immediately prescribed him with some anti-anxiety pills; something to take the edge off, he said. Mike, as you'd expect, was reluctant to rely on medication, so didn't take it immediately. But after a couple of days, with no respite in his anxiety, he acquiesced.

Almost immediately, the pills seemed to have the exact opposite of the desired effect. Mike's anxiety became heightened. His heart raced. It was almost as if he'd been pumped full of adrenaline. I wondered if his body's unfamiliarity with any kind of unnatural or chemical interference meant that he was more susceptible to undesirable side effects. It got to the point where he almost forgot how to breathe. He would lie in his bed and be acutely aware of his breathing difficulties, such that he had to really concentrate on what should be a natural behaviour. Lying down became too traumatic. Any kind of cover on his chest, even the lightest sheet, just added to the feeling of compression. He would wake up in a panic, barely able to catch his breath. He took to sleeping in his reclining chair instead.

The doctor was called out again. His answer to Mike's adverse reaction to the medication he had been prescribed was to up the dosage. He gave Mike some stronger pills and advised him to continue with the existing ones. Mike, who hadn't had a decent night's sleep in some time by then, did as the doctor told him with the hope that he could get some rest. But he got even worse.

Mike's sleep patterns became chaotic. He would drift in and out of fitful sleep, plagued by vivid nightmares. He stopped eating regular meals and was clearly uncomfortable. As much as he needed a good eight hours of sleep, he would doze for maybe an hour then spend the next five in a state of semi-consciousness.

One evening when I was doing a quiz at a bar in Mold, Laura phoned me. She was scared. Mike wasn't doing well. I left immediately and hurried to Number 34. Mike was sitting in his chair, and seemed neither awake nor asleep. He appeared to be hallucinating and was talking without really saying anything, muttering and moaning. He would fall asleep for a moment then start awake, struggling to catch his breath. I sat with him all night, afraid for him, not knowing what to do.

When morning came around we phoned the hospice in Wrexham. We'd been talking to them for a few days already. Mike had suggested that there might come a point when Laura would need a break from caring for him, and the hospice had all the necessary facilities. There was also a doctor there who was better informed about motor neurone disease than Mike's GP or the hospital. I had told him about the medication Mike had been prescribed. He was horrified and said Mike should stop taking the pills immediately. But the damage was done. That morning when I phoned, I described Mike's symptoms. The doctor told me Mike was experiencing respiratory failure. He wasn't getting enough oxygen into his system and wasn't expelling the toxins. The medication had made him worse. He needed to go to hospital. Immediately.

We got Mike dressed in his jogging bottoms and a jumper while we waited for an ambulance, which got there within half an hour. Mike was barely conscious by the time they loaded him into the back. When he was awake, his mouth gaped open as he tried desperately to draw in air. And he was afraid. We all were. The paramedics put him on oxygen straight away and put the blues on as we all raced to Wrexham Hospital. The doctor who worked at the hospice also ran a surgery at the hospital, and he met us at the ambulance bay. Mike urgently needed a breathing assist machine.

It took a few agonising hours. Laura and I sat by Mike's bedside on the ward, helplessly watching Mike struggle. He lay in the bed with his head lolling to one side. He blinked his heavy-lidded, half-closed eyes slowly at us, as if he had been sedated. The machine, when it came, was a mask that covered Mike's nose and gave him a boost of extra air when he breathed in, and then assisted his exhalation to start to remove the toxins. Within ten minutes Mike became almost normal again. The transformation was dramatic and incredible. He was still exhausted, but he could breathe again.

This all took the best part of the day, so Mike needed to stay overnight. I sat in the chair next to his bed and hoped in vain that he might get some sleep. The ward was anything but conducive to rest. The horrible white lights were blazing until 3 a.m. and there was barely a moment that someone didn't cough or moan or call for a nurse. At one point it seemed like everyone had quietened down, but then the nurses appeared with a great trolley full of medications and shattered the short-lived peace. Mike needed sleep. He needed rest. And he couldn't get it there. He was already getting lethargic again, his breath catching. He was relapsing.

I managed to get hold of the doctor at the hospice and explained how Mike was struggling to recuperate on the busy hospital ward. He offered us a bed there and, within the hour, Mike was back in an ambulance being transferred to the hospice. But he was getting worse. Again. There was another doctor there who knew a lot about breathing assist machines. She came to see Mike and quickly informed us that the mask he was using wasn't enough. Mike's nasal cavities were collapsing. The cartilage had weakened to the extent that it wasn't strong enough to keep the passageways open. It's a common symptom of motor neurone disease. Because of the restriction to his nasal passageways, the mask wasn't able to do its job properly. He needed a full face mask that covered his mouth as well. But they didn't have any on site that would fit.

Faced yet again with a potentially fatal wait for a piece of medical equipment, I felt the panic rising in me. I was watching Mike slowly suffocating to death and couldn't do a thing about it. He was getting worse by the minute. I started googling and searching for a way to get hold of the kind of full face mask that he needed. I managed to locate one a couple of hours' drive away. I was just about to race out of the hospice, get in the car and tear off like a lunatic when the doctor turned up with the kit Mike needed. She had been doing the same as me, frantically calling around to find a mask.

She replaced it with the one that wasn't adequate, and almost instantly Mike started to regain consciousness. He began to slowly improve. His breathing levelled out. The recovery wasn't as quick as before. It took a few hours before he was alert again, but he was still very weak. The whole experience had physically and mentally knocked him for six. It was several days before he was back to being himself again, but the weakness didn't leave him.

Every part of him had taken a hit. His arm strength was depleted. Swallowing was harder. Eating was difficult in several ways. Mike began to rely on the mask to assist his breathing, and was glad of the quick relief it provided after having to remove it to eat. Solids were soon a scary prospect, filled with the threat of choking. He just didn't have the strength to cough properly. He couldn't clear his throat. He would try, and a thin rattling sound would come out of him, a sound that haunts me to this day.

We were introduced to a cough assist machine. It was separate to the breathing assist, and far more aggressive. Once attached, the wearer would take in as much air as they could, and you would press a button as they exhaled and it would suck air violently out of the lungs, ideally clearing any blockages to the airways. There were a couple of issues with this machine. Firstly, it needed to be used sparingly. Every time it's used, it weakens the lungs. It was counter

253

to our philosophy of trying to prolong what strength Mike had left. Secondly, I was worried that if it was used to help with choking (as was suggested) it could potentially suck what little air Mike had left in his lungs out without clearing the blockage. Feeding Mike became terrifying for me. I would watch him out the corner of my eye, petrified that any of the mouthfuls I gave him could be potentially fatal. I hated that machine and what it put Mike through. I tried it on myself, as did Laura, to gain an understanding of what it did. It was horrific. The way it completely empties your lungs is far from a pleasant feeling, even for someone with normal functions.

For a while he could eat softer foods like poached eggs or pasta or bread dipped in a sauce of some kind. As fabulous as the staff at the hospice were, the food left a lot to be desired. Especially given the healthy regime Mike had become accustomed to. He couldn't cope with salt or sugar and was used to everything being organic. Even a slightly salty sauce with his pasta would aggravate his throat. This was the start of me continually making soups for him that I would take in and warm up in the kitchen there.

We were all working on the assumption that Mike was only at the hospice until he was strong enough to come home. We took turns being with him. We all got trained in the breathing machine, and learned how to use a hoist. Claire showed us massage therapy that could help him. We never doubted for a minute that he was going to regain enough strength to be able to leave the hospice. About six weeks in, I was in Cardiff doing an appearance at a convention; the chance to earn a little doing a quick Q&A and signing a few photos wasn't something I could pass up. While I was there, Laura phoned me up. Distraught.

She had been called into an office at the hospice and casually told by someone who wasn't even a doctor, just an administrator, that Mike was dying. He was at the end of his life, and they were providing palliative care, making his last days as comfortable as they could. Not for a minute did they consider that Mike was ever going to leave the hospice. Laura couldn't believe that she was being told this, especially in the absence of me, or Dad or Mandy. I told her to set up a meeting for me, and raced back from Cardiff.

When I got there, intent on ripping someone a new one, I pointed out firmly that not only was their reading of Mike's situation completely wrong, but the way they had delivered their opinion to Laura had been absolutely unacceptable. The doctor, who was always so helpful and wonderful, apologised for the manner in which the information had been disclosed, then went on to add his professional opinion. He had seen several people come through the hospice with motor neurone disease and was familiar with the progression of the disease and its symptoms. In his opinion, Mike was experiencing acute respiratory failure and had maybe a month left to live.

I couldn't believe what I was hearing.

'Fuck you. We're going to prove you wrong.'

I don't remember if I actually swore at him, but whether or not I actually said that at the time, that was wholeheartedly how I felt.

One month!

Skyward (Again)

I'm asked my name.

'Royd,' I answer. 'Like Roy, but with a d.'

I'm being weighed again. This seems to be a regular occurrence. Any time I have to do something remotely dangerous and leave terra firma, I get weighed to make sure that whatever is keeping me from plummeting to my death is fit for purpose.

'You going as well?' Drew is asked. He has finally manned up and is joining me for this task. 'What's your name?'

'Drew,' he smirks. 'Like Rew, but with a d.'

Drew's next to be weighed, and he's certainly heavier than me, so at least I can take comfort that if it's safe enough for him, I should be absolutely fine. We're going up into the mountains again. And this time we are going to paraglide off them. From the highest commercial launch site in New Zealand. It's not my first time taking to the air on this journey. On the way down to Queenstown I got to fly a vintage Tiger Moth over Lake Wanaka, and I've been up in three helicopters on the South Island.

◆

After we crossed the mountains from Kaikoura we headed down to Franz Josef, a quaint town on the western side of the South Island.

With a population of only a few hundred, there's little more to Franz Josef than a couple of cafés, a few shops and a particularly busy heliport. The main attraction there is the glacier.

Unlike many glaciers, the Franz Josef is remarkably accessible. It descends from the mountains to less than a thousand feet above sea level. Māori legend has it the ice was formed from the frozen tears of Hine Hukatere after her lover was swept to his death by an avalanche. Notwithstanding the risk of further rock fall or the perils of walking on ice, we piled into a helicopter and flew up the valley to a flattish spot on the ice flow. It was a breathtaking flight, but the panorama from the ice was equally rewarding. The ridges and crevasses of the vast dirty whiteness concealed the other groups of hikers that had been visible on the flight in, and our guide was careful to maintain the illusion that we were all alone out there. Not that we were ever likely to bump into another party. The glacier is about seven miles long and several wide.

With massive crampons fitted to our boots, we set off carefully across the ice, getting used to walking on the huge spikes. The landscape there is constantly changing, so we were cautioned to follow closely in the footsteps of our guide. The weather was clear and bright and surprisingly warm. After a foray into an ice tunnel I was asked if I wanted to try a spot of ice climbing. I leapt (figuratively) at the opportunity. After being harnessed up and tied on, I rappelled down into the kind of crevasse you really wouldn't want to stumble into accidentally, then climbed back up using a couple of vicious looking axes. It was a new kind of climbing for me, and I loved it.

Drew asked the helicopter pilot to make our return flight down the valley a bit more 'emotional'. Kiwis don't need a lot of encouragement in that regard, so we soon found ourselves hugging the craggy rock face that reared up from one side of the ice, banking sharply and dropping like a stone back towards the verdant flatland. It was exhilarating.

In Queenstown, it got even more exciting. I got to see the Remarkables up close and personal, in a doors-off helicopter flight. Strapped in and holding on tight, we swooped and banked and hovered all around the peaks that crowned the Queenstown area. You could almost imagine a column of hobbits, dwarves, elves and men trudging perilously amongst them on a journey of immense importance. As we neared the airport and the end of our flight, we had to hover for several minutes over a mountain while we waited for a plane to land. That was weird. I had felt no fear buzzing around, banking close to jagged cliffs and soaring over rocky ridges, but just hovering brought home how unnatural and precarious being up in a helicopter can feel. It's not like a plane. If something happens to one of those rotor blades you're not going to glide gracefully to safety. You're going to drop. Hard and fast. Like a sack of spuds.

We didn't. Obvs. We waited a bit longer, then beetled our way back to the heliport area of the airport. And I was back there a day or two later for my third helicopter ride, this time with mountain bikes strapped to the side of the bird. We flew up to a grassy plateau among the peaks and unloaded the bikes. Kitted out with GoPros, I watched the chopper abandon me (with a guide) and saw Drew grinning at his chance to get some aerial shots.

The last time I had enjoyed being on a bike was with Mike.

Before Mike's downward turn, before he needed oxygen, Mandy booked us all a week at Center Parcs. Mike was in an electric wheelchair by then, struggling with that particular newfound blow to his independence, and was less than thrilled at the prospect. While Mandy wanted to do something as a family, to rally around Mike and really enjoy each other's company, Mike was apprehensive of being treated as disabled. I wasn't convinced either, but appreciated the spirit of the venture. It might be alright, I tried to tell myself. Mandy and Chris had Megan and Jacob with them, and Edan was going as well as Laura.

When we arrived, as if to cement Mike's fears, the accommodation was overbearingly disabled friendly. There was a big ramp up to the entrance of Mike's room, and his bed, one of two singles in the room, was coated in plastic sheeting and surrounded by grab bars. It felt a bit clinical, like a hospital. Mike's face was a picture.

We all hired bikes for the weekend, and rode around alongside Mike in his wheelchair, suddenly equal to him in our mode of transport. His chair was sleek and fast, and we all zipped around with big smiles on our faces, while Mike tried to knock us off our bikes. It didn't matter where we were. We were all together, and we were having fun. Edan got to hang out with his cousins, and race quad bikes. We played board-games and hung out. It was a wonderful break, one that we ended up wanting to repeat. But Mike started deteriorating soon after that, and we never did.

Cycling down the mountain was something Mike would have loved. Thankfully, it was a fairly benign descent, more about appreciating the landscape than thrill-seeking, and I didn't have to pedal too much. Which was a huge relief. Have I mentioned my bad knees? I did another cycle ride back on the North Island, around the rotten egg stench of Taupo's bubbling hot sulphur springs, and it was more than my knees or my nostrils could cope with. The only bits of that I really enjoyed involved either freewheeling or stopping altogether. At one point our guide pointed out a silver fern, the plant that symbolises the New Zealand national identity. I had learned a little about this plant on my overnight foraging adventure, and happily explained how Māori hunters and warriors had used the pale silver underside of the fern to find their way home. The fronds would catch the moonlight and illuminate a path through the forest.

We came down the mountain into Arrowtown, a charming one-street mountain community that is relatively unspoiled by the commercialisation that Queenstown has unavoidably succumbed to. Drew was waiting there, the camera on his shoulder. He'd been in the village for a while and had splashed out on a greenstone pendant for girlfriend (now wife) back home. This whole trip had forced a postponement of their plans to bring a little life into the world, after the pain of a miscarriage, and the hei-tiki necklace he had found promised its bearer improved fertility. Spoiler: it worked.

◆

Drew's next to me now. We're standing on a grassy slope high above fields and forests, harnessed and helmeted and somehow each tethered to someone that has at least a little experience in leaping from mountainsides. As has become usual for this kind of thing, I'm kitted out with GoPros, but Drew reckons he can operate the smaller, but decent, 'B' camera while he tandem paraglides next to me. Neither of us has ever done this before, so I'm not sure how he's decided that. I think he just wants to share this experience.

I did an interview this morning on the banks of Lake Wakatipu with *Seven Sharp*, a New Zealand news programme, and they've sent a couple of camera operators up here to get additional footage for their report on my ongoing journey. So it's a mini media circus up here on the hillside. I'd better not mess up and die.

I have no real idea how this is supposed to work. Apparently all I have to do is run as fast as I can down this slope until I can't run anymore. Until the massive parachute I'm dragging behind me lifts me, legs still pumping, up and into the relative safety of a nice thermal. But what if I don't get enough speed up? What if I come to the end of this fairly gentle slope before I take off? It's not exactly a cliff edge we are hurling ourselves from, but the land does drop away pretty sharpish. What if there isn't enough wind?

And then I'm running. I'm doing it. And all those questions are zipping around my brain as my legs churn beneath me. I feel like I'm running through treacle, like something is holding me back. I'm running and running and getting nowhere. Except nearer and nearer to tumbling down the side of this mountain. I suppose my tandem partner is running behind me too. How are we attached again? Why do I keep doing these stupid things? One day something is going to go horribly wrong. Maybe that day is today. Surely we're not going fast enough to get airborne? And if we don't go up, then we can only go down. About five thousand feet down a rocky steep slope. Is there a way to abort? I have a sudden palpable fear that this escapade is going to be on *Seven Sharp* for all the wrong reasons.

And in a heartbeat I realise that I'm running on air. Then we're floating upwards. The mountains drop away into a receding model landscape and we're up in the big blue sky with nothing but the gentle sound of the wind ruffling that wonderful parachute above us. I probably should have mentioned that Drew took off first so he could film my launch from the air. But just because he didn't die, it didn't mean I wasn't going to.

This is possibly one of the most serene and beautiful things I have ever done. I'm a condor soaring over mountain tops. I'm being softly cradled by the canvas above me, lovingly carried on a warm breeze, perfectly safe. It's impossible not to smile. I even have a little canvas seat to support my weight so I'm not just hanging here. There was a slight moment of panic when I settled into that; my partner pulled a cord, dropping me a few inches into a comfortable position. The jolt was enough to make my heart skip a beat, but since then I've been in heaven.

Drew glides along to the side of me, casually pointing his camera at me. I can't imagine that, behind the lens, his beardy face isn't all smiles too. I wave at him joyously and he waves back. This is amazing.

After a while I see Drew and his partner turn into a tight spiralling descent. I know enough to not be alarmed by what looks pretty catastrophic. Corkscrewing is just a faster means of descent. He needs to get down before me so he can film my landing. Saying that, it also looks hideously unpleasant. I wonder how many Gs he's pulling!

'Do you want to do that?' my partner asks me. Aside from the fact that it would make Drew's sacrifice pointless if he isn't ready to film my arrival, I have no desire at all to make my descent anything other than graceful, smooth and slow. I politely decline. Instead we descend in huge wide circles, gradually getting closer to the ground, until eventually we drift down the last few feet and, just like that, I am standing in a field with the parachute folding silently to the ground behind me.

I feel liberated. I still can't help smiling. Drew, who clearly survived his corkscrew, lowers his camera and grins back at me. A slight nod of the head is enough to know that he loved it as much as I did. I've found an activity on this adventure that, given the chance, I would happily do again and again.

Number 1

If there was ever any doubt that Mike was going to leave the hospice, which there wasn't, the grim one-month sentence passed by the doctor there served only to galvanise our collective determination. Mike was absolutely going to get out. He was going to go home. We never regarded his stay in the hospice as anything other than a road to recovery. The only question was how long that would take. Mike needed to be comfortable with being moved. He felt secure in that environment, safe in the knowledge that medical professionals were at hand. We all needed to be intimately familiar with the workings of all the specialist equipment we would need to care for him at home.

I had nothing against the hospice. On the contrary, I thought it was an amazing place. And the alternative to Mike being there would have been an extended stay in hospital, something that would no doubt have seen his condition decline far more rapidly. Yes, the hospice was intended as a place of palliative care, but we didn't see it that way. While Mike recovered slowly and we strove to understand the level of care he needed, the staff were always delightful. Whether during the day or in the middle of the night, they would greet us with cheery smiles and offer us cups of tea and sandwiches. They could see we were hands-on with Mike, and were completely supportive. Mike's time there wasn't as grim as you might expect. His room had patio doors that opened out onto a well-kept garden (though I always worried about wasps getting in and stinging him). It was clean and comfortable and he had a constant stream of people coming to see him. Dad and Mandy were there a lot of the time. Story would visit. So would Ali and other mates of Mike.

But Mike's condition was changing. He was weakening. He was wearing the breathing assist more and more. The aim had been to use it only when he needed a boost, not to rely on it. Eating was the most noticeable change. To begin with he would eat comfortably, and not need the mask, but after a short period of time it was hard to get through a meal without replacing it, not least because having food in his mouth made breathing all the more difficult. And attaching the mask, previously a light-hearted affair with Mike joking about not being able to breathe, became a more critical and scary endeavour.

The mask needed cleaning every few hours and it got to the point, when Mike was more reliant on the breathing assist, that we had to be incredibly clinical about removing, cleaning and replacing it in a timely fashion. It took co-ordination. There were two straps that went over the top of Mike's head and the back of his neck to pull it airtight to his face. It required a confident but gentle approach, a swift movement that had to be executed in such a way as to not pull at Mike's head, since his neck was becoming weaker. And the machine needed to be switched off at the same time. All these steps had to be on point and I made sure I became an instant expert.

While I cleaned the mask, wiping away the unavoidable build-up of spittle and whatnot that would accumulate in it, I would watch Mike out of the corner of my eye and wait for the understated urgency of his nodding to indicate that he wanted it back on as soon as possible. Replacing it was equally fiddly. After carefully attaching the straps around Mike's head, it had to be pulled down over his face, ensuring it was airtight, and the button on the machine pressed at the same time. If the button wasn't pressed, activating the assist, putting the mask over his face would have been much the same as covering his mouth and nose with a hand. Horrifying. Sometimes, the mask still didn't sit right, and there would be a hissing leak of air coming out the side, and of course this meant it wasn't giving the optimum amount of breath for Mike. So I'd have to perform the sequence of moves to take it off and put it straight back on under the added pressure of Mike not having a full breath because of the leaking. I absolutely hated myself if I didn't get it a hundred per cent right first time. Despite the stress and fear that my inability to get it perfectly right would cause him, he would still manage to helpfully make light of my ineptitude with a roll of his eyes. Often, he'd beckon me to come close to his mouth and breathe out, 'dickhead!'

Hoist training was another sharp learning curve. Mike had become too weak to use any of the methods we had previously employed so the nurses at the hospice used a hoist to move him. We immediately went on a course to learn how to gently manoeuvre the sling under him, attach the hoist, then lift him to transfer him from the chair to the bed or vice versa. Sometimes we used it just to lift him up from the chair to adjust his position and make him more comfortable. The hardest thing about moving Mike was being able to do it without hurting him. His whole body was becoming weaker and he found it harder and harder to get comfortable. We also tried every kind of mattress on offer at the hospice – hard, soft, undulating, ribbed, you name it – but sleeping in the bed there was proving difficult for Mike, even with it raised up. Mike took to sleeping in a big armchair next to the bed with a wall of pillows around his head, which he was struggling to hold upright. His arm

265

would rest on a pillow and he'd have an extra blanket over his feet to keep them warm.

There wasn't a daily routine as such. Mike's stay in the hospice was all about convalescence, so we'd quietly celebrate every bit of sleep he could snatch, every moment of comfort that would aid his improvement. If he slept during the day, we would sit there in silence beside him, glad that he was able to get some much-needed rest. Everything we did was with the view to him getting out of the hospice and returning home.

◆

Before Mike went into the hospice he lived at Laura's house, 'Number 34' as we called it. Dad had installed a special toilet there, one that washed and dried you after use, a help in preserving Mike's dignity when nature called. Even before the hospice, going to the toilet wasn't an easy procedure. Mike needed to be manoeuvred into his wheelchair, then via the kidney board onto the toilet. If I was helping him, I'd give him a big towel to hold in his teeth that hung over his chest to his knees. I'd have him lean on my shoulders as I lifted him up to remove his joggers before lowering him onto the toilet again. All behind the cover of the towel.

'You alright?' I'd ask him.

He'd nod.

'You sure?'

He'd nod again and wave me away. I would wait outside, too worried about him to venture much further, and let him do his business.

'You might want to give it five minutes,' he'd joke. As emasculating and difficult as the whole process was for Mike, there was never a sense of doom and gloom to the complicating of such an essential routine. There was always banter.

As time progressed in the hospice, it became increasingly clear that Number 34 just wasn't suitable for his growing needs. Aside from the special toilet, its carpeted floors and layout meant it wasn't kitted out for wheelchairs and hoists. Mike, before the hospice, had sat in the garden there and looked at a bungalow being renovated next door. He had jokingly suggested that he should rent it. We began to realise that perhaps that flippant suggestion was more viable than we'd thought.

I approached the man who was busy refurbishing the house. It had belonged to his parents, and he was preparing to put it on the market. I explained Mike's situation and he agreed to rent it to Mike.

'Number 1' needed additional work done to it before Mike could move in and the man had agreed we could do what was needed. But that was fine, as we were still honing our hoist skills and acquainting ourselves with the breathing and cough assist machines. Mike wasn't quite ready either, although he'd already proved the doctors wrong and lived longer than the month they had given him. Knowing that when he got out he would either be in his wheelchair or the hoist, with its small wheels, a lot of work needed to be done to make sure there were no bumps between rooms. All the carpets were removed. The floors all needed to be hard and smooth, and it needed a wet room.

I got in touch with a builder friend of mine, Dylan, who had done my roof and some work on Mike's previous house years before. Built like a rugby player, and a black belt in some kind of martial art, Dylan is as tough as they come, but he has the heart of an angel. He immediately offered to do anything and everything he could to help, and we set about working on the new house. Dylan did the bits I didn't have the time for, like widening the driveway so there was room for Mike to be able to transfer from car to wheelchair, and building a ramp to the front door.

I spent hours making the threshold level, laying tiles in the little porch so that Mike's wheelchair could all but glide into his new house. I did the same between every room, using tiny wedges and making infinitesimal changes to tiling and flooring so that every transition between rooms was seamless and smooth. If Mike was in the hoist, we needed to be able to move completely unhindered between rooms. Dylan helped me build a wet room, and I painstakingly tiled and grouted it. We fitted the toilet and the shower and I made sure the threshold between the wood floor of the bedroom and the tiles of the wet room was perfectly level.

Once the building work was done we prepared the rest of the house for Mike. We put his television in, his bed, his chair, his pictures on the walls, unpacked his clothes and made everything perfect, ready for him to move in. We also made sure Edan's bedroom was set up and ready for when he came to stay. We made it feel like a home. We were determined he'd be there before Christmas so we could all spend it there with him. And when we were confident that we could provide the care he needed, that we knew how to operate the machines and the hoist, that we could take care of Mike and make him comfortable, when Mike was ready for his own space, we booked an ambulance and Mike left the hospice. He'd spent three months there, and having been told in the first couple of weeks that Mike would likely only live for a month, that his care there was palliative, here he was moving into a new house. It was just September, well ahead of Christmas.

I'd given Mike updates about the house and showed him pictures of the work in progress while he was in the hospice, but it was still a magnificently special moment wheeling him up the drive and up the ramp to his new front door. Saying that, it was also a somewhat tricky operation. We had to move his breathing assist machine in first, and get Mike, who was basically holding his breath, inside nice and sharpish so he could be hooked up again in the living room. But once he was comfortable and had his breath back we gave him a piecemeal tour, showing him the bedroom and the wet room. I carefully pointed out all the delicate and loving work I had done to make his life easier.

'So what?' he grinned at me.

Mike was back.

Heart of Darkness?

If you look at a map of the south-western tip of New Zealand's South Island, you could be forgiven for thinking you're looking at the coast of Norway. It's not called Fiordland for nothing. Despite the name given to the area, clearly derived from the Scandinavian 'fiord', the Kiwis don't call the deep glacially formed channels 'fiords'. The wide, steep-sided waterways that conjure up images of Viking longboats rowing out to sea, oars sliding into glassy water to the slow rhythm of a hide drum, or (for me) memories of Mike fishing from a rock, are here known as 'sounds'. Fiordland is by far the largest national park in New Zealand, and is remote, almost impenetrable and sparsely populated. Historically even the Māori only travelled here seasonally, to hunt, fish and collect the greenstone from the clear waters of the many rivers that feed into the sounds.

That's where I'm heading. And, happily, my task is to do a spot of fishing. From the wording of the task, this is intended to be purely recreational. It does, however, present me with possibly my last chance on this journey to complete another task give to me weeks ago, back on Waiheke Island: to catch and cook a fish.

Mike and I loved fishing. Much of our time in Norway was spent in that pursuit. Before we went, we would always go to a local tackle shop and marvel at the variety of spinners and lures on display. I didn't know what I was doing, but it was fun to stock up on all the gear. I didn't know what lure or bait I needed for a particular fish or circumstance. I barely even knew what fish was what. Beyond the more obvious ones, like salmon, mackerel, trout, carp and bass, I couldn't even name another kind of fish. My fishing technique was random, utterly devoid of skill or learning. And, unsurprisingly, I rarely caught anything. Mike, more patient and dedicated than me, was deservedly more successful.

On a previous trip to New Zealand, while overseeing post-production on a film I was producing, I took every chance I could, almost every weekend, to go fishing. I sent Mike photo updates of my cumulative failure to get so much as a nibble over eight or ten trips. I knew he'd be sitting there and rolling his eyes at my typical inability to catch a thing. On my last long weekend I made it to the top of the South Island, determined to catch a salmon and cook and eat it on the banks of the river.

Using my random, unskilled technique I cast into the river, confident only in my assumption that there weren't even any fish there. As I reeled my line back in, I got a bite. Victorious, I pulled up a small fish, just big enough to not throw back, that had taken my bait. I managed to light a fire and fashion a basic spit for the fish. Of course it then fell off and ended up gritty and covered in sand and ash and was utterly inedible. It was horrible: a disaster, a complete failure. Mike tasking me with catching and cooking a fish is absolutely him having a laugh at my almost legendary capacity for fishing failure, but also a way of willing me to succeed. So succeed I must.

Thus far, I have let him down. I've had a few opportunities already, and come up empty-handed every time. There was a glorious spot on the way to Raglan, where Story is now, where the road crosses a beautiful stream. He, Andy and I stopped there and stood on the bridge looking down into the crystal-clear water. We could see the fish. Easy pickings, we thought. Surely. For a good hour, Andy and I dipped our spinners and flies and bait into the water, and got increasingly bemused by the lack of interest from the fish. Story, who had been quietly observing us and the fish, asked me if he could have a go.

'Sure, whatever,' I said as I handed him my rod. With all my experience of fishing (albeit mostly without success) in various countries, I was pretty sure that if I couldn't get a bite then Story, who had little to no experience, surely wasn't going to catch anything. I watched as he lowered the line to the water. Then, instead of plopping it in like Andy and I had been doing, he started dancing it over the surface, mimicking the movement and behaviour of a fly. Within a minute, he'd hooked a big trout. Absolute beginner's luck!

'I don't see what the big deal is,' he said with a smile as he reeled it in. 'That was way too easy.'

Oh, the arrogance of youth. Paternal instinct prompted me to chasten him just a little by insisting on a ritual that Mike and I had always followed in Norway. The first fish you catch, no matter how big or small, you have to kiss and throw back.

'Give me the rod,' I asked Story after he had casually kissed the trout and released it to its watery home. 'I want another go.' If he could do it, then so could I. Not that I'm a competitive dad. I copied his technique, which had seemed brilliant, so obvious and simple.

Nothing. We spent another hour on that bridge, me jerking my wrists and doing everything I could to convince the fish that my lure was a distressed fly that desperately needed to be eaten. But no, they weren't falling for that trick a second time.

I had another couple of attempts up near Nelson on the North Island. Mike had sent me on a bushcraft course to learn some more survival skills. The prevalence of spiders during my earlier foraging adventure meant that I was wary of the task at the time, but it turned out to be mercifully free of arachnids and an enjoyable day learning from an expert called Ian. The key tool in bush survival is a good knife. Ian showed me how to sharpen even a cheap blade until it is razor sharp, able to drop easily through a piece of paper. Ian showed just how important and versatile a keen edge was. It can be used to prepare kindling, to start a fire, to strip flax leaves into strands that can be woven into cordage to make snares, fishing lines, netting and more. With Ian's guidance, I made a pair of tongs from a couple of twigs we found, using my knife in various ways to fashion the pieces, then cord to lash the closed end together. I learned how to build static or sprung snares for rabbits or possums, and we ate apples and nuts from trees on his land. I spent an hour or two sitting in a field, cathartically weaving strands of flax into a bracelet that I am wearing now. And in the evening, as dusk fell all orangey over the New Zealand bush, I stood on the smooth rocks in the middle of a bubbling stream that ran by Ian's house and completely failed to catch a fish. I woke up early the next morning, as we stayed the night in his annexe, and tried again in the dawn light.

Not even a nibble.

◆

The light is already fading fast when we arrive at our accommodation in Fiordland, a big bed and breakfast up on a hill right on the edge of Fiordland, overlooking Lake Manapouri and the mountains beyond. After settling into the comfortable room, I venture out onto the back lawn to enjoy a cigarette and watch the end of the sunset over the lake while I try to contain my excitement about the day's fishing I have ahead of me in a landscape that would have had Mike salivating.

I can barely stand to smoke half of it; the place is swarming with a cloud of sandflies. I hurriedly retreat inside, beating at the air and scruffing the little monsters from my hair and face.

I'd been warned about these little critters. Although still tiny, they get bigger and bolder the further south you go on the South Island. Fiordland, it turns out, is a notorious hot spot. Second only to penguins, sadly in short supply in my immediate vicinity, their favourite sustenance is the blood of humans. And their bite hurts. They're not like mosquitos. They don't just suck blood through a nice neat proboscis. Without the precision and cleanliness of nature's equivalent of a hypodermic needle, sandflies actually slash painfully at your skin with tiny blade-like mandibles and then lap at the pool of blood that bubbles up there. In a country that prides itself on having nothing nasty in nature (aside from the odd immigrant spider from Australia, as Andy discovered), these miniature vampires are New Zealand's worst resident and best-kept secret. They've been annoying settlers, residents and tourists since 1773, when Captain James Cook described the feverishly scratched bites on his crew as resembling ulcers from smallpox, and presumably the Māori for long before that. So that's why the Māori only travelled here seasonally. They even have a legend that tells how the goddess of the underworld, deeming the fiords too beautiful to be sullied by humanity, released a swarm of sandflies to act as a powerful deterrent.

And it works. I hide inside, behind netting and doors, and rinse the broadband watching YouTube videos.

Tomorrow is going to be hideous.

The next morning is bright and clear. I tentatively venture outside and am relieved to find that sandflies seem to prefer the evenings. The air is free from them. I'm not sure whether they will be more of an issue at water level, but for now I can enjoy my morning coffee and cigarette without the incessant whine of hungry insects in my ears and the fear of being eaten alive.

And I can finally enjoy the view. It is spectacular. The lawn slopes gently down towards a steeper, wooded slope that descends rapidly into the still, mist-covered waters of the lake. It reminds me of a place Mike and I once stayed, on one of our trips to Norway. The autumn sun, still low in the sky behind me, is warming up and I can see the mist gradually beginning to recede and reveal the landscape in front of me. I'm back to hoping this is going to be an amazing day. This is absolutely somewhere Mike wanted to come. We talked about it several times and, just looking out across this untamed wilderness, I can imagine that, of all the places I've been in New Zealand, this is where Mike would feel most at home. This is somewhere, irrespective of sandflies, that Mike might well have settled. A surge of happiness washes over me, picturing Mike here in this place, in his element, a place of splendid isolation that would have suited his soul. It feels like home. And then, behind that wave, comes a pang of sadness. I wish he was here now. I feel his absence and his presence in the same moment.

I've brought Mike here with me in a sense. I have his hooded top that he took to Norway. And I have his green Tilley hat. I painfully went through his Norway kit a while ago, knowing that some task on the list involved the hat, and when I pulled it out of his pack I held it to my crying face. It still smelled of him. It was his favourite hat, the one he wore all the time in the fiords, fishing and camping. He looked way cooler in it than I ever could, and I've never even dared put it on. But now, that's what he wants me to do.

'You could wear my Tilley hat,' the task states. 'See if it brings you luck to catch a fish for once.'

Cheeky sod.

But he's right. I need all the luck I can get. And yet I have a feeling that if there's any place in the world right now that I might actually be able to catch something, this is it.

◆

We find our guide down on the banks of the Waiau River, close to the small town of Te Anau, a little north from our accommodation. We load fishing gear and camera kit onto the small metal hulled boat that will be our home for the best part of the day and push out onto the still water.

The mist is still clinging to the river as we motor around the first bend and open up the throttle a bit. Trees lurch out of the gloom as we pick up pace and I sit at the front of the boat gazing into the swirling white and the wilderness, feeling like Martin Sheen in *Apocalypse Now*. The boat glides effortlessly through the shallow water, the roar of its engine dulled by the fog around us. In moments we are isolated and wonderfully alone. It's just us and the river and the trees and the sun slowly burning holes in the mist. It's perfect.

Mark, our guide, shuts off the outboard and we drift. I look over the edge of the boat into water that is so clear it is difficult to tell how deep it is. I can see the bottom and the rounded edges of all the well-worn pebbles that cover the bed. And I can see fish.

I cast my line, repeatedly, sending it out to a little area under the overhanging tree branches where I feel certain there are fish.

I let the current carry my spinner before reeling it in and casting again. Mark comments on my cast, saying it's the best he's seen among people he has taken out fishing. I don't reveal that, despite my deft wrist action and unerring accuracy (I have got pretty good at being able to land my spinner on a fairly precise bit of water), I can barely catch a cold. He tells me the river is teaming with trout and salmon. Big fish. The bigger fish come out towards the end of the day, often to feed on mice that drink at the water's edge.

'Mice?' I ask, incredulously. I had seen some weird mice-shaped lures in a tackle shop in Queenstown but thought they were a joke. It turns out that mice are prolific in Fiordland, so the trout have taken to catching any they can.

'I caught a massive trout a few evenings ago,' Mark tells me. 'When I cut it open I found twelve mice in there. Twelve!'

Surely I can catch something here.

I pull out Mike's Tilley hat, not just because it might bring me luck but mainly because I really don't want to catch a fish and not be wearing it. I can smell Mike as I pull it onto my head. In my mind's eye I can see him, sitting on a rock away from the shore in Norway. He's at peace, content, in his element, confident and cool. If I look half as good as he did in it, I'm doing well. I'm wearing his grey hooded top under my waterproof too. In an odd way, I feel like Mike is almost here, as close as I've ever felt him.

I cast once.

Twice.

A third time. And I get a bite.

I've got one. I can barely believe it. I reel it in carefully, pulling out a net to lift a decent-sized trout from the cold water. It worked. The hat worked. I grin, entirely to myself, lost in the moment, imagining Mike proudly beaming down at me.

I did it, bruv.

I give the trout a big kiss and let it slip back into the river.

Wanting a moment to myself, I ask to be let ashore on a small rocky island in the middle of the river. I take my rod, Mike's hat and my tobacco with me. Drew, respectful of my needs, asks Mark to take him upriver for a bit so he can go ashore and get some nice establishing pan shots of the boat careening around a bend. Or something. I don't care. I just want to be by myself.

And I am left alone with just the gentle chiming of the river as it bubbles over wet rocks to break the silence, alone in the wilderness with head and heart full of Mike. I am so nearly done here. This is nearly the end of the list. It certainly feels like it. I feel closer to Mike than I have ever felt on this journey, as if he is sitting here beside me. Just like we used to sit for hours fishing together, not needing to talk, just revelling in the landscape and the calm wholeness of our world.

I clutch Mike's hat while I smoke a cigarette. I imagine him looking at me, smiling, his eyes bright with pride.

'You lucky bastard,' he'd say. Then he'd probably go off and catch a bigger fish just to show me up. Not only that, he'd probably throw it back in expectation of an even bigger one.

I miss the banter.

I miss Mike.

I don't want the list to end. It ties me to him. When it's gone, somehow so is he. Those few words of the tasks, kept secret from me all this time and now nearly all completed, are the closest I get to him talking to me. I want to hear his voice.

But I still need to catch another fish. And cook it.

◆

I get back on the boat. We head to a different part of the river and amazingly it isn't long before I catch a fish I can keep. In a wider section of the river we pull the boat up onto a bigger island with driftwood on its beach. I spot some flax growing on the opposite bank and ask Mark if he can take me over to pick some. He offers to get it, and I set about gutting and cleaning my trout. Ian, the bushcraft master, kindly gave me one of his cheap but razor-sharp knives that he swears by; it makes short work of the fish as I butterfly it.

I peel the flax into strands and weave them into a short length of cord, which I then use to lash together a framework for the butterflied trout, a technique I learned on a course Mike and I went on before one of our Norway trips. I gather some wood and get a fire going, and I cook the fish.

As banal as all that sounds, I am loving every minute of this. So I am going to repeat myself. Every second is infused with this heart-swelling awareness of my surroundings. Not only am I in this place of exceptional beauty, of tranquillity, of unsullied nature at its best, I am also cooking (over a fire I started from scratch) a fish that I caught in this river less than an hour ago, a fish that I then gutted, cleaned, butterflied and tethered to a tool of foraged wood that I bound together with cord I made from leaves that were, until not long ago, happily growing beside this river. I needed to reiterate that. It's the most natural thing in the world, man as hunter-gatherer, living off the land. But it's nearly all stuff that most of us have forgotten about, stuff that has been regrettably replaced with technology and noise and materialism.

But this . . . this is Mike. Through and through.

A colleague of Mark's arrives in another, swankier-looking boat. These boats are designed for high speeds, happy on deep water but also fast and resilient enough to power over sandbars and shallows in the tributaries at a ridiculous rate of knots as well. After Drew and I wolf down the delicious fish, we clamber aboard for a thrilling blast along the river and out onto Lake Te Anau, a huge body of water that feeds into the sounds to the west. And we float there quietly on the deep, deep water for a while, circled by the jagged purple silhouettes of the Southern Alps.

It's heavenly.

Drew and I are allowed take the helms of the two boats, and we race them back across the calm water towards the river mouth and the rapidly approaching end to my adventure.

The Garden City

There's a slight sense of malaise about the long drive from Queenstown to Christchurch. For a while we keep the Southern Alps to our left as we head north-east, stopping occasionally to enjoy panoramic views of huge lakes and the receding mountains, last lingering looks at the epic landscape that has, in all its roller-coaster glory, been home for several weeks. Then we turn more to the east. The land, and the mood, begins to flatten as we near the coast. Fiordland is still fresh in my mind, and I wish I could have spent longer there.

We find our accommodation at the clean and comfortable Jucy Snooze near the airport. It's still a bit of a drive to the city itself, and not an area exactly oozing soul. It's functional and industrial. There are a few generic eateries nearby, and several roundabouts.

Walking around downtown Christchurch makes for sombre viewing. It's six years since one of the strongest ever recorded earthquakes in an urban area struck the city. Its epicentre was barely seven miles from the centre of town and its effects were devastating. Many of the buildings in the business district are boarded up and smeared in graffiti, some hiding behind huge chain-link fences. Behind more of these fences are great plots of bare earth where condemned buildings have been demolished, one by one. There are entire blocks of the area that are impassable and uninhabited. Almost every street reveals a bleak reminder of the disaster suffered by 'The Garden City'.

I spend an hour perusing a museum dedicated to this relatively recent chapter in Christchurch's history, a sobering insight into the calamity. The city had already been weakened by an earlier quake, stronger but further away, several months before the big one in February 2011. So when that one hit, several buildings collapsed and many more were weakened beyond habitation. Great areas of the city's suburbs became affected by liquefaction, a weakening of the subsoil that left swathes of land unsafe to rebuild on.

I can't tell how much of my emotional reaction to Christchurch hinges upon my own sense of loss from having nearly completed Mike's list, but there definitely seems to be a sobering air to the place. From a couple of conversations with staff at the museum I learn that a lot of people left the city in the months and years following the disaster. They moved elsewhere in the country or emigrated to Australia. Or further afield. It's been six years and there is little sign of rebuilding. They haven't even demolished all the condemned buildings yet.

As I explore further I am relieved to see it isn't quite all doom and gloom. A large market area has sprung up among the rubble. Huge brightly-coloured metal shipping containers have been upcycled into retail units and street food outlets. The market is brimming with people buying clothes and crafts, and the air is heavy with the combined aromas of a dozen different cuisines. There is an element of defiance here, a will to persevere in the face of the harshest odds, a refusal to be moved on or beaten by the cruel power of nature. I am reminded of humanity's desire to survive.

◆

Over lunch in Christchurch's Botanic Gardens, I meet Doctor Claire Reilly, who in many ways personifies that drive and fight for life against the odds. Claire was diagnosed with motor neurone disease in 2006 and was given the usual gloomy prognosis of two to three years to live. Despite the fact, she tells me, that having picked out the coffin she wanted to be buried in early on, which she still keeps in her house as a reminder of her mortality, she has made every effort to not succumb to this horrible disease. She now works, and has done for a while, for the Motor Neurone Disease Association (MNDA) New Zealand. This is the reason I'm here in Christchurch. To talk to Claire.

I was worried about how I'd react when I met her. Since Mike passed, I haven't been around anyone with MND. I haven't been able to watch or read or see anything to do with suffering or terminal illness. I didn't want our conversation to be stymied by a flood of painful memories. I was afraid emotion would get the better of me and I would be unable to cope with talking to someone else in the grip of the disease that claimed Mike. I've been corresponding with Claire via email for a while, in anticipation of getting to Christchurch, but a face-to-face meeting is something else entirely.

The reality is, happily, that I feel completely comfortable sitting here with Claire and her partner/carer. She does remind me of Mike, but not in a way that makes me want to crumble into a teary mess. She has the same sharp sense of humour, the same fight and determination. She has refused to let her condition dictate terms to her. Yes, she is confined to a wheelchair, but she has still managed to tick off some items on her own bucket list. She finds ways to travel and enjoy her life at the same time as raising awareness about MND and providing a platform for sufferers to share experiences and advice and find valuable support, something Mike had wanted to create in the UK. Claire is a remarkable woman, inspirational and easy to talk to.

Her hands remind me of Mike, but she's not on breathing assist. I have a surge of anxiety when I watch her eating, remembering the perils of swallowing. Please don't choke. I watch her in readiness, trying to appear like I'm not watching. But I don't need to worry. She is fine. She asks me about Mike, about my journey around New Zealand, and about the documentary. The whole point of the documentary, and this book, is to raise awareness of MND, and hopefully even generate a little revenue that can be put towards research and facilities. At the beginning of this journey, back in Auckland, I met another representative of New Zealand's MNDA and mentioned a desire I have to put on a charity auction in Wellington at the end of my tasks, so I discuss this idea with Claire. The MNDA here is much smaller than the UK version, and I want to do anything I can to raise both awareness and money.

◆

Back at the Jucy Snooze, it's Drew's last night. We've finished the main shoot of the documentary and I can tell he's more than ready to make the long journey home to his broody girlfriend. He's flying up to Auckland in the morning, then it's just a short hop across the Tasman Sea to Australia, a slightly longer hop to Dubai, then a final one back to London. Right at this moment in time I don't envy him that odyssey. I'm going to fly up to Wellington and spend some time there before I go home. I have the charity auction to host there, and just a couple of tasks left to tick off before I get to the last one. The last one isn't a mystery. I know what it is, and I'm not looking forward to completing it. In truth, I'm just not ready to go home. The longer I can spin this out, the more time I get to share with Mike. In a way.

Drew and I splash out on a burrito at one of the generic eateries a short walk from the hotel. I might even treat him. It's been nearly three months since I first met the hirsute camera guy, but we've been breathing the same air day in and day out every day since, and I'd say we've become firm friends, and I can see this is a friendship that'll last our lifetimes. We have things in common; we've both lost a brother, for a start. But it's not just his empathy for what I'm doing that connects us. He's actually a cool guy and I really like him, though of course I don't tell him that, and I certainly don't tell him that I'll miss him. He's been a key part of this adventure, and I'm glad and thankful that he became part of my journey.

After our brief and slightly downbeat dinner, I give him a manly hug and wish him well for his homeward trek, then shuffle off back to my room to pack for Wellington.

PART FOUR

NOT THE END

Buckets of Ice

I'm in Number 1. But there's something different about it; the layout doesn't feel quite right. Mike's eyes widen at me. Something is wrong. His breathing assist isn't working. The machine has stopped. I panic. I pull his mask off. Without the machine functioning, the mask is far more of a threat on than off.

'Don't worry,' I tell him with as much calm as I can muster. 'I'll get the spare machine. I'll be ten seconds.'

I run through the house and into a room that I know is there but that I don't really know or recognise. Spare equipment, back-up kit, a secondary machine. It's all in here. And it's a mess. Why has nobody tidied in here? Why didn't I organise it better? I can't see the machine. I start frantically pulling at bits of equipment, throwing them back over my head, scrabbling around to try and find the only thing that will save Mike's life.

I can hear him, his breath rasping, a horrid sucking sound as he tries to get oxygen into his lungs. But it won't work. It can't work. Not without the machine.

I am swimming. The clutter folds around me like a sea. I am drowning in an ocean of masks and tubes and hoists, everything except the one thing I need.

The one thing Mike needs. To stay alive.

◆

The same vivid nightmare. Over and over.

As wonderful as it was when Mike got out of the hospice and moved into his own space, into Number 1, I was in an almost constant state of anxiety. There were so many things that could go wrong. It was a world away from his time at Number 34. There he was still eating solid food, poached eggs and the like that I would make him, and he didn't need the mask. There we had been able to shuffle him from the kidney board onto the toilet. There he had been stronger, and in less discomfort.

We learned how to care for Mike while he was in the hospice, learned how to use the breathing and cough assist machines and how to operate the hoist safely. In the hospice, if anything had gone wrong, there were always medical professionals seconds away, ready to swoop in and help. But in Number 1, we were left alone to care for Mike. It wasn't that I didn't trust myself maintaining his equipment and doing everything in my power to make him comfortable and safe. There was just the dread of something going wrong that I couldn't deal with. I was terrified of being rendered helpless. Helpless in the most critical time, when someone I love might need me. This living nightmare would ultimately become a reality.

Mike was already reliant on the breathing assist. We had a spare mask and a secondary machine if anything went wrong with the first one, but what if that wasn't enough? I lived in fear of a power cut. I never showed it. I manifested an outward appearance of calmness and fun. Even when I was adjusting Mike's mask for the tenth time in an hour. Sometimes a hair would get stuck inside the mask, and I'd need to take it off and clean it, study it under bright light and try to get rid of the offending follicle. I'd wipe it out and urgently reattach it, not wanting Mike to be without it for too long. If I hadn't managed to get the hair, I'd have to repeat the process. This could happen several times in a row, and each period Mike was without the mask was fraught. He'd need a while to get his breath back before I could try to adjust it again. Aside from the odd pesky hair, Mike's mask would still need adjusting frequently. There was always condensation building up on the inside, and in the tubes. For full-on cleanings we would utilise the spare mask, but I would still be in the kitchen, a sense of urgency about my scrubbing and sterilising, worried about the spare one failing.

Mike lived in his wheelchair, largely immobile, and while he never developed bedsores or pressure ulcers from sustained sitting, he was rarely comfortable for long. He would slide forwards in his chair, or slump to one side. He lacked the strength to pull himself upright, so we needed to do it for him. All but the slightest of movements required the use of the hoist, a machine on wheels which fastened to a harness. We kept the harness on Mike's chair, under him, so that we just had to lift up the five points of contact that hooked onto the hoist arm. We had to be sure that the harness wasn't trapping any part of his body that would cause him pain, all the time being careful not to dislodge his breathing assist. It required a keen awareness of everything around Mike, and a serious degree of co-ordination. Having gathered the eyelets of the sling together, I would hold the controls for the hoist in my left hand, and push my knee gently into Mike's thigh before raising him slowly and pulling him towards me.

There was only so long Mike could bear to be suspended like that, and in that brief time I would quickly adjust the cushions on his chair to make it comfortable again. Lowering him required the same co-ordination. Without pulling his painful shoulder, I'd need to exert slight pressure on him to pull him towards me and to his left. Mike tended to slump towards his right, so I'd try and start him a little the other way so it would be a slightly longer time before he needed adjusting again.

That needed doing probably every half an hour. In between adjusting the breathing assist mask. Toileting took a long time as well. He would need to be lifted with the hoist onto the commode. Just getting to that point could take fifteen minutes. It was all laborious, but I never felt self-pity. I felt for Mike. My poor dear brother. Everything was an ordeal for him.

I couldn't complain. I wouldn't have dreamt of it. No matter what stress I was feeling, no matter how overwhelming the fear sometimes was, no matter how hard it was to maintain my positivity, it wasn't me in the mask, confined to a chair, in pain. He also had to endure daily injections for deep vein thrombosis. In the hospice, his legs had become swollen and he was booked in for an ultrasound. I didn't know at the time what the treatment for DVT was, but Mike did. And he was terrified of what the test would reveal. He did indeed have clots, and he returned from the scan horribly down. He needed to have an injection every day for the rest of his life.

It's a long needle, inserted into the stomach. And Mike, as I've mentioned, had a crippling fear of needles. I learned how to give the injection, and administered it nearly every day (sometimes Laura did it), trying to vary the spot where I pushed the needle in, as the flesh tends to harden if overused. Mike never got used to it, never found a way to not break out in a cold sweat at the thought of it. And why would he? It was the equivalent of Mike handing me a spider to hold every single day.

Once Mike was settled, comfortable and watching something on the TV, I would nip outside with a coffee and a cigarette and keep half an eye on him through his living room window. Before long there was an ever expanding Venn diagram of dark rings on the window ledge where I would set my coffee cup. I'd mindlessly indulge in Candy Crush while I smoked, until I saw movement from within, at which point I'd dart inside and ask Mike what he needed.

I could have done something more productive with those moments, like learn a language. Something other than Candy Crush. My thumbs ached after a while and Mike would roll his eyes at my childishness. But that was the point. It was mindless. It was my reset. A simple moment or two where I could switch off my scared brain.

I'd make Mike soups all the time. I'd started that while he was in the hospice, but it hit a new level in Number 1. I would make regular trips to a farm shop near us, well stocked with delicious organic produce, and well attuned to providing food for people with specific dietary requirements. Mike and Laura would go online and order other ingredients, with regard to flavour as much as health benefits. Solid foods were off the menu. Even the Farley's Rusks that Mike had for breakfast had to be blitzed and sieved into a fine liquid. To begin with I had just soaked them, but even the slightest hint of texture soon caught in Mike's throat. The soup was the same, sieved and thinned into an easy-to-swallow liquid. But he still had perfectly working taste-buds, and he liked flavour and variety. I would watch him nervously when I fed him, scared that at any moment swallowing would prove too much for him. And when I was in the kitchen, preparing his soups, I would pause every two minutes to check on him in the living room.

Claire came once a week and massaged Mike, and in between her visits we would do what she had showed us. In a quiet moment, I'd ask Mike if he wanted a foot massage. I'd remove the blanket from his legs and pull off his slippers and his thick hiking socks and his flight socks, then apply organic coconut oil. Often, halfway through, he'd need adjusting. I'd rush off and wash my hands before going through the hoist procedure and making him comfortable again before continuing.

Dad was there most mornings before I got there. Generally I spent the days with Mike, often until nine in the evening, when Laura would settle in for the night shift. Dad being there before I got there gave her a chance to go and get some sleep. Many times I walked in and saw Dad sitting there with Mike, gently massaging his hands. It was heartwarming and heartbreaking at the same time.

We were changing as a family. Before Mike got ill, we rarely hugged each other. Even more rarely would we say 'I love you.' If anyone said anything remotely gushy they would quickly be derided. As close as Mike and I were when we were younger, we wouldn't embrace or display affection for each other. But that all changed. I would walk in every morning and thread my arms carefully around Mike and give him a big hug and tell him I loved him. Same every evening, before I went home.

Edan, who was around eleven at that time, would do the same when he visited. We'd done up a bedroom in the house just for him, with a TV and a gaming system. He'd come in and hug his dad and tell him about his day at school. He is such a beautiful compassionate boy. He'd sit there and massage his dad's hands, or rub the coconut oil into his legs, and watch TV with him. Mike adored his son, and those moments with him.

As grim as daily life might come across in these pages, we made it as normal as possible. We made it fun. There was always banter, and the laborious tasks were glossed with humour and silliness. I may have veneered my anxieties with a smile, but there were still lots of good times. I wasn't in a rush to get home in the evenings, even though that was my time to unwind and rest before starting all over again the next morning. More often than not I'd sit with Mike and watch TV well into the evening. We loved the Red Bull channel and soaked up all the extreme sports and misadventure. You'd think that Mike wouldn't have wanted to watch people doing the things he desperately wanted to do again, the things he would never get to do again, but he loved it. We watched snowboarding, wakeboarding, downhill cycling and the rest. We watched comedy shows like *8 Out of 10 Cats Does Countdown* and *Would I Lie To You?*, and drooled over cookery programmes like *The Great British Bake Off* and *Man v. Food*. I think if Mike had recovered, he would have gone on a blowout of all the kinds of food he had spent his life avoiding. He never got the chance to bite into a big American burger, or stuff his face with pancakes. Yet, somehow, seeing them on the screen was more consolation than torture.

Even sitting there, watching TV, I always had half an eye on Mike. I'd frequently ask him if he needed anything. I'd hoist him up and fix his chair and adjust his mask. And when I got up to go home, for as long as he was able to talk, weakly on an out breath, he'd apologise to me. He'd apologise for the fact that I was there, with him, looking after him, dealing with him. And it cut me to the bone every time he said it. I waved it aside. He had nothing to be sorry for.

'What are you on about? I'm having a great time with you,' I'd tell him.

But he continued to say sorry. Most days. And he'd thank me too. I didn't want or need his thanks. His love was enough.

'I love you bruv,' I'd say before I went home to my bed.

To my recurring nightmare.

◆

The Ice Bucket Challenge, designed to raise awareness for motor neurone disease was, at this time, becoming an internet sensation. In America, MND is known as ALS, amyotrophic lateral sclerosis. Or Lou Gehrig's disease. Lou Gehrig played for the New York Yankees back in the 1920s and 1930s, and his big hitting earned him the nickname 'The Iron Horse'. The disease that was later named after him struck him in his mid-thirties. He retired from professional baseball in 1939 at the age of thirty-six, and died two years later. It took another baseball player diagnosed with the disease, Pete Frates, to inspire the spread of the Ice Bucket Challenge as a means to raise money and awareness.

So, at Number 1, wheelchair-bound and reliant on his breathing assist, Mike decided he wanted to do it. I hadn't even considered that as a possibility. You can't throw water over someone hooked up to a breathing assist machine. And the shock it could deliver to his body was surely a risk not worth taking. But he was adamant. He knew that the Tolkien name could add traction to the drive for awareness and donations. There was a feeling that a lot of people were just jumping on a viral bandwagon without really understanding what it was they were supposedly raising awareness and money for. Mike wanted people to see him in his mask, to see what it was to have MND, to bring a visual awareness to the campaign. He also thought it would be a good laugh.

It took a while to plan. We figured out that we could put the breathing assist on an extension cord so he could get to the front door. That would be the safest place to do it, and we could remove the mask for as long as it took to empty the bucket over Mike, then quickly dry him off and replace the mask. We also decided that the bucket should be full of ice rather than ice water. The cubes of ice would more than have the desired effect, but they would be less of a shock to his weakened system than a deluge of cold water. It would be easier to brush them off Mike, and easier to get him warm again.

On the day, I got a bit dressed up. I put on a jacket and tie and prepared a little speech. I squatted down in the doorway of Number 1 next to Mike in his mask and introduced both of us. A few times. Mike turned his expressive eyes to me every time I mentioned him and opened them wide, making me laugh. Eventually I managed to get a clean take, and explained that Mike had MND. Then, off camera, we removed his mask.

I emptied the ice over his head. At the bottom of the bucket, some of the smashed ice had turned into a freezing dust that was little better than water. I brushed it from where it had landed on his head, and we promptly got a towel on him and replaced the mask. The shock and spasms you get from being suddenly immersed or covered in ice water is an insight into the loss of control endured by those with MND. For Mike, it was like doubling down. For Mike, risk aside, this was an exercise in thrill-seeking as much as it was a powerful visual for raising awareness. He loved the excitement of it. There had never been a thought in his mind that it could be too traumatic or dangerous for him, or that he couldn't or shouldn't do it. Once his mind was made up, that was it. It was a reminder of who he was before this horrible disease took hold of him.

When it came to my turn, I buttoned up my jacket and steeled myself. But Mike had other ideas. He had sent Laura around the charity shops to find an outfit for me. I was shown a bag of clothes and told to go and change.

'It's what Mike wants,' Laura goaded me with an evil laugh. 'Whatever's in the bag, you have to put on.'

So, of course, I did.

I re-emerged into the already cold day wearing a skimpy red dress with a pink faux feather boa, clutching a fistful of big red chillis that I was instructed to eat.

'It's already cold,' I grumbled, then bit down into several chillis at once. As the heat began to spread through my mouth, I pulled a silly pose and readied myself for the shock. Story and his best friend, Calum, emptied three huge buckets of ice cold water over me. Mike, towel over his shoulders, just inside the open front door and safely outside the splash zone, smiled through his mask. His eyes laughed.

It was a great day. It was a change in the routine. We weren't just sitting watching TV in Mike's living room. For him, it was like a day out. He had the thrill of doing the challenge himself, the satisfaction of knowing how potent a force for awareness that was, and the joy of watching me. Me with a mouth full of chilli heat, squeezed into a red dress, being bombarded by gallons of freezing cold water.

◆

I'd arranged a local charity screening of the second Hobbit film, *The Desolation of Smaug*, the previous year, at Theatr Clwyd – yes, the film I was cut from for the theatrical release, much to Mike's ongoing amusement. As December rolled around again, the final instalment, *The Battle of the Five Armies*, was ready for release. Again, ahead of the national release, I was permitted to arrange an advance charity screening. Unlike the year before, this time there was no way Mike could attend.

I decided to incorporate a silent auction in the evening, and set about sourcing a variety of exciting items that guests could bid for. We had Sir Ian McKellen's prosthetic Gandalf nose holder, signed by him. A friend of mine, Jonny Duddle, who'd illustrated some of the Harry Potter books, gave a signed drawing of Snape. Ed Sheeran even signed and donated a guitar. Peter Jackson sent through a collection of behind-the-scenes stills from the production that we had printed as posters and set on easels in the foyer. Video messages of support came in from Peter, Martin Freeman, Orlando Bloom, Luke Evans and others. I was able to give goodie bags to all the guests containing generously gifted chocolates from Whitakers in New Zealand, *Hobbit*-themed pens from Air New Zealand, Merino woollen socks and more. I had a local band called The Joy Formidable perform an acoustic set. They were hugely successful, even touring with the Foo Fighters in America. The evening was a resounding success, but a few items didn't quite reach what I had hoped. Mike stepped in to up the bidding, and ended up with a few of them. He and Laura clubbed together and won the signed Ed Sheeran guitar to give to Story for Christmas.

When Christmas came around, we got to do what we had set out to do months before. Despite the earlier pessimism of the medical staff at the hospice, Mike was home, and we could all have Christmas with him at Number 1, just as we had planned. I normally deplore tackiness, but Christmas is the one time of year that I actively embrace every bauble and kitsch decoration with unbridled enthusiasm. Even if nobody sees my house over the festive season (and few people do, generally), I festoon every room with fairy lights and decorations that I have accumulated or inherited over the years. I get the biggest tree I can that will fit inside and cover it in tinsel and baubles and decorations. I love it.

Mike loved it too, and he wanted that Christmas to be as sparkly and tacky as possible. I got him the tallest tree I could for his living room and dressed it in lights and sparkly things. Mike had a three-foot-high crystal with LED lights in it that slowly changed colour, reflecting into the crystal's own beautiful colours. And he had scented flickering electronic candles on his mantlepiece. When the tree was up and illuminated, his living room became like a fairy grotto, bathed in the warm and beautiful glow of all these soft lights. It was as Christmassy as it comes.

I don't know if Mike felt that would be his last Christmas with us, but he certainly went all out in terms of gifts. He sat for hours with Laura at his laptop, carefully choosing thoughtful and generous presents for all the family. The first Christmas after he was diagnosed, he had given me a Links bracelet that sadly came apart not long after the move to Number 1. He gave me a new one which I haven't taken off to this day. Story got Ed Sheeran's signed guitar, and Mike sat happily watching Edan open his presents on the floor in front of that glorious tree. He got so much joy from seeing happiness on faces as people unwrapped his gifts. Sadly there wasn't a lot we could get Mike that we would normally have got him. He had to make do with practical things: extra comfortable pyjamas, a nice pillow, a blanket, new slippers and a giant pot of organic coconut oil for his massages.

It was a beautiful and memorable Christmas. Everyone turned up throughout the day. Dad was there. So was Mandy and her husband and kids. Laura's mum, Dolly, was there. She, like Dad, would visit most mornings by way of support for Laura. I cooked a big Christmas lunch and a specially requested sprout soup for Mike. Mike inevitably got tired in the afternoon, so we wound the celebrations down a little and put on a film. Despite the circumstances, and despite the fact that Mike still needed his regular adjustments in his chair, his injection, his mask cleaning, toileting and feeding, it was one of the best Christmases I can remember, a Christmas filled with laughter, love and happiness.

Dragon's Gold

I was having a smoke on the street outside the Roxy cinema, a gorgeous and lovingly restored art deco theatre in the Miramar area of Wellington. I'd been back a few days and was there for the charity auction I was putting on in aid of New Zealand's MNDA.

I started the ball rolling back in Auckland at the beginning of this trip, and had spent the last few months gathering whatever I could to be auctioned. Rob Hamill and Rachel offered up a day's sailing on their catamaran. There were paintings from a local artist and friend of mine, Rieko, and also from Weta prosthetic artist Gino Acevedo, another friend of mine. My biggest coup, and the main lot of the night, was the orc mask I wore when I roared in Peter Jackson's face not long ago. Richard at Weta was more than happy to part with it for a good cause, and even had it specially mounted on a head stand.

I had plenty of help. Thankfully. I'd been a little busy cavorting up and down New Zealand doing Mike's bucket list, so every bit of assistance was crucial. I'd been corresponding with Jodie O'Doherty for some time. Jodie works for the MNDA here and her mother has been diagnosed with the disease. She was invaluable in co-ordinating the event. So was Belindalee, our amazing NZ producer and fixer for the documentary. And we wouldn't have been there at that awesome cinema, the Roxy, without the help of Richard Taylor and his partner Tania Rodger, who own it with Jamie Selkirk, one of Peter's business partners. There were loads of people there that night who need thanking. Jed Brophy kindly offered to emcee the event and brought along his wonderful wife, Yolande, with him. Another dwarf from the Hobbit films, Peter Hambleton, was there. And so was my orc-face brother, Shane Rangi.

Yes, I did have to give a speech. And no, I hadn't planned it. I was just hanging about outside, sucking on a cigarette and enjoying having my date, Jesse, there with me. I was suited and booted and ready to raise some money.

Yes, I know. I said, 'date'. Back up, Royd.

Remember that stand-up comedy gig I did here in Wellington? Remember how I talked about swiping left and right on Tinder and how I had to rush off after my few minutes of humiliation glory and go on a date? Well, Jesse was that date.

I need to contextualise. I haven't been in a relationship for years. Lots and lots of years. While Mike was ill I had no time and absolutely no inclination to be involved intimately or otherwise with anyone else. And after he died, until this trip, until now perhaps, I felt no capacity at all to connect with another person on a romantic level. Losing Mike made me petrified of getting close, of having to feel loss again, or the potential loss of a relationship gone bad. I was in a rut.

This trip, this odyssey around New Zealand, offered a chance for me to move on. I came here vaguely open to the prospect of meeting someone. I felt almost ready. Tentative, but almost ready. I began on Tinder, not for sordid reasons, but because it felt a bit easier than having actual conversations. Meeting someone face-to-face would still be a challenge, but the filter of an initial textual conversation seemed a safer way of building up the courage to open myself up, even the tiniest bit, to a stranger.

So, after exchanging a load of messages, we arranged to meet. And it went well. She is funny, engaging, ambitious, beautiful and great company. It was weird but refreshing to spend time with someone outside of the bucket list and the documentary that were dictating almost every move I made. We chatted and laughed and we ended the night with a little kiss. I left for the South Island shortly afterwards, thinking that was that, but we continued messaging. We met up again when I got back from Christchurch and got on even better. I don't want to sound conceited, but having her there with me and with my friends and people I know, as part of an evening that was really all about Mike – it was a big deal. A few months ago I couldn't have even comprehended lowering my self-erected barriers enough for someone to be involved in this part of my life. But I let her in. And that was a huge step for me.

I was proud of myself. I was proud to be there with Jesse, and proud that the evening was happening. The support I had from both the MNDA and the filmmaking community here, many of whom are great friends of mine, was overwhelming. I was back in speech mode, feeling like I wanted to thank everyone. The turnout was great, better than I had dared hope for. I had been surprised when I'd gone in earlier, as I'd been outside then too, watching people dribble in. The place was packed.

I chatted to Jed and Shane for a while before I noticed a man in a wheelchair, surrounded by his family. I immediately knew that he had MND, and I wanted to talk to him. His name is Mike. Of course it was. I struggle talking to anyone called Mike as it is, let alone someone who has the same disease that claimed my brother. I overcame my apprehension of talking to someone with MND when I met Claire in Christchurch, so I wasn't going to pass up the opportunity to talk to this man. I knew how much of an effort it must have been, in his situation, to get there, and how difficult it can be to be in a crowd of able-bodied people. I wanted to make him feel welcome and comfortable. I wanted to talk to him. I needed to talk to him. I walked over and apologised for interrupting, then introduced myself. To avoid obvious confusions, I am now going to refer to him by his full name, Michael.

Squatting down next to his wheelchair, I talked to Michael for nearly an hour. He smiled a lot, and was a fun and lovely man, and clearly thrilled to be here. He was loving the occasion. His family were delightful and so loving towards him. It was heartwarmingly familiar to see them bonded around him. Eventually, knowing the auction couldn't be far off, I excused myself and announced I was popping outside for a cigarette. Michael laughed. It turns out he used to be a big smoker, and he was chuckling enviously, gutted that MND had put paid to a bad habit he had thoroughly enjoyed, but happy to indulge vicariously through me.

'Royd, it's starting.' I was summoned inside.

◆

I took the microphone and prepared to deliver my unprepared speech.

'I've got to thank my brother for setting this in motion. He sent me on this journey, and without him and the terrible suffering he went through and that other people go through, I wouldn't have realised how important certain things are.'

Family. Support. Love. Positivity.

'Just get out there and make a change. Make a difference. Enjoy life. My brother enjoyed life, despite what he was going through.' I saw Michael, who I met not an hour before, watching me with a big grin on his face. Inspired by him, and memories of my brother, I continued. I wanted to inspire. I hoped he wouldn't mind, but I wanted to draw attention to Michael and his family. I pointed him out. Him being there was what that night was all about.

'It breaks my heart but it also mends it, meeting people like you.' I looked at his smiling face while I talked. To him. 'And when I meet people like you it reminds me why I'm doing all this.'

And it does.

I bumbled on for a bit longer then handed the stage back to Jed and to the auction, during which I squatted next to Michael's wheelchair. Michael had his heart set on a piece of purloined dragon's gold that Jed offered up for auction. A piece like the one he gave me, the one that went in Mike's coffin.

I gestured to Jed when it came up, and we made sure that Michael won it.

◆

It's barely a month since that night at the Roxy, and I'm on my way back to Wellington. From a funeral. Michael, who I met at the auction, passed away a few days ago.

I couldn't believe the news. Yes, he was in a wheelchair. But he was so alert. He was smiling, happy to be there. That's the thing about MND; it's your body that fails you. Michael's mind was as bright as I imagine it had ever been. Brighter even. In his eyes, he was full of life. And when I talked to him that night, that is all I saw. I looked past the devastating effect the disease was having on his physicality. So I was shocked. Shocked and upset.

I got in touch with the family and respectfully asked if it would be okay if I came to the funeral. I wasn't sure how it would go, since the last funeral I'd been to was Mike's. I didn't want to just break down, overcome by my own grief for Mike and the memories of his funeral that being there might hurl back up at me. But I wanted to go. So did Jed when he heard the news. Jed spent much of that evening talking to Michael as well, and has been active in helping the MNDA in New Zealand, so felt as strong a need as I did to go.

The family welcomed us coming. They told me how much Michael had enjoyed that evening at the Roxy. So we went.

The turnout was huge. Michael was a popular man who had clearly touched the lives of many. I spent time talking to the family, learning more about the man they had lost. I contained my emotions and felt honoured to be involved in paying tribute to a wonderful man who I had only got to meet once.

Driving back to Wellington, I feel broken. All the emotion I pushed down inside me during the funeral is bubbling up. I remember the aftermath of Mike's funeral. I can almost feel that crushing emptiness again. And I grieve for Michael's family, knowing exactly what they are going through and what they will go through. It's not just a matter of losing someone you love. It's the gnawing nothingness of having your very being ripped from you. It's not just the absence of your father, brother, son, husband or friend. It's the gap that is left behind when you no longer have that person to care for, day in and day out. It's the complete vacuum of focus. Of purpose. Like I did for so long after Mike died, they will feel utterly lost. They will, perversely, miss and yearn for what drove them to get up each day for the time that Michael had been sick: the chance to give everything to care for someone you love.

It's a horribly perfect limbo, a stagnant stasis of emotion.

I am thankful to Mike for giving me the focus of this bucket list. It is my way out of that limbo. I must finish the list and find my way back to life.

Pounamu

In the course of this journey it was revealed to me that, among this epic litany of tasks that have inspired in me the full gamut of emotions – from terror to reflection, from sadness to joy – there was a gap. A blank. A missing item. A number that contained no instructions from Mike. A place on the list that he hadn't had the time to fill. Or maybe he'd left it blank for me to fill in?

Back in Queenstown, during my interview with *Seven Sharp* on the banks of Lake Wakatipu, I invited viewers to propose ideas for that missing task. I wanted it to be something particularly pertinent to New Zealand. In the end, despite a slew of suggestions including the usual extreme sports and Kiwi madness as well as things like sheep shearing, I went with an idea put forward by Shai, who I'd been strapped to when I went paragliding.

Carve a greenstone.

It turns out that greenstone, or Pounamu to the Māori, is pretty much exclusively found on the west coast of the South Island. The Māori used to brave the sandflies of Fiordland to collect it and fashion tools and jewellery from it. Jewellery powerfully imbued with the mana, the spiritual life force, of the carver.

But I'm back in Wellington. Nowhere near Fiordland or the west coast. Or even the South Island. It's just as well, then, that I've been put in touch with Owen Mapp and his wife Hanne.

They live in Palmerston North, a town a couple of hours north of Wellington, where they make jewellery, and lecture at the local university.

Owen predominantly works with bone, but is also an expert in greenstone. Result. 'It's jade,' Owen corrects me. 'Greenstone is just a name we use to sell it to tourists.' Owen, in his seventies now, has been working with jade for his whole life, so he knows what he's talking about. He has a studio here, in his house, and an impressive collection of bones and stones. His house and his workbenches are stacked high in the materials he works with and loves.

We sit around a table and I tell Owen why I'm here. I tell him about Mike. About the documentary. I have an idea for something I'd like to make, a pair of pendants that fit together, two halves of a whole. I want to give Edan something that will represent him and his dad. I have an idea that at some point in his life, Edan might want to give one of the halves to someone significant to him.

Owen listens carefully. He asks lots of searching questions about Mike. About Edan. About their relationship. Then he tells me about how Māori chieftains used to carry wooden staffs bearing cumulative carvings that represented their lineage and history. They were passed down through the generations, each making their own marks in the wood. The staffs, in an almost literal sense, became family trees. They would have protrusions jutting out that represented individual people.

We settle on a simple design of two rectangular pieces, one with a protruding edge and the other with a corresponding indent. The two pieces will join perfectly together, becoming one. One will represent Mike, and the other Edan. Perfect. All I have to do now is make them. Owen has a good stash of bits of stone, much of it gifted to him over the years. A lot of it is offcuts from other projects, but I only need a small bit. You can't collect or trade jade now, so most jewellery you find has been made from old stock. I find a rough cut slab maybe five inches by three that will suit my purpose, then draw the shape of the pendants on it.

Owen takes me into his studio, where all his cutting and sanding tools are, and shows me how to operate the cutter, how to change the blade and switch between the cutters, grinders and sanders. He makes a start, cutting the stone, but I soon interject and ask if I can have a go. That's why I'm here, after all. I sit down and carry on cutting. Owen didn't know how confident I'd be operating the machine, or how easily I'd take to it. It's a sharp diamond blade, fed by water to keep it cool, and I guide it carefully and slowly along the line. Owen is quickly satisfied that I have the hang of it and leaves me to it.

I'm there a while. It's slow-going, but immensely therapeutic. I break for a delicious meal and some wine with Owen and Hanne and relish every minute of their hospitality and excellent company. But I want to get back to it, so I excuse myself and work into the night. They have kindly made up a spare room for me, and I eventually go to bed, long after them, and wake early the next morning to get back to work.

It takes me several of these visits, each time overnighting with Owen and Hanne, to carve the two pieces. I make one side convex and the other concave, giving each rectangle a nice smooth curve. I carefully cut, grind and sand the two parts so that they slot together perfectly. When I have done all I can with the machine, I take to gently sanding and rubbing the pieces by hand. Owen impressed on me a real sense of perfectionism. Jade jewellery takes as long as it takes. It has to be perfect. It is only then that it is ready. It is only then that it will be fully imbued with your mana.

And when it is done, I find myself looking at the offcut from my bit of stone. It's maybe four inches by an inch, and it's speaking to me.

'Would you mind if I use that as well?' I ask Owen. I want to cut it into five smaller pieces and make other pendants for other people. He thinks it is a beautiful idea. It's the same bit of stone as the ones that will go to Edan, so there's a link between all of these pieces, between all the people I will give them to. I decide to make them for Dad, Laura, Mandy and her daughter Megan, and one for Jesse.

Owen introduces me to a friend of his called Steve, who is an expert in making jewellery cordage and lashing. Steve shows me how to use a special hand machine to weave strands of cordage and how to carve and cut the tiny horn sliders that adorn it. I use his magnifying spectacles to carve my initials in miniature on the sliders. I set about putting the finishing touches to all the pieces I have made.

The whole process is long and slow. I probably spend the best part of a week at Steve's place and at least two weeks in total at Owen and Hanne's, spread over the course of a couple of months. And I have loved every minute of it. I have poured my love, my spirit, my mana into these gifts. I can take them home and give them to the people I love. I can give them a little part of this crazy journey that I have been on. A little part of New Zealand.

And for Edan especially, a little part of his dad.

Of Mike.

◆

It's nearly Father's Day back home.

Story has ended up managing that coffee shop in Raglan, but he's made time to come to Wellington to visit his old man for a long weekend, and I couldn't be happier. I've enjoyed my extra time here, spending time with friends, leading an unusually (for me) active social life. I've grown close to Jesse too.

But, speaking of Story, or my story . . . the only thing I haven't done, which I was supposed to do, is write. That, not nurturing a blossoming relationship, was meant to be the main purpose behind extending my stay in New Zealand. Before I came out here there was already interest from a couple of publishers in my story, in Mike's story. So I got myself a literary agent. I'd had an investment trailer put together for the documentary by my good friend Jonno, husband of Reiko who donated the artwork for the Roxy event: a short piece with existing clips of Mike and me, that set out what this journey was likely to be like. The *Metro* newspaper in London ran a story about it and I was approached about doing a book as well.

The plan was, after the bucket list was all but finished, for me to spend a bit of time getting stuck into that book here, in Wellington. And I started well. I found a perfect spot in the lovely house I'm staying in, a breakfast table in a bay window that beautifully catches the morning light. I pictured myself sitting there, in beams of golden sunshine, a mug of steaming coffee beside me, beavering away. I went out and bought notebooks, pens, pencils, and pads of Post-it Notes. My agent had told me that whatever I did, whatever I wrote, I should always be asking myself *why*. *Why* am I writing this? Everything needs a why. So I wrote 'WHY?' on a Post-it Note and stuck it on the table next to my shiny new writing gubbins. Definitely a good start. Then I went for breakfast. And I met some friends. I didn't write anything else that day.

That's a couple of months ago now, and all those morning sunbeams have shone emptily through that window, completely fading the word 'WHY?' from the Post-it Note. It suddenly occurs to me that I'm not sure I'm actually capable of writing this book. I'm too close to it all. I'm going to need help. If I can just think of someone who can write, who has been a part of this journey, that possesses the necessary empathy and gets my sense of humour, someone who has perhaps filmed me and will edit the documentary . . .

Anyway.

I do all the things with Story that I always do with people who don't know Wellington. I take him to the Chocolate Fish Café. Of course. We sip lattes and look at the water, like Mike and I did. We have a bite to eat there and watch the most amazing sunset I've ever seen. The sky glows fire red. I take a photo of it, but it doesn't look real. It's like I've put a bit of red gel over the lens. We go out for the night and meet some friends of mine, and get predictably wrecked while I happily take Story on a pub crawl.

Late in the afternoon on Father's Day, Story and I travel around the coast. We've had the most perfect weekend. We end up across the peninsula from Miramar, near Seatoun, on a rocky little outlet, far away from any houses. We walk right out onto the point and sit and look at the bay. We just sit there, barely talking, like Mike and I would have. At one point we spot the hump of a whale in the distance. I pull out the bottle I tried to throw into the sea at Black Sands Beach, the bottle containing the childhood picture of me and Mike. I love hugs. That one.

I say a few words, private words, and hurl the bottle as far as I can into the deep water.

And I hug Story.

Thunderclap

I phone Mandy and barely get a handful of words out before I burst into tears. I can't help myself. I've just been told I could die.

◆

I booked my flight when I realised my visa was fast running out. I don't want to overstay and compromise being able to come back here again. I needed that incentive, and I needed something to push me into moving on, something to defeat the eternal procrastinator in me. I know what the last part of the bucket list is, and I know it requires me to leave New Zealand, to leave my friends and the contentment I have found here with Jesse. I am finally enjoying my life. And yet, I do want to go. I'm ready. I think.

I made the most of my remaining time here with Jesse. And it was in the middle of doing so that I was assaulted by the most sudden and excruciatingly painful headache I have ever experienced. I stopped what I was doing and collapsed in agony. For an hour or so, my head felt like it would explode. The pain eased a little, but lingered throughout the evening. It was bizarre and unpleasant, but, despite (and perhaps because of) Jesse's obvious concern, I fobbed it off as a freak occurrence. Nothing to worry about.

After that experience, I was cautious for maybe five days before the same thing happened again. One moment I was fine, better than fine, and the next . . . it felt like someone had smashed me in the head with a hammer. This time the agony lasted several hours and lingered into the next morning when I awoke.

This time, on Jesse's insistence, I went to see a doctor. He took my blood pressure and ran a few basic tests. Then, frowning with concern, he decided he wanted a second opinion. Everything, he explained carefully, seemed to be indicating that I might have had a brain haemorrhage. He phoned a neurologist at the main hospital in Wellington and explained the symptoms and what had happened, and the neurologist's advice was for me to call an ambulance and get to hospital immediately. I needed a brain scan, and I needed one right away.

I felt okay at that point, but opted not to argue. The sense of urgency wasn't lost on me. I did decline the ambulance though, and drove myself to the hospital. When I checked in, the neurologist was waiting for me. The attention I was getting from the medical profession started to alarm me. I was smartly wheeled into a room and given a CAT scan. The headache was barely a dull pain at that point. Surely nothing to worry about.

The scan results came back quickly. And everything appeared perfectly normal. As I thought. But there was one problem. Apparently a CAT scan only shows recent bleeding on the brain. It had happened about a week before, and the headaches were the lingering aftermath of it. It was still possible, the neurologist explained to me, that I had indeed suffered a brain haemorrhage, but that the evidence of it was now in my spinal fluid. And the only way to check that was to perform a lumbar puncture.

A lumbar puncture.

I mean, you couldn't write it. I, of course, immediately recalled the traumas endured by Mike when he had to undergo this procedure, both as a child with suspected meningitis and as an adult facing an official diagnosis of MND. And here I am, on the cusp of completing Mike's bucket list and this is what I've been told I need.

'Do I have to?' I asked the neurologist and the nurse pathetically. But I know the answer already.

'Of course you don't.'

I wait for the 'but'.

'But you'd be taking a huge risk.'

The big issue here is that I am due to fly home in a few days. With altitude comes pressure. If I have had a brain haemorrhage, even a tiny one, the altitude could trigger it again. If that happens, there are only two outcomes for me. I will either die, probably quite quickly, or I will end up in a permanent vegetative state. Death or catatonia. Hardly a war cry, is it? A lumbar puncture will reveal whether or not I have had a haemorrhage. If I haven't then I am good to go. If I have, then I will need to be rushed into theatre straight away so they can cut into my skull and save my life. Hopefully. I don't even know what the chances of making it through surgery are.

All I know is I don't want a lumbar puncture.

'Can I have a few minutes to make a phone call?' I asked.

'Of course,' the neurologist nods.

◆

Mandy tells me I have to do it. If I don't, she tells me bluntly, I'll probably die. I half agree with her, and hang up. I wipe the tears from my eyes and dial Story.

He doesn't answer.

I cancel the call. I shouldn't have tried to call him, I realise. What was I going to tell him? I'm relieved I haven't put that burden on him. He would have jumped straight into his car and driven south like a lunatic. By the time he could have got here, I'd either be fine, dead or in surgery. He doesn't need a six-hour drive with that kind of worry and fear barrelling around his head.

I phone Jesse at work to tell her. She threatens to walk out and come here to be with me.

'No, no, it's fine,' I tell her, playing it down. 'I'll be okay. Everything's good.'

Everything is not good.

Between phone calls, tears, chain smoking and soul-searching, I've probably been out here for forty minutes or so. I summon up the courage to go back inside. The neurologist and nurse are where I left them. They haven't moved. They've waited for me.

'I'm so sorry,' I mumble. 'I thought you'd be doing something else.'

'Honestly, it's perfectly fine,' the neurologist smiles at me. Then presses me. 'Have you made a decision?'

I tell them I'll have the lumbar puncture. He nods, satisfied. Everything is already prepped. They really aren't taking any chances. And barely moments later I am lying on a bed in a foetal position, in an open backed hospital gown, getting a local anaesthetic. This is happening. I dig deep for bravado.

It's not like Mike's experiences. It doesn't really hurt because of the anaesthetic they give me but didn't give Mike. I feel the big needle going in. I feel it inside me. Inside my spine. It's a weird hollow feeling. They extract some fluid and patch me up. It's done. They rush my sample off to be tested. I am alone, still curled up in a foetal position. I pull the blanket tight around me and clutch it, white knuckled, to my chin. I think of Mike, of him going through this, comprehending what he must have felt at the time. This long journey, the journey he sent me on, has finally culminated in a moment of shared experience with him. It's almost like a circle

316

closing. I am aware that, in a matter of minutes, I could well be rushed into emergency brain surgery and an unknown future. But I am also lost in remembrance. Of Mike. Of us.

I let go.

I sob.

I cry like a baby.

◆

Only twenty minutes pass, and my results are in. There is no blood in my spinal fluid. I'm okay. I am safe to fly home.

Goodbye

Mike went downhill after Christmas. He got weaker, and the pain in his shoulder intensified. He could barely stand to be without the mask, even for short times. We would try and pass a straw through the side of the mask so he could at least stay hydrated. Still wanting flavour, he liked cold coffee. But he wasn't getting enough fluids. And that was making him weaker.

Being confined to his mask, while vital, was having a detrimental effect. In order to make sure the seal was airtight, I would shave him every few days. But the accumulated dampness around the corner of his mouth, and the difficult act of shaving around the ingrown hairs that began to appear led to Mike getting an infection. He needed anti-inflammatories for his arm and shoulder, he needed fluid and he needed antibiotics.

There was no way he could take a normal course of ibuprofen. He couldn't swallow it. He would have struggled swallowing children's liquid ibuprofen too, but the sugar content alone was enough to rule that out anyway. His body wouldn't have coped with it. We looked into suppositories as an option. It's a far more effective way to administer medication. At the time, so we were told by Mike's doctor, suppositories weren't available on prescription in this country. I spoke to my cousin, Rachel, who lived in France, and she was shocked. She could just walk into any pharmacy and get pretty much anything she wanted as a suppository. After talking to the doctor at the hospice, it turned out that we could get suppositories here after all. We'd been given the run around yet again.

Anyway, they helped. For a bit.

The lack of fluid was more concerning. Mike had little or no strength left in his neck. His head would loll to one side and he would need constant support from an array of pillows. Hoisting and adjusting his chair several times an hour became an even more complicated procedure, as Laura would need to hold his head while I did the lifting. He couldn't wear a neck brace as it would have choked him and been uncomfortable on his skin. And it would have affected his mask. He needed liquid.

I asked the doctor about getting a saline drip, a way of getting fluid into him intravenously, as a matter of urgency. I was met with resistance. It seemed to be the opinion of the medical profession that Mike was nearing the end and there was no point in prolonging his discomfort. We were supposed to let him go gracefully. No. Just no. Mike was in distress and was desperately thirsty. The breathing assist machine sucked moisture from Mike as well, and his throat was uncomfortably dry. He just needed some fluid. We resorted to rubbing small frozen cubes of coffee on his lips through his mask, anything to get him some moisture.

A nurse finally came out with an antibiotic drip to fight the infection. Despite the expected difficulty of finding a viable vein that wasn't collapsed, she was eventually able to get a cannula in place. As the liquid fed slowly into his bloodstream, Mike became visibly more energised. It was working. I again asked if, since the cannula was there, he could have a bag of saline added to the drip once he'd finished the antibiotics. The nurse had one in the car, but couldn't attach it without permission from a doctor. I faced repeating my earlier conversation.

I went outside, my phone hot against my ear, and begged for help. 'You've got to let this happen,' I wanted to shout. 'You're killing my brother,' I was ready to scream. It was unfathomable that there was such a reluctance to permit the nurse to use the saline that was already here. Eventually, I managed to persuade the doctor, and rushed inside to give the nurse the thumbs up.

Mike again responded well. He perked up enough to be able to drink a little liquid through a straw. I felt like he could turn a corner again, like he had when we got him out of the hospice. He would get stronger again. He just needed to fight off the infection and keep getting fluids.

The problem with IV drips is you can't rely on one vein for ever. The nurses had to reposition the cannula from time to time. They switched hands, changed veins, pushed more saline into Mike. And every time, he improved. He was a little more alert.

◆

It was a Tuesday evening. I had stayed a little longer than usual. When I hugged Mike to say goodbye and 'I love you, bruv', he found the strength to push his head against mine again. I got home at about half nine, exhausted. I grabbed some food and watched something mindless to zone myself out. I slept.

The next morning, Wednesday, I was ready to go again. I was just pulling away from my house in the car to make the fifteen-minute drive to Number 1, when a text came in from Laura.

How long will you be?

I sent a quick reply, telling here I'd be there in ten. I figured she'd had a rough night and really needed to go to sleep. I'd be there soon enough.

Hurry, came the one word reply. I didn't know what that meant, but assumed she needed help with something. Maybe Mike needed the toilet. That was a two-person job by then. Whatever the cause of the apparent urgency, I instinctively put my foot down and got there as quickly as I could. I screeched to a halt outside the door and rushed inside.

Laura was waiting for me outside the living room. Dad was in the kitchen with Story. Laura's mum was there too.

'Mike's not responding,' Laura said, her voice hushed.

And I didn't know what that even meant, but I went briskly into the living room and saw Mike. He was there, mask on, breathing assist machine still doing its thing, propped up against the usual tower of pillows, unmoving, with his eyes open. It crossed my mind that he might still be asleep. He hadn't been able to close his eyes for several days and had taken to sleeping with them open.

'Mike,' I said softly. Then again, a little louder, 'Mike?' It still looked like he could be in a good deep sleep. I called his name louder again, shouting. I turned to look at Laura, and recognised on her face the feeling that was unmistakably ballooning rapidly inside me.

Fear. Panic.

'Shall I call an ambulance?' Laura asked me.

I nodded frantically. 'Yes!'

They will come and they will do something that will make him wake up, I told myself. I didn't know what that something was, but I was sure they'd have the answer. Maybe it would be a drip, maybe something else. I didn't know.

Dad must have heard my voice, or something in my voice, something in the way I shouted 'Mike'. He came into the living room, and I look at him desperately. Helpless. Scared.

'Mike's not responding,' I told him, and watched the colour flood from his face.

Dad pushed me aside to get to his youngest son. 'No,' he roared in disbelief or denial, his voice replete with unimaginable pain. 'Mike,' he began to call, over and over. We all tried to wake Mike.

The paramedics got there fast. The first responder swept in, calm and confident. He asked quick clear questions while he stuck ECG pads all over Mike and took his pulse. It was weak, but it was there. Mike was still alive. Still there. The ambulance turned up, all noise and flashing blue lights.

They wanted to get him onto the floor to work on him. He was already sitting on the sling, so while Laura put blankets on the hard floor, I hooked the hoist up and began lowering him out of his chair towards them. I knelt on the floor, cradling Mike in my arms as I lowered him. But it didn't feel right. Mike hadn't lain flat for months. Maybe a year. I was sure that straightening him out, stretching him out flat on a hard floor, no matter how vital whatever the paramedics needed to do would be, was a bad idea. I knew it would cause him even more injury and pain. There had to be another way. I made my feelings known, and set about putting Mike back in his chair. They needed to tend to his needs in that position.

And they did.

For a short time.

And then he was gone.

I was in a living nightmare, swallowed by my deepest fears. I was broken.

I went outside to call Mandy. I couldn't get the words out. But she understood, and raced over as fast as she could.

Back inside, the breathing assist machine was still working, still trying in vain to help Mike breathe. I turned it off. And I took Mike's mask off. Without the machine on, it oddly felt to me like the mask would somehow suffocate him. That was the moment. I knew, from all his time in the hospice and there at Number 1, that the mask and the machine had kept him alive. Turning that off was my acknowledgement that he had actually gone.

And the pain that brought was indescribable.

Story was a calming presence amidst the chaos. As I removed the mask he stood quietly, with his hands lightly resting on Mike's head. Whatever he was doing for Mike, it helped me. It gave me strength.

Two coroners came. One of them was impatient, like he had a long list of house calls to make that day, but one of the policemen who had also turned up took him aside and had a quiet word.

'Take as long as you want,' he told me, knowing we were still waiting for Mandy to get there.

We all took our turns to say goodbye to Mike, having a moment with him, and Mandy arrived and had hers. I walked into the back garden then, not wanting to see him taken away by the coroners. And we all stood around in tears, in a numb kind of limbo, shocked and emotionally ill-equipped to even begin to comprehend the loss we had just suffered. It seemed like time itself had stood still. How would we ever move on from this?

It was late morning by the time the coroners and all the emergency responders had left. We went to Edan's school and waited in the office for him to be pulled out of his lessons. He bounced in, a quizzical smile on his face, innocently wondering what was going on. I could barely stand. I could barely talk. It was taking every fibre of my being to not collapse into a puddle. I felt like I had failed him.

'I'm so sorry, but your dad's passed away.'

◆

Laura told me that it had been a normal night, apart from Mike wanting a constant stream of ice cubes. He had consumed tray after tray as the hours passed. In the early hours of the morning, Mike had remained still for a while, and she had felt able to rest. Mike had a device that would fit between his body and his elbow that would beep if squeezed. It was a simple way for Mike to alert any of us to the fact that he needed something. When Laura woke up, early that morning, she realised she had woken up by herself, not in response to a beep. But something was different. She told me she had felt like Mike's presence had shifted and his sleep had deepened. Concerned, that was when she messaged me.

She told me Mike had waited until I got there.

My brother had waited for me to say goodbye.

Home

Leaving New Zealand was a wrench, but it felt like the right time. I loved my time there, but with my visa due to expire and the drama of my thunderclap headache and lumbar puncture, I was ready to go home. I left Jesse with the hope that we could continue to make the burgeoning relationship work. I love New Zealand and I'm sure I'll be back there soon enough. Long distance love rarely works, and New Zealand is about as long distance as you can get, but I wasn't ready to give up on what was the first semblance of a relationship I'd had in years.

I had to leave Story there too, of course. For now. I flew up to Auckland from Wellington and had a good few hours layover there before the flight to Los Angeles. Story offered to drive up from Raglan and see me in Auckland, at the airport, but I dissuaded him from that idea. I knew it would be too upsetting to say goodbye in person. He was settled and happy and enjoying his New Zealand adventure.

I phoned him from Auckland airport though, and we talked for ages. As ready as I was to leave, I was miserable at the prospect. The whole odyssey around New Zealand, the bucket list adventure, was an emotional link to Mike. And that chapter was coming to a close. As much as I needed to move on, I was leaving something behind that I didn't want to lose.

I sat on the plane in a numb limbo. Air New Zealand had generously upgraded me to Premium Economy, but I was still feeling fairly dejected. I had zero inclination to talk to anyone. I just wanted to sit there for the thirteen or so hour flight and wallow in my own wretched thoughts. Then do more of the same for the eleven hour flight to the UK. There was a girl sitting next to me, who I soon learned was called Kirsty. The cabin crew kept approaching her and asking her if she was okay, if she needed anything. They were attentive and caring, but Kirsty clearly wasn't happy. She wasn't okay. I wondered if she had lost someone. My empathy warmed up and made me want to help, to comfort her.

'Is everything alright?' I eventually leaned over and asked her. We'd reached cruising altitude.

I soon learned that it was Kirsty's first time in an aeroplane. She was emigrating to England for work and leaving her family behind in New Zealand. And she was thoroughly petrified of flying. She was in the grip of a crippling fear. I spent that entire flight, and the next one, talking to her, trying to take her mind off her horror at being eight miles up in a big metal tube with wings. And I mention this not because of how magnanimously I reached out to her and did my best to alleviate her terror, but because it was really her that helped me. Chatting away to her, I forgot my malaise, my own sense of loss. So by the time I saw Dad, I was truly happy to be home.

◆

Dad meets me at Manchester airport, his strong face filling me with joy. I throw my arms around him and tell him I've missed him.

'She still runs,' Dad indicates my car, Mike's old car. 'I've turned her over every week.'

I've been away a long time.

'Do you mind if I drive?' I ask. I have no issue with him driving. I just want to be behind the wheel.

'Sure, son. So, tell me about your trip.'

'I will but right now I want to hear about you,' I say. 'What have you been up to?'

'Oh, you know, the usual.'

I want to hear about the 'usual', the day-to-day of these long months I have been away. I drive us to Chester, to his house, talking all the way. Then I do the last twenty minutes of my journey on my own.

Home.

It feels good being back in Wales. Strange, but good. I feel oddly light, like a horrible pressing burden has been lifted from my shoulders. The litany of tasks are all but behind me. The list ties me to Mike, and finishing it saddens me; but it also releases me. I am happy to have fulfilled Mike's wishes and far happier than I was at the beginning of this journey, when the fear of what lay ahead of me and the weight of making sure I did Mike proud hung heavy on me. Six months I've been away, but the unchanged familiarity of the roads that take me home comforts me and welcomes me. The sun beams down through the windscreen as I turn into the little lane that leads up to my house, and my heart soars. As much as leaving New Zealand felt like leaving Mike behind in some way, he is here too.

I have a kind of shrine to Mike in my house. When he died I didn't want anything of his. We were faced with the prospect of going through Number 1 and deciding what to do with everything. I didn't want to see any of it. I didn't want to see the cushions that propped his head up, or the black New Zealand scarves that I used to tie his arm to the hoist to keep it raised when he was on the drip. Everything, at the time, seemed too steeped in painful memories. And I didn't want to remember. Not then. But fortunately there was no huge rush to clear his house. When we did go back, I found that I absolutely wanted those things. I'd bottled up my response to losing him and pushed away any notion of keepsake. But when I walked around his house I realised I needed to face the grief. I needed to be able to look at these inert objects and see them not as painful memories of misery, but as bits of Mike that would forever be a reminder of happier times, when he was still here. So they now live in my downstairs bedroom and I say good morning to him every day. And goodnight, and goodbye. And hello. And when I'm feeling a little lost and the pain of missing him is a little too sharp, I hug the pillows that he would rest his head on. And it helps.

I push open my door and breathe in the musty air of my long empty house. I'm home. And Mike is here waiting. I go to his shrine and say hello, and I stand looking at it for an age. There are a couple of pictures of him here, smiling back at me. There are his dog tags from our Norway trips, his rings and beads, and the scarab beetle Dad got him. There's the envelope of forget-me-not seeds that everyone was given at his funeral, that have been scattered and sprinkled in all corners of the world. The pictures he printed are on the walls of my house. And I still have some of his ashes.

I made sure I would be home early enough to be able to dump my bags and drive to Moel Famau, where the majority of Mike's ashes were scattered. Before I went to New Zealand, I went up the mountain every single day to spend time with him. And I want to go there now.

It's not a long drive, and again the old familiarity of the route warms me. I park in the car park, not begrudging Mike the two quid it costs me, and take the well-trodden path up the mountain, then off-piste to our special place. And I sit in the dappled sun under the tree where we scattered him and pour myself a coffee from my flask. It's quiet. Serene. I sit for an hour or two, smiling through occasionally misty eyes while I reflect on the last six months.

In some ways it's like I never went away. Everything here is just as it was the day I left. It's as if I've blinked and imagined this epic journey, but I'm still here. But things are different. I'm different. There is a peculiar sensation I haven't felt in ages. I think it might be contentment. I feel at peace. And I feel like I've done something, achieved something. Mike asked me to do all these things, and I've done them. For him. And for me. And as much as I love coming up here, being in the peaceful embrace of Moel Famau, I won't go back to making it a daily pilgrimage. I can't. I need to move on. It is enough to know that the mountain is here, that Mike is here.

'Thank you,' I whisper out loud as the sun intensifies for a moment, 'and I miss you, Mike.'

◆

Jesse texted to say it wasn't going to work. It shouldn't have been a surprise. We're twelve thousand miles and twelve hours apart. Her morning is my evening. My day is her night. And I should have seen it coming. In the last couple of weeks in New Zealand she pulled away a bit. I'm sure she knew then, consciously or otherwise, that only a little soul-searching would tell her that staying together on opposite sides of the planet was going to be a tall order.

I suppose I was caught up in the unfamiliar but wonderful feeling of having opened up enough to let someone in. For the first time in years. I blithely said I wanted to find a way to make it work, not because I thought we could, but because I didn't want to lose what I had newly rediscovered; a connection.

So her decision to end it cut me to the bone. As happy as I am to be home again, and even despite the contentment and peace I felt up the mountain, I am still far from emotionally intact. The last six months, though edifying, have been raw. I have confronted my grief for Mike and laid some demons to rest, but of course I still hurt. I still feel loss. So I cried. I cursed myself for being stupid enough to get into a relationship, for laying myself open and vulnerable. The one reason I shy away from letting people into my life, and my heart, is the fear of loss.

But she was right. It was never going to work. And, looking back at it now, a couple of weeks after the hammer blow of her rejection, I can honestly say that I don't regret any of it. Yes, I feel the loss deeply, but I am better for the whole experience. She enabled me to get out of the funk I was in. Out of the relationship rut I had created. She teased me out of myself and into a more sociable and open frame of mind. Maybe, just maybe, she has helped me realise that to love and be loved is worth the risk of potential loss.

Inside the Mist, the Tears

I always knew I'd end up in Peru. More than anywhere in the world, Mike wanted to come here. And he wanted to see Machu Picchu. A friend of his had been and had ignited in Mike a fascination that filled his adult life. He never got to go. Not physically. But he's here with me now, a portion of his ashes kept safe and dry in their small wooden casket hanging around my neck.

I flew into Cuzco a few days ago, walked out of the airport to the breathlessness that an elevation of eleven thousand feet gives you, and took a cab to my hotel. I was greeted with a hot cup of coca tea, an infusion of coca leaves that is meant to alleviate altitude sickness. I'm not sure it helped. If anything, it made me feel even more light-headed. I spent a couple of days slowly exploring the city, often pausing to catch my breath, marvelling at the stunning architecture. Once the capital of the Inca empire, Cuzco is an eclectic mix of styles. The Spanish conquistadors brought with them smallpox, often endemic in Europe. The indigenous population, with no acquired immunities to the disease, dropped like flies. The Spanish also destroyed most of the buildings and built their own on what was left of the stone walls built by the Incas. The great blocks of stone, lovingly cut and shaped to fit tightly together in a dry wall process called ashlar, whetted my appetite for the ruins of Machu Picchu.

A lot of the locals seem to dress in traditional Peruvian clothing in Cuzco, all colourful and vibrant, and there were a lot of street vendors selling what I assumed would be relatively overpriced knick-knacks. The blankets and clothing and jewellery all looked great, but I felt sure that they would be more authentic a little off the tourist trail. I was approached by several women wanting to be remunerated for a selfie next to a llama. If I want one of those, I'll find my own llama, I quickly decided.

Three days later, I took a bus down the mountain from Cuzco into the Sacred Valley. It was a terrifying few hours, winding back and forth on a barrier-less road that, by some miracle, hadn't fallen into the valley thousands of feet below. I'm not sure if the driver was reckless, supremely confident or had just had some devastating news that rendered him suicidal, but we hurtled down the mountain with scant regard to other buses that ascended from the opposite direction in an equally precipitous manner. Mercifully, the humidity steamed the windows up and I was spared from witnessing the full horrifying extent of the driver's cavalier descent.

I breathed easier once we'd reached the bottom, as much from relief as the dramatic reduction in altitude, and we headed up the Sacred Valley. The landscape was spectacular. The Andes rose up sharply around us, their lower slopes often fashioned into dramatic agricultural terraces. Along the way we passed through a few villages, one of which notably featured a large smiling statue of a guinea pig. We stopped for a while, no doubt with the intent of providing custom to the various stalls that lined the side of the road. More tourist trap trinketry.

Domesticated five thousand years ago in these parts, guinea pigs (or 'cuy' as they are called here) are everywhere. And they are primarily a food source, so much so that they are revered; there's even a painting of the Last Supper in Cuzco's cathedral that features Jesus and his disciples preparing to chow down on one of the unfortunate fur balls for the main course. And among the tourist stalls on the side of the road in the middle of the Sacred Valley, there were cooked cuy readily on offer. The poor rodents, apart from being speared from arse to mouth and seared over an open flame, were otherwise intact. Their twisted and meatless limbs jutted out from their charred torsos, and their dead gaping mouths revealed blackened verminous incisors. Let's be honest, it's basically a burnt rat on a stick. I'm not one to denigrate something that's been integral to a culture for five millennia, but they looked absolutely rancid. I'm sure they probably taste just like chicken, as most unpalatable and debatable delicacies are often said to, but I wasn't having any of it.

The bus journey ended at a train station, again surrounded by street vendors and resplendent in a myriad of vibrant colours. I took the train to Aguas Calientes, the village nestled among the foothills beneath Machu Picchu itself. The train followed the path of the Urubamba River and my view was again often stymied by misty windows, but this actually began to add to the growing mystery of this beautiful landscape. It was a steep ascent through the streets of the town up to my hotel, and I was becoming increasingly focussed on the real reason I was here.

I barely slept. I was excited. I imagined how thrilled Mike would have been. I've made this long journey across the ocean and up into the magnificent Andes in Peru, and was a short distance from this almost mystically imbued heritage site that Mike had been desperate to visit. I woke up several times in the night, sleeping in short bursts between checking the time on my phone. I didn't want to miss the bus, and my anticipation was growing by the hour.

It was dark when I left the hotel this morning. The aim was to be in the ruins when dawn broke. I thought I'd beat the rush, but as I got to the place where the bus was due to collect me, the gloom was full of hundreds of tourists intent on the same plan. My heart sank as I joined the seemingly endless queue, predictably lined with stalls selling the usual curios, but also waterproofs and coffee. I glumly figured I'd be there a while. I'd miss the sunrise. But then the queue started moving, and it moved fast. A great convoy of buses filled up and left one by one, and in no time at all I was on my way up here to Machu Picchu, peering through fogged-up glass at the lightening sky.

◆

After a short wait at the entrance, I am inside Machu Picchu. Nearly everyone in front of me takes a right turn at a fork in the path, presumably to descend gently into the midst of the ruins. I follow the minority, and go left. Uphill. I climb as swiftly as I can. I want to get away from any people. I want privacy. I want to find a special place, away from the eyes of tourists and away from the most trodden pathways. Mike's ashes are in a waterproof bag on a lanyard around my neck. He hangs close to my heart, as he has done since I arrived in Cuzco. In the pack I carry on my back I also have a small box given to me by Mandy that I am to unwrap here.

I manage to get away from the few people that turned left, and find myself on a high point. I get my first glimpse of some ashlar walls and wonder if I would normally be able to see the ruins spreading out beneath me from here. I wonder, because I am now above a blanket of low cloud that has obscured my view and the sunrise. The wall I am near vanishes into the mist not far from me. I follow the path and come to some steep steps carved out of the stone of the mountainside, weather-worn and worryingly slippy, that descend ominously into the cloudy veil. The morning is quiet around me. An occasional voice drifts through the murk, but there is nobody near me. Maybe down these steps is where I need to go.

I begin a cautious descent, tentatively putting one boot after the other and feeling like I'm disappearing into a cloud. I'm wearing Mike's old hiking boots and a pack on my back and I soon realise that I can't risk walking down these steps forwards. I have no idea what the wispy whiteness that clings to the mountainside hides. It could be perfectly safe. Or it could be a cliff face a few thousand feet high. I turn side-on and manoeuvre my way down, one step at a time, until I reach a grassy ledge. It's about two metres wide and follows the contour of the hill. I can see that it opens out a short distance to my right into a grassy area that looks perfect for what I want.

I'm in the cloud now. Looking up, I see the stairs disappearing into nothingness. I nervously edge my way along this grassy path with no clue as to what is beneath me. It's level and I'm confident that I won't fall off it, but I have no idea how solid it is. As well as the anxiety I have about the path giving way and hurling me into an abyss, I can feel the rising emotion of knowing that I am about to do what I came here to do. This is the end. And I don't even know if I can do it.

I make it. And I sit. I feel tears stirring in the corners of my eyes. I get out the box Mandy gave me and take off the lanyard containing Mike's miniature casket of ashes, and I place them on a rock in front of me. And I sit. In the perfect stillness, in the mist shrouded quiet of this Peruvian mountainside, my mind is a cacophony of confused voices. Everything is perfect about this location. Surely it is just as Mike would have wanted. And yet I am besieged by doubt. I have been for the last couple of days. As much as this is what Mike wanted, I am struggling to find it in myself to scatter his ashes. This may be the perfect place, shrouded in mist and mystery, on top of the world, but something isn't right about the here and now. I don't feel right being here on my own. I don't feel worthy of this solitary ceremony. I want to share this farewell with other people. With people who loved Mike. People he loved. Edan should be here. Dad and Laura too. And Mandy, although she won't fly, so I can probably rule her out. Story could be here. Mike's best mate, Ali, could be here. Not just me on my own.

Tears filling my eyes, the gravity of what I am here to do weighs heavily on me. Besides feeling that I shouldn't be alone in this moment, I simply don't feel ready to end the journey. I don't want it to be over. I need some help, some support. So, briefly amazed that I have full reception on my phone, I call Mandy.

'Just spread the ashes, Royd,' she tells me after I mumble my way through my concerns. 'It's what Mike wanted. Just spread his ashes. You didn't go all the way to Machu Picchu to not spread them, did you?'

I hang up, my head no less muddled. I call Dad.

'Just do what you think is right, son.' His voice, soft, strong and kind, folds around me like a blanket, reassuring me.

He's right. It's up to me. I call Edan, Story, Laura and Ali. Not for advice. I want their voices here with me, with Mike. Maybe that will help me know what to do.

It doesn't.

I sit.

But I can't simply sit here for ever, so I get out the box Mandy gave me, and unwrap it. The first thing I see is Mike. Looking right at me. It's a passport photo, one Mandy always carries with her. And he's staring back at me, at my red-rimmed, tear-filled eyes.

And I break down, the tears beginning to flow freely. It's perfect, Mike looking at me, eyes bright and half of his mouth turning up in a cheeky smile he probably shouldn't have had for a passport photo. And it's perfectly painful too. I'm here for you, Mike. I made it. I'm in Machu Picchu. You're in Machu Picchu. I hold his gaze for a while, feeling him with me, unashamed of my tears, open to my pain.

Eventually I bring myself to open the box. Inside is Mike's Stussy bracelet. Mike spent years obsessively collecting beads from all corners of the world, scouring the internet for new ones. Dad got him some. So did Mandy. And he built a bracelet out of the beads, each etched with a different motivational phrase. Love. Live. Remember. That kind of thing.

Struggling to make out the letters through my tears, I read some of the words. And, in doing so, I realise that I have made my mind up. I look up, out into the quiet nothingness of the swirling cloud that clings to the side of this mountain, and I rationalise my decision. I don't know what the view here is. For all I know, there's a McDonald's perched on the sides of the mountain across the valley. And Mike doesn't need to be looking at that every day. And anyway, I'm not going to be pressured into doing it for the sake of a documentary.

I'm not going to spread his ashes.

I can't. And I don't want to. I want to be here with Edan when he is a little older. And Story. I want to properly share this moment of saying a final farewell to Mike. I want other people who loved him to say goodbye too, to make the journey here and see exactly where it is that part of Mike will remain.

I'm not going to spread his ashes.

I know Mike would have wanted Edan here too. I know he'd understand my decision. If he were here in my place, I'm certain he would come to the same conclusion. Now is not the time. There's no timescale on the list. I can come back later and do it.

I'm not going to spread his ashes.

That's that. And, resolute, I feel a weight lift from my shoulders.

I sit there for another hour, drinking in the quiet and the solitude. And as the morning sun creeps up over the mountain tops it begins to burn off the mist. The cloud parts and I find myself staring into the abyss. I peer over the edge, seeing a cliff face that falls thousands of feet straight down. There is nothing below me. Looking out, I see the Andes. I see mountains and valleys and trees. And as much as I reel at how perilous my arrival on this grassy clearing actually was, and how much scarier my return clamber along that narrow path and up those slippery steps will be, I am also touched by the beauty of my surroundings. In a while I'll scramble back up those stone steps and I'll be able to see all of Machu Picchu spread out beneath me, a picture postcard of one of the most amazing places in the world.

But, for now, I am happy to sit on top of this cliff, on the side of this mountain, revelling in the glory of nature.

Just me.

And Mike.

My brother.

It's only right that he should have the last word. His bucket list, lovingly bequeathed to me, ends with these words, painstakingly spelled out, letter by letter, with his beautiful bright eyes:

> *Love you and thank you, bro. I hope you've had the time of your life. My life wouldn't have been the same without you. Live to the max. I live through you. I'm still with you in spirit, always. xxxxx*

Afterword

Thank you. You've ploughed through hundreds of pages of me wittering on, so it seems only right to air Mike's voice. I've taken the liberty of rearranging the order slightly, to reflect the chronology of the book, and have also made the odd comment below some of the tasks, but here is the bucket list he left me . . .

1. The Funeral Trip. Please make a tit of yourself before you speak, trip over and make it really dramatic. Make everyone laugh for me and lighten the moment.

2. Snowboarding. Any recall of a leopard-print thong, cuffs, sunglasses and a cowboy hat? Course you have . . . Hope it's not too chilly.

Mike did actually specify a place to do this task in New Zealand but, given that the bulk of the tasks were scheduled for the summer there, snow was going to prove difficult. I was going to Avoriaz anyway, to spread Mike's ashes, so it seemed fitting to take advantage of the slopes.

3. The last time we went to New Zealand I was struggling with my walking, using a cane to help steady myself. Get in to the spirit of this journey by dressing up as Gandalf who also carries a cane. Embrace the character. Tell people they shall not pass constantly and block their path with your wizard staff.

4. You need to invite people to have a picture with you. You must get thirty-nine photographs. You need to capture no less than thirty-nine laughing faces please. Thirty-nine, the number of years I loved you, bro.

5. You need a new tattoo. I think you know what you need to do here Royd, a reminder of me . . . eternally.

6. Your hair's too long – shave it off. And whilst you're at it go and have a lovely soothing leg wax, or if you'd prefer to keep the hair on your head – add a back, sack and crack wax to the leg wax and keep your hair on your head . . . oh choices :)

As reluctant as I was to shear my locks, that was really the only choice available to me. There wasn't a lot to be achieved with a back, sack and crack wax. If you get my hairless drift! And, though it's not mentioned in the book, I did have a leg wax. And it hurt.

7. Go back to Black Sand Beach on the west shore. I wrote something on the TV for you, remember that moment, it meant the world to me. Write it down and put it in a bottle and send it out to sea. Before you send it, take a photograph and have one hundred A6 flyers printed.

8. Your boat skills leave a lot to be desired. Remember Norway? Why don't you remedy this by learning to sail properly.

9. Kayaking at Cathedral Cove. Thank you for loving me and looking after me the way you did, I'm with you always.

10. Auckland – SkyJump and SkyWalk.

11. Drive a V8 race car.

12. HOBBITON. You are an artist. There should be an outfit waiting for you, and an easel. Offer to paint Hobbiton visitors or dress as Mr Baggins and open the door to noisy passers-by, asking them to hush as you're trying to sleep. I love this place and our time here. I'm with you and I'm everywhere, I love you bro.

I went for the artistic option here. In retrospect I wish I had done both.

13. Skydiving in Taupo.

14. *You need a new face.* We had a great time visiting Weta Workshops. Why don't you see if they have a spare Orc mask lying around. It can only be an improvement.

15. *Nature's Larder.* Remember the book I started to write? Go foraging and brew up, sit and enjoy the forest, just be in the moment and feel my spirit with you. I thought of this when I pictured you here:

'The wind is silent and so we reflect, the earth turns, yet we are still, our bodies may weaken but our minds can find solace. Just be mindful and enjoy the moment. We are energy, we are love, we are one.'

16. *Is Wellington Zoo looking for volunteers to entertain the kids?* Volunteer for the day and dress up as they wish to entertain the kids. As you love spiders, please try your best to help clean out the tarantulas or at least handle them.

17. *You think you're funny.* Find an open mic comedy night and see how many laughs you get.

18. *Random acts of kindness.* Find people to help, even in the smallest way. Give flowers to people, hug strangers, buy lunch for the homeless, leave positive messages on sticky notes, go and talk to the old person on the bench, smile at people and brighten their day.

19. *Dress as a hippie* and spread some love, hand out the flyers. You have to be really happy when you do this and feel the love and hugs.

20. *Street love.* Start conversations with strangers, your mission is to obtain kisses from them, trouble is you can't tell them that verbally, you have to act that part out.

21. *Hey Man.* You approach people, pretending to know them, your mission is for at least one of these people to acknowledge they remember you and shake your hand or take your number. Or get one person to take you home with them for tea.

22. *Half-Day Lost World. Abseiling.*

23. *Black-water rafting/tubing.*

24. Swim with the fur seals.

25. Swim with the dolphins and raise awareness for them. The Maui's dolphin lives off the coast of New Zealand, with only fifty-five animals alive today, they are considered critically endangered by the IUCN. The biggest threat is entanglement in fishing gear. The Hector's dolphin inhabit the coast off NZ and are on the endangered species list with approx. only 7,000 alive. I don't know if there are implications of swimming with them, check before.

I love dolphins. I think there are implications. And the tourist industry in Kaikoura was shattered. I wish I hadn't gone out and swam with them as briefly as I did before I realised how wrong it was. The sea is their environment, not ours. I am sure Mike would agree with me, and I hope that my reluctance to indulge in this activity is a small nod in the direction of raising awareness.

26. Past Life. I wonder if you had a past life regression, have we known each other before? There's nothing to fear, just see what happens.

27. River sledging.

28. The Fox.

Not only did I do this, I did the swing as well. Twice. So there.

29. Spread some love and happiness. Set up an amp, microphone, music in a town centre and offer to dance with people to make them happy. You need to get at least ten people to interact and dance with you no matter how long it takes.

30. Stage fright. Karaoke, not letting you off that lightly. Two choices:

Wear a dress and act like a girl, you're good at that. Sing a girlie song in a soft velvet voice. A little dance maybe? Just for me.

Or,

Wear what you like, choose a really sad song and get really emotional, tissues at the ready, sob REALLY loudly.

342

Due to the handy availability of a huge ukulele group, this ended up being me learning a song and performing it with them. Live! I am certain Mike would have approved of this interpretation.

31. Find a dance group. Learn and perform a piece with them and don't forget to dress the part: baseball cap facing backwards, baggy pants etc.

32. Take a yoga class – the teacher's late and you volunteer to step in. Tight Lycra pants please.

33. You are a famous UK ceramic artist/potter, you offer your services teaching art students how to turn a pot on a wheel. Dressed in your white apron with clay splattered all over it, you are told this two minutes before you enter the room. Enjoy.

34. Auckland Bridge climb and bungy jump.

35. Nevis Highwire. Wear a pink tutu please and hold on tight to your fairy wand!

36. Tandem paragliding/hang-gliding.

37. Fly a plane yourself.

38. Guided glacier walk.

39. We didn't get to view New Zealand from the air did we. Go for a doors-off helicopter flight – soak it up, with you all the way bro.

40. Heli-biking.

41. Thermal bicycle trail.

42. Do a spot of trout fishing in the fiords. You could wear my Tilley hat, see if it brings you luck to catch fish for once. Make a fire (the Norway way), cook a fish and enjoy. I'm with you always so if you get the fire to light, I'll take credit for that.

43. Bushcraft/survival. One-on-one training.

44. Carve a greenstone.

This filled the one gap Mike left in his list.

45. Stand-up paddleboarding in grass skirt and coconut bra.

I kind of did this, actually. It was a simple matter to get hold of a paddleboard. The grass skirt and coconut bra? Not so easy.

Production did manage to find a luminous lime green mankini, but I flatly refused to deviate from Mike's express wishes. It was only when Andy offered to go with me in just a thong (which Rachel produced from somewhere) that I eventually acquiesced. The resulting scenes, in which poor Andy had to sit behind me, wobbling around on the board, and watch as the glowing Borat-style swimsuit delved insidiously further and further into the crevice between my buttocks, didn't make the documentary. And rightly so. And it didn't make the book either. Nobody wants to see, or imagine, that. Sorry.

46. Visit an active volcano.

I did actually go on a day trip to White Island and walk around the active crater there. Since then, and before the writing of this book, several tourists were killed there when the volcano erupted. Out of respect for them, I have chosen not to include this task in the book.

47. Hukafalls jet boat ride.

There wasn't a whole lot to say about this. The terminal for the jet boat is right next to a shrimp farm, which at the time I would have preferred to visit. But the boat ride was fun. Ridiculously fast, wetting and an adrenaline rush. The boat, expertly piloted by a beautiful Kiwi woman, spun on a dime and flew over the water. I'd do it again, if only to marvel at her skills.

48. Attend an audition, acting, singing, dancing. Whatever is offered to you first, do.

It's just the nature of these things that not everything finds its way into a book. I did attend an audition, for *The Merry Wives of Windsor*, in Wellington. I'm not an actor, and Shakespeare is Greek to me, so it was certainly a challenge. But I nailed it. So I thought. I enjoyed a few moments of worrying how I'd turn down the part (due to being really busy) when they offered it to me, before it was revealed that the audition was a sham. The production was already live. The actors I thought had been there to audition alongside me were already cast.

49. You have a gift from me, I'd like you to have it. If you're seeing this, you're near the end of my list. Shame we had to tweak the original plan, but look on the bright side, I'm still amazing and you're still a dick! Some things will never change.

Mike's Stussy bracelet was the gift.

50. You're not going home just yet, you're going to take me to Machu Picchu. It would be amazing if Edan could meet you there to fulfil my dream.

Love you and thank you, bro. I hope you've had the time of your life. My life wouldn't have been the same without you. Live to the max. I live through you. I'm still with you in spirit, always. xxxxx

Acknowledgments

On behalf of Mike, the family and I would like to thank everyone who selflessly gave everything to surround Mike with the warmth, love and happiness that was so important.

And to the people who helped, and are continuing to help make this journey possible, from the bottom of our hearts, and his, thank you.

About Royd Tolkien

As the great-grandson of J. R. R. Tolkien, Royd grew up on a diet of storytelling and entertainment, with the characters of *The Hobbit* firmly entrenched in his imagination.

Following acting roles in Peter Jackson's *The Lord of the Rings: The Return of the King* and *The Hobbit: The Desolation of Smaug*, Royd was inspired to become a producer. He went on to produce two films and was developing more when, in 2012, his younger brother, Mike, was diagnosed with motor neurone disease. Royd put everything on hold to care for Mike until he passed away, on 28 January 2015.

Since then, Royd has completed *There's a Hole in My Bucket*, a feature-length documentary that follows his journey around New Zealand fulfilling the bucket list bequeathed to him by Mike. He lives in Wales.

About Drew Cullingham

Born in Berkshire, Drew has always had a keen interest in literature. Having studied English at university, he (perhaps foolishly) declined an offer of a place on a prestigious creative writing MA course under the then Poet Laureate, Andrew Motion, and instead spread his wings.

Going on to live in Ireland, America and Italy, he worked in the legal profession in Belfast and was a professional musician for years before finding his way into the film industry. As well as being a proficient technician, Drew has written, directed and edited several feature films and is working on his first novel.

He lives in Northamptonshire with his wife, Victoria, and their daughter, Indiana.